The Politics of Gender
in Early Modern Europe

Habent sua fata libelli

Volume XII
of

Sixteenth Century Essays & Studies
Charles G. Nauert, Jr., General Editor

ISBN: 0-940474-12-3

Composed by NMSU typographers, Kirksville, Missouri
Cover Design by Teresa Wheeler, NMSU Designer
Printed by Edwards Brothers, Ann Arbor, Michigan
Text is set in Bembo II 10/12

The Politics of Gender

in
Early Modern Europe

Jean R. Brink, Allison P. Coudert
and Maryanne C. Horowitz,
Editors

Volume XII
Sixteenth Century Essays & Studies

This book has been brought to publication with the
generous support of
Northeast Missouri State University

The United Library
Garrett-Evangelical/Seabury-Western Seminaries
2121 Sheridan Road
Evanston, IL 60201

Library of Congress Cataloging-in-Publication Data

The Politics of gender in early modern Europe / Jean R. Brink, Allison P. Coudert,
and Maryanne C. Horowitz, editors.
   p. cm. -- (Sixteenth century essays & studies ; v. 12)
Papers derived from the Sixteenth Century Studies Conference, held in Tempe,
Ariz. in 1987.
   ISBN 0-940474-12-3 (alk. paper)
   1. Women--Europe--Social conditions--Congresses. 2. Women--History--
Renaissance, 1450-1600--Congresses. I. Brink, J.R. II. Coudert, Allison, 1941- .
III. Horowitz, Maryanne Cline, 1945- . IV. Sixteenth Century Studies Conference
(1987 : Tempe, Ariz.) V. Series.
HQ1149.E85P65 1989
305.42'094'09031--dc20

89-26669
CIP

Table of Contents

Acknowledgments

This book was brought to fruition because of the remarkable industry of Robert V. Schnucker, ably assisted by Paula Presley and Trey Hoffman, and because of the continuing support of Northeast Missouri State University. For this particular volume, it is a privilege and a pleasure to express appreciation to Kobe University of Japan. Dr. Fumiko Takase, Director of Women's Studies at Kobe College, has encouraged and contributed to the Sixteenth Century Studies Conference by acting as the international editor for Japan of the Historians of Early Modern Europe, by presenting her research at the annual conferences, and now by supporting the project of bringing together essays on gender that derive from the Sixteenth Century Studies Conference at Tempe in the fall of 1987.

General Introduction

THIS COLLECTION OF ESSAYS is made with the goal of broadening the level of discourse in gender studies. In its earliest phases, scholarship on women embarked on a quest to identify the overlooked contributions of forgotten women, hoping to recover a neglected "Emily" Shakespeare. This process of reexamining the canon for female worthies has made us increasingly aware that the process of identifying great figures or major works requires continual reevaluation. New figures and new kinds of discourse have been added to literary anthologies. More recently, gender as a concept has furnished fresh perspectives for examining texts in the canon and for reexamining historical assumptions about the relations between the sexes and the structure of the family, contributing to the development of the field of family history.

Part One of this volume uses the concept of gender to explore the complex factors that combined to establish the witch as a focus and outlet for misogyny in the early modern period. Misogyny, the hatred and distrust of women as a group, found an outlet in a virulent persecution of witches in the early modern period. The background to this persecution was complex. The learned, celibate clerical tradition of the Middle Ages helped to set the intellectual stage for this outbreak. Attacks upon and defenses of women were an established literary genre. Against images of the ugly, demonic witch, defenders of women promoted images of the busy and productive housewife, but a housewife remained subordinate to her husband's governance. Patriarchal hierarchy was not threatened by the celebration of women in subordinate roles, but at the beginning of the early modern period, forces were at work that challenged the established intellectual principle of male superiority. The witchcraze was one response to that challenge.

In popular culture of the late sixteenth and early seventeenth centuries, especially in the drama, we find numerous instances in which the figure of the "witch" becomes a focus for anti-female sentiment. While we would expect the cross-fertilization of theological and institutionalized political views of the inferior status of women to be reflected in the drama, the characterization of the witch offers an important perspective on the problem of misogyny. The drama, because of its public character and its traditional associations with liturgy and ceremony, figures as an important source for reconstructing public views of the witch. By analyzing the witch as a cultural symbol and by illuminating the witchcraze, the essays in Part One attempt to throw light on gender specific traditions and events that need further examination.

The essays in Part Two return to issues posed in the first phase of gender studies, the consideration of female worthies. These essays focus for the most part on individual women, but they do so to illustrate how female aspiration was perverted, subverted, ignored, or marginalized by mainstream culture. Part Two also shows that female achievement was by no means entirely suppressed. While the images of female worthies were being rendered suspect, their less threatening sisters were laying claim to what later was to be labelled the private sphere. These women established conventions relating to gender that asserted female ascendancy within the domestic sphere and that nourished forms and traditions that affected the canon far more than has been acknowledged.

The two sections of this collection bring together well-defined approaches to gender studies, suggesting the importance of recognizing the interrelationship of various levels of discourse:

1. the intellectual history of woman as a symbol that can illuminate a complex of intellectual, social, and even emotional assumptions about gender;
2. the social history of women as an aggregate of individuals defined by gender;
3. the biographical records of individual women in history whose experiences were shaped not only by gender and class, but also by unique and particular facts of nature and nurture.

These essays focus on women, but not to claim recognition for an overlooked group. This collection is intended to add to the growing literature that examines gender as a symbol, as a political and social concept that must be informed by historical understanding.

Part One:
The Figure of the Witch as a
Focus for Misogyny

Introduction to Part One

ALTHOUGH SCHOLARSHIP ABOUT EUROPEAN WITCHCRAFT seems to proliferate less rapidly today than it did a decade ago, studies such as the four
essays in Part One continue to furnish valuable increments to a scholarly
corpus which subtly changes shape as it grows. Each of these essays adds
something slightly different to our available stock.

As an anthropologist, James Brain offers information from non-European
societies in order to illuminate two very different aspects of European
witchcraft: why witches were ordinarily women, and whether more mobile
societies may be less prone to witchcraft accusations. Even for curmudgeons
like me who remain skeptical about how far non-European keys will open
European locks, this essay contains stimulating suggestions about female
pollution and the image of the succubus in its first part, and about the
remarkable freedom from witchcraft among small-scale societies which
move frequently and practice immediate-return economic systems in its
final section.

Viviana Comensoli focuses on the stage to illuminate attitudes towards
women accused of witchcraft. When scrutinized with proper care, a text
like *The Witch of Edmonton* reveals more complexity than expected. The
playwrights as sociologists implicitly argue that village communities, not
private individuals, created witches; they even introduced an "enlightened"
judge who warns against village superstitions. Yet in the end convention
triumphs; as Comensoli notes, both the witch and the murdered wife in
the play's subplot die at the moment of maximum assertiveness, when they
exceed conventional gender behavior.

Sigrid Brauner uses a new lever to pry open an old chestnut, much
debated during the *Kulturkampf* a century ago: did Luther bring any "modern"
attitudes to the problem of witchcraft? Using Luther's biblical exegeses
plus a few plays written by his followers, she demonstrates the relative
modernity of Luther's gender-bound housewives when contrasted with the
black-and-white woodcut misogyny of the *Malleus Maleficarum*. Much, of
course, depends on the terms of the comparisons being made: a devil's
advocate might argue that Luther and his followers should be compared
not to the *Malleus* but to some of their Catholic contemporaries, like the
select committee of the Spanish Inquisition which set down guidelines for
cases of witchcraft in 1526, showing more gentleness (if no less patronizing
attitudes towards women) than any Protestant authority ever demonstrated.

Allison Coudert's essay is the most ambitious of the four. Is her
somewhat "perverse" plan "to resurrect the old thesis that the witch-craze
was more severe in Protestant than in Catholic countries," an attempt to
raise the dead that would make Doctor Faustus envious? Her argument
resembles a three-pronged pitchfork: (1) the Devil was more threatening

to Protestants; (2) Protestant ideology about women created more tension than its Catholic counterpart; and (3) Protestants had no great ecclesiastical or secular courts which could implement gentler policies towards accused witches. One can raise objections to each prong: (1) probably exaggerates the extent of millenarianism among Protestants; (2) underestimates the extent of "covenant theology" pacts among Catholics; and (3) merely reflects the accidents of European politics–there is no logical reason why Protestantism never developed appellate courts as large and sophisticated as the *Parlement* of Paris or the Mediterranean Inquisitions. But, all objections aside, it constitutes an unusually stimulating exercise in historical revision.

William Monter
Northwestern University

An Anthropological Perspective on the Witchcraze

James L. Brain

OUR UNDERSTANDING OF HISTORICAL ATTITUDES TOWARD GENDER may be illuminated by a comparative cross-cultural approach to witchcraft.* Two issues are especially important: the reason for the near universality of the image of woman as witch, and the idea that geographic and spatial mobility may be an important and overlooked factor in the absence of witchcraft accusations and in the decline of their frequency.

The Image of the Witch

Anthropological and historical evidence shows that the specific details of beliefs about witches and their behavior will vary according to the concerns of a particular society. There are, however, two universal constants about witch beliefs that cut across cultures: witches represent people's deepest fears about themselves and society, and they represent a reversal of all that is considered normal behavior in a particular society. This has been documented for small-scale societies,[1] but the situation in Europe needs to be examined. Norman Cohn discusses the European witchcraze in terms of "collective fantasies," "obsessive fears," and "unacknowledged desires" in the minds of sixteenth- and seventeenth-century men and women.[2] Margaret Murray and, to a certain extent, Carlo Ginzburg locate the origins of European witchcraft beliefs in pre-Christian religions.[3]

It would be unfortunate if we were to revive Murray's hypothesis. The beliefs about witches can be explained without reference to pre-Christian religions, if we assume that witch-like behavior is a simple reversal of normal and socially accepted behavior. In Catholic Europe, the Church demanded attendance at mass in the daytime on Sundays; the predominant color there was white. By reversing this, one can easily predict that witches will celebrate their own sabbath at night, and that black will be the predominant color in their community or congregation – hence the term "black mass." Reversal also predicts that whatever ritual or service is

*I am grateful to Professor Alan Jacobs for information on the Massai. I should also like to thank Professors Allison Coudert, Sigrid Brauner, and Viviana Comensoli for the inspiration I gained from their work.

[1]M. Wilson, "Witch Beliefs and Social Structure," *American Journal of Sociology* 56 (1951), 307-13; Lucy Phillip Mair, *Witchcraft* (New York: McGraw Hill, 1969).

[2]Norman Cohn, *Europe's Inner Demons: An Inquiry Inspired by the Great Witch-Hunt* (New York: Basic Books, 1975), 258-63.

[3]Carlo Ginzburg, *The Night Battles: Witchcraft and Agrarian Cults in the Sixteenth and Seventeenth Centuries* (Baltimore: The Johns Hopkins University Press, 1983); Margaret Murray, *The God of the Witches* (New York: Oxford University Press, 1970; first published by Sampson Low, Marston & Co., 1931).

performed will be a reversal of the Christian mass – the recitation of prayers backwards, the reversed cross, and worship of some form of Antichrist. The Church demanded acceptance of the doctrine of the Trinity, in which subliminally one can perceive that Mary is made pregnant by her own son in the shape of the Holy Ghost; the reversal of this doctrine makes profane incest an attribute of witches. If there was a sacred act of ritual cannibalism in Holy Communion, then witches could be expected to take part in some blasphemous form of cannibalism. The belief in Jesus' conquest of death and decay manifested itself in the idea that the bodies of saints do not decay at death; in witch beliefs, this finds its reversal in the belief in vampires that do not decay. If heterosexuality is the extolled norm, then homosexuality will be seen as witch-like, and if chastity is the ultimate condition of holiness then obviously one should expect witches to engage in sexual orgies.

This point can be carried even further: if patriarchal authority is divinely ordained, as Saint Paul insisted, then any attempt by women to subvert or to assume that authority can be seen as an illicit reversal and hence as witch-like behavior. The first example of the subversion of divine authority, of course, is attributed to Eve in her disobedience. Both Protestants and Catholics were concerned with issues of authority and women. Martin de Castañega's treatise on superstition and witchcraft (1529) answers the question of why women are more prone to be witches than men thus: "The first reason is because Christ forbade them to administer the sacraments and therefore the devil gives them the authority to do it with his execrations."[4] Here we see not only the reversal of normal, i.e. God-given authority, but also the idea of the administration of blasphemous, heretical sacraments. Additional reversals occur in his explanations of how and why witches, like angels and Christ, can fly; how and why they, like Christ can walk on water; and how and why they, like Christ and the devil, can become invisible or change their shape.[5] In the pattern of inheritance D. H. Darst records another reversal. Instead of passing on inheritance from father to son, witches inherit their discipleship to the devil from mother to daughter, from aunt to niece, or from grandmother to granddaughter.

To the issue of authority, feminist anthropological scholarship offers very cogent insights.[6] Authority is always legitimate; power may be, but often is not. Where women are denied authority, they inevitably seek their ends by the manipulation of the power they possess: by denying sex, food

[4]D. H. Darst, "Witchcraft in Spain: The Testimony of Martin de Casteñega's Treatise on Superstition and Witchcraft (1529)," *Proceedings of the American Philosophical Society* 123, no. 5 (1979): 298-322.

[5]Darst, "Witchcraft in Spain," 306.

[6]Michelle Z. Rosaldo, "Introduction and Overview," *Woman, Culture and Society*, ed. Michelle Z. Rosaldo and L. Lamphere (Stanford: Stanford University Press, 1974), 1-42.

or nurture; by failing to perform household tasks, by outright disobedience, or by passive resistance in the form of sulking, scolding, and gossiping. All of these possibilities subvert legitimate male authority and can, therefore, be seen as evidence of witchcraft. One can conceive of a sliding scale: the less authority – or responsibility – women possess, the more manipulation of power will occur, and vice versa. Thus we can confidently expect to find the paradox that women are often extremely powerful in societies in which they are denied any authority; in these social organizations they develop strategies to attain their ends outside the legitimate parameters of authority.

This paradigm has great relevance to women in Renaissance Europe in terms of the generation of misogyny. As Lamphere demonstrates, the image of women in patrilineal and patrilocal societies is invariably negative: women are believed to be deceitful, untrustworthy and manipulative.[7] This negative image is a direct result of marriage practices: the men are all related by blood; the women, because of rules of clan exogamy, are all strangers both to the men and to each other. In a large extended family, the men will have the solidarity of kinship; the women will lack any solidarity. In such societies the only possible way for a woman to achieve her goals is for her to manipulate those who possess legitimate authority – her husband and her sons. Lamphere contrasts this inevitably negative image of women with the very positive image enjoyed by Navajo women. In that matrilineal society marriage is often matrilocal, so that it is the husband who moves to his wife's family. Here he is the one surrounded by strangers and must depend on his wife to negotiate concessions for him. Under these circumstances women are viewed as competent managers and good negotiators. This shows that the locality of marriage is crucial in determining the image of women. While it is true that in northern European societies bilateral descent was the norm, most marriages probably have demanded that women move to join their husbands. If manipulation of power is the only available route a woman can follow to achieve her ends then inevitably her image will be that of a manipulative bitch – as the *Malleus Maleficarum* makes abundantly clear.

There is little doubt that a contributing factor to the denigration of women in European thought was the legacy of Aristotle by way, particularly, of Augustine. "Conceiving of the soul as possessing nutritive, sensitive or appetitive and reasonable faculties, Aristotle saw women's souls as deficient in all three aspects, but especially in the faculty of reason."[8] Acceptance of

---

[7]L. Lamphere, "Strategies, Cooperation and Conflict among Women in Domestic Groups," *Woman, Culture and Society*, ed. Michelle Z. Rosaldo and L. Lamphere (Stanford: Stanford University Press, 1974), 97-112.

[8]E. Robertson, *An Anchorhold Of Her Own* (Knoxville: University of Tennessee Press, forthcoming).

this idea leads inexorably to the dicta of the *Malleus* about the predisposition of women to be witches because of their manifold weaknesses (Question 4).[9]

Not only was the woman's soul seen as inferior; her body was too. "In Aristotelian and Galenic terms, woman is less fully developed than man. Because of lack of heat in germination, her sexual organs have remained internal, she is incomplete, colder and moister in dominant humors. She has less body heat and thus less courage, liberality, moral strength."[10] That these ideas may appear absurd to us has to be tempered by their legacy and persistence in more recent times. Darwin believed that women were less evolved than men because of their childlike skins and softness,[11] and the Freudian doctrine of penis-envy surely owes something to them.

The denigration of the body leads into another area germane to the witch stereotype and one that has been much explored by anthropology. The question of ritual pollution is used widely to "prove" that women are inferior, and doubtless has much to do with latter-day disputes about the ordination of women. All bodily emissions are considered polluting or, in our modern idiom, disgusting. Among others, Mary Douglas seeks an explanation for this attitude.[12] In her opinion, all such substances are considered threatening because they are liminal, because they have "traversed the boundary of the body" and are thus of the body but yet not of the body, and thus do not fit our standard categories. While I do not dispute this point, I have argued elsewhere that what makes these substances so deeply threatening is that they remind us of death.[13] It is no coincidence that they are often sought for and used in magic intended to bring about the death of the victim. Of course, both men and women produce polluting emissions, but only women menstruate, give birth messily, and lactate. Customarily women take care of small babies who, like animals, are uncontrolled in their excretions, and the association with babies makes women additionally polluting. The issue of pollution throws additional light on why midwives were disproportionately often accused of witchcraft. Because they assisted at birth, they inevitably became contaminated with polluting substances. It should also be recalled that midwives traditionally laid out the dead and were contaminated by death, the ultimate pollutant.

[9]Heinrich Kramer and Jakob Sprenger, *Malleus Maleficarum,* tr. Montague Summers (New York: Dover, 1971).

[10]Robertson, *Anchorhold.*

[11]B. Dykstra, *Idols of Perversity* (New York: Oxford University Press, 1986), 167-73.

[12]Mary Douglas, *Purity and Danger* (London: Routledge and Kegan Paul, 1966).

[13]Brain, J. L. "Sex, Incest and Death: Initiation Rites Reconsidered," *Current Anthropology* 18, no. 2 (1977): 371-84.

Women's very physiology therefore makes them appear more polluted and polluting than men. Even in regard to the sexual act itself, a man can more easily be cleansed since his genitals are external and can be readily washed. A woman cannot be so readily cleansed, since her own polluting bodily fluids have been augmented by the deposition of the man's semen. Pollution alone would not make a witch, yet the *Malleus* makes clear that pollution is a primary aspect of sexuality. Sexuality is allied to temptation, and the Devil is the great tempter. Nowhere is this more powerfully demonstrated than through the medium of lust for women –"though the devil tempted Eve to sin, yet Eve seduced Adam" (*Malleus:* Part 1, Question 6).

Although the *Malleus* is obsessive in its misogyny and loathing of sex, it seems to deal only indirectly with one sexual matter – the nature of semen. Literary references of the Shakespearian period show that this was a subject that exercised men's minds. In some ways, this belief is still widely held as part of folk beliefs even today in the United States. The basic assumption of this belief is that marrow and semen are the same substance; the skull is the largest bone in the body and the brain is its marrow. Therefore any emission of semen depletes a man's life force and intelligence. "As the main storehouse of bone marrow, the brain is the source of semen, via the spinal cord. The supply is limited. . . . Loss of manhood, power, and ultimately life itself results from the 'spending' of the life force, which is a finite capital."[14] Francis Bacon wrote in 1626 that "The skull has Braines, as a kind of Marrow, within it;" and even Leonardo da Vinci apparently believed in a duct connecting the brain to the penis via the spinal cord.[15] Understanding the belief that semen and marrow were one and the same gives point to the many references in literature to the danger of expending a man's marrow. If we grasp this unfounded fear, we can well understand yet another aspect of the witch image: that of the succubus and its terrifyingly debilitating potential.

Claude Levi-Strauss suggested that the primary pair of oppositions is that of nature versus culture.[16] Sherry B. Ortner claims that universally women are perceived as being, if not *part of* nature, at least as *closer to* nature than men, who are perceived as the generators of culture.[17] This position

[14]Weston La Barre, *Muelos: A Stone Age Superstition* (New York: Columbia University Press, 1984), 130.

[15]Ibid., 115-18.

[16]Edmund Ronald Leach, *Claude Levi-Strauss* (Harmondsworth: Penguin Books, 1970), 35.

[17]Sherry B. Ortner, "Is Female to Nature as Man is to Culture?" in *Woman, Culture and Society,* ed. Michelle Z. Rosaldo and L. Lamphere (Stanford: Stanford University Press, 1974), 67-87.

has been challenged,[18] but it is convincing. It generates the following sets of oppositions (always unequal in value):

Nature – Culture
Women – Men
Darkness – Light
Left – Right
Disorder – Order
Death – Life.

It is significant that in many languages the word for left is synonymous with female and right with male.[19] One should note that "right" as in side or hand and "right" as in correct or "the right to" are not merely homonymous. The same is true of "droit" or "recht." Perceptually, witches are always believed to do and to be everything that is the reverse of normal and right. Similarly, all the other characteristics in the left column are applicable to the witch stereotype.

The link between women and nature suggested by Ortner was hardly an unfamiliar one in Renaissance Europe. Bacon in particular took the view that the mission of science was the subjugation of nature. Moreover, he participated in the "rhetoric that conjoins the domination of nature with the insistent image of nature as female."[20]

That the image of witch as woman (or vice versa) is extremely widespread in the world is beyond doubt. Elsewhere in the world, and in Europe before the association of witchcraft with heresy, witchcraft was considered bad but of minor importance. During the witchcraze a new doctrine emerged that linked witchcraft with devil worship and hence with heresy. This change in doctrine made the image of woman as witch lethal to women. The change did not occur in a vacuum, and there are many powerful reasons why the witchcraze occurred.[21] The witchcraze ended, but misogyny and gynophobia are still alive and well at the end of the twentieth century.

[18]C. McCormack and M. Strathern, eds., *Nature, Culture and Gender* (Cambridge: Cambridge University Press, 1980).

[19]James L. Brain, "Handedness in Tanzania," *Anthropos* 72 (1977): 180-92.

[20]E. Fox-Keller, "Feminism and Science," *The Signs Reader,* ed. E. Abel and E. K. Abel (Chicago: University of Chicago Press, 1983), 116.

[21]See the three chapters following this one: "Luther on Witchcraft: A True Reformer?" by Sigrid Brauner, "Witchcraft and Domestic Tragedy in *The Witch of Edmonton,*" by Viviana Comensoli, and "The Myth of the Improved Status of Protestant Women: The Case of the Witchcraze," by Allison Coudert.

*Mobility as a Factor in the Non-Existence
or Decline of Witchcraft Beliefs*

Examining non-Western small-scale societies, one discovers a rather startling fact. Societies with the simplest technologies of all – hunter-gatherers such as the San of the Kalahari, the Mbuti pygmies of the Ituri Forest, and the Hadza of northwest Tanzania – are quite unconcerned about witchcraft and do not think that it occurs in their societies.[22] They do, however, impute it to their sedentary agricultural neighbors.[23] When they themselves are forced into a sedentary way of life, "witchcraft fears are rampant."[24] Why fears of witchcraft are unimportant to such peoples is described by several authors. Of the San peoples, L. Marshall writes, ". . . the composition of a band is fluid – marriage takes individuals from one band to another, and whole families move from one band to another; bands split and disband completely."[25] Similarly, Richard Lee notes that "hunters have a great deal of latitude to vote with their feet, to walk out of an unpleasant situation."[26] In J. Woodburn's description of conflict resolution in these societies lies the key to the absence of witchcraft beliefs. When conflict arises, people move, giving an ecological reason. Thus, "they solve disputes simply by refusing to acknowledge them."[27]

It is significant that all these African hunter-gatherers possess negligible property and practice bilateral descent. The situation is very different in societies that practice unilineal descent. In his essay, Meyer Fortes suggests that unilineal descent is characteristic of societies in which property rights are acknowledged.[28] Such societies invariably subscribe to a belief in sorcery or witchcraft or both. Unlike their African counterparts, Australian hunter-gatherers practice unilineal descent. They claim ownership over totemic

[22]L. Marshall, "!Kung Bushmen Religious Beliefs," *Africa* 32, no. 3 (1962): 221-52; C. Turnbull, "The Importance of Flux in Two Hunting Societies," in *Man the Hunter*, ed. Richard B. Lee and I. DeVore (Chicago: Aldine, 1968), 132-37; J. Woodburn, "An Introduction to Hadza Ecology," in ibid., 49-55.

[23]C. Turnbull, *The Forest People* (New York: Simon and Schuster, 1961), 228; J. Woodburn, "Egalitarian Societies," *Man* 17 (1982) 431-51; Richard B. Lee, *Kalahari Hunter-Gatherers* (Cambridge: Harvard University Press, 1976), 127-29.

[24]J. Woodburn, "Social Dimensions of Death in Four African Hunting and Gathering Societies," *Death and the Regeneration of Life,* ed. Maurice Bloch and Jonathan Parry (Cambridge: Cambridge University Press, 1982), 187-210.

[25]L. Marshall, *The !Kung of Nyae* (Cambridge: Harvard University Press, 1976), 180.

[26]Richard B. Lee, "Work Effort, Group Structure and Land Use among Contemporary Hunter-Gatherers," in *Man, Settlement and Urbanism,* ed. B. Ucko and R. Trimingham (London: George Duckworth and Co., 1972), 182.

[27]J. Woodburn, "Introduction to Hadza Ecology," 156, and J. Woodburn, "Minimal Politics: The Political Organization of the Hadza of N.Tanzania," in *Leadership: A Comparative Perspective,* ed. W. A. Shack and P. S. Cohen (Oxford: Clarendon Press, 1979), 244-60.

[28]Meyer Fortes, "The Structure of Unilineal Descent Groups," *American Anthropologist* 55 (1953) 17-41.

sites and believe in evil magic, as evidenced by accounts of "bone-pointing."[29] All the accounts emphasize, however, that only men are involved; that the practice is thought to be rare. It is also believed that "the professional worker of magic is always to be found in another tribe."[30] Woodburn suggests that the crucial factor that differentiates African from Australian hunter-gatherers is "the relatively tight control which men exercise over women" among the Australians.[31] This point has relevance to the European witchcraze. It is also important that Woodburn describes the African hunter-gatherers as having an "immediate return system" of economics, whereas the Australians, more like sedentary peoples, have "delayed return systems."[32] A comparable people, the Ona (or Selk'nam) of Tierra del Fuego, are a hunting-gathering people. Anne Chapman describes them as inegalitarian, oppressive to women (unlike the African hunter-gatherers). They put an "emphasis on patrilineality, and patrilocality [and] the preeminence of territoriality. . . ."[33] Like the Australians, they change campsites frequently; like them they believe in sorcerers; like them they claim that sorcerers belong to another tribe.[34]

If we turn to the nomadic pastoral peoples, we should, according to my hypothesis, find a situation similar to that found among the Australians and the Ona/Selk'nam, since all pastoralists practice patrilineal descent, and own property, but move fairly frequently. This proves to be the case. There is no mention of witchcraft among the Fulani (Peuls) of the Sahel region of West Africa,[35] while among the pastoral Somali "magic, witchcraft and sorcery play a small part."[36] The same is true of the Turkana and Dodos of Northern Kenya,[37] and the Karamojong of Northern Uganda,[38] where

[29]N. W. Thomas, *The Natives of Australia* (London: Archibald Constable, 1906); B. Spencer and F. J. Gillen, *The Northern Tribes of Central Australia* (London: Macmillan, 1904), 462-63; idem., *The Native Tribes of Central Australia* (London: Macmillan, 1899 reprinted 1938), 553; Adolphus Peter Elkin, *Australian Aborigines* (Sydney and London: Angus and Robertson, 1938), 203-5; M. J. Meggitt, *Desert People* (Chicago: University of Chicago Press, 1962), 139, 176.

[30]Elkin, *Australian Aborigines,* 203.

[31]Woodburn, "Minimal Politics," 258.

[32]Woodburn, "Egalitarian Societies," 258.

[33]Anne Chapman, *Drama and Power in a Hunting Society* (Cambridge: Cambridge University Press, 1984), 63.

[34]E. L. Bridges, *The Uttermost Parts of the Earth* (New York: Dutton, 1949), 213, 373.

[35]D. Stenning, *Savannah Nomads* (London: Oxford University Press, 1959) and "The Pastoral Fulani of Northern Nigeria," *Peoples of Africa,* ed. J. L. Gibbs (New York: Holt, Rinehart and Winston, 1965).

[36]I. M. Lewis, "Shaikhs and Warriors in Somaliland," *Peoples of Africa,* ed. J. L. Gibbs (New York: Holt, Rinehart and Winston, 1965).

[37]P. Gulliver and P. H. Gulliver, *The Central Nilo-Hamites* (London: International African Institute, 1953), 86.

[38]N. Dyson-Hudson, *Karimojong Politics* (Oxford: Clarendon Press, 1966), 40.

"in theory, witches are never found in one's own settlement but always in a different group from one's own."[39] The closely related Jie, their neighbors, have adopted a partially sedentary mode of existence. They diagnose witchcraft as the cause for a sequence of misfortunes, and their "normal procedure [then] is to move to a new homestead to avoid the evil influence."[40] Similarly, the nomadic pastoral Maasai of Kenya and Tanzania believe that one can learn the techniques of sorcery, but "they have no conventional category of supernatural 'witches'. . . and they often make fun of their Bantu neighbors who they know do possess such beliefs."[41] Their linguistically and ethnically similar sedentary neighbors, the Arusha (il Arusa), on the other hand, are very concerned about witchcraft.[42] The same holds true for the closely related agricultural Nandi and Kipsigis in Kenya,[43] and for the related Lango and Teso of Uganda.[44] The ethnically different, click-speaking Sandawe, not far away, who were probably formerly hunter-gatherers, now practice agriculture. Predictably, G. W. B. Huntingford says of them that "witchcraft is prevalent and illness and death are attributed either to it or to the anger of ancestral spirits."[45]

The ethnographic data show that in societies with total mobility and little attachment to property and with consequently little development of hierarchy and authority, there are no fears about witchcraft. Where there is considerable mobility but some attachment to property – often expressed by the presence of unilineal descent – we can expect to find a belief that witchcraft exists. The assumption is, however, that it is located in some other group and can easily be avoided by the move of a homestead. As dwellings are temporary huts in a thorn corral or something similar, this is not considered a particularly serious matter. When we turn to the sedentary peoples of the non-industrial world, however, we can expect always to find beliefs in witchcraft. The details of the beliefs may vary, but, as I have already mentioned, there is a remarkable consistency about some aspects of the beliefs.

[39]Gulliver & Gulliver, *Central Nilo-Hamites,* 49.

[40]P. Gulliver, *The Family Herds* (London: Routledge and Kegan Paul, 1955), 104.

[41]Alan Jacobs, Professor of Anthropology, Western Michigan University, personal communication, 1985.

[42]P. Gulliver, *Social Control in an African Society* (Boston: Boston University Press, 1963), 21.

[43]J. G. Peristiany, *The Social Institutions of the Kipsigis* (London: George Routledge, 1939), 94-95. Michael Langley, *The Nandi of Kenya* (New York: St. Martin's Press, 1979), 10, 62.

[44]J. H. Driberg, *The Lango* (London: T. Fisher Unwin, 1923) 241ff.; J. T. D. Lawrence, *The Iteso* (London: Oxford University Press, 1957), 182; and Gulliver & Gulliver, *Central Nilo-Hamites,* 26.

[45]G. W. B. Huntingford, *The Southern Nilo-Hamites* (London: International African Institute, 1953) 137-38.

At the same time, it is manifest that particular forms of social organization or socio-political situation can generate more or less acute fears of witchcraft. Siegfried Frederick Nadel shows convincingly that two peoples that are almost identical ethnically, linguistically, and culturally can demonstrate radically different attitudes to witchcraft.[46] One society was rife with fears and accusations; the other had none. The only difference between the two societies is that the former has three age grades; the latter six. To move into the next higher grade, men had to forego the privileges of the age group they were relinquishing. Where there are six grades this presents no problem; where there are only three, suspicions and accusations proliferate between the young men and those in the middle grade – who are understandably reluctant to assume the mantle of old age and to eschew sexual activity and other privileges. Comparably, J. C. Mitchell shows that even in the circumstances of a modern tobacco estate in Zimbabwe (then Rhodesia), relatively well-educated permanent staff members constantly suspected their colleagues of evil magic directed against them.[47] Uneducated casual laborers on the same estate who in their home areas might well have been anxious about witchcraft, were quite unconcerned during their temporary sojourn on the estate. The more highly educated workers were in constant contact with one another and were always in competition for the favors of the white management.

Let us turn now to Europe. That virtually everywhere people believed in witchcraft from time immemorial until the eighteenth century is well established.[48] Why, then, was there the enormous surge of accusations during the Renaissance period? And why did the craze draw to a close? As Thomas notes of the decline in belief and the acceptance of a more rational viewpoint, "the ultimate origins of this faith in unaided human capacity remain mysterious." Thomas accepts that "the decline of magic coincided with a marked improvement in the extent to which the environment became amenable to control."[49] Better food supplies and conditions of health, the cessation of plague,[50] better communications and banking services, insurance, better fire-fighting – all these factors undoubtedly contributed to a greater sense of security. While it is true that the human impulse to seek scapegoats remains with us in the twentieth century, we have, in the

[46]Siegfried Frederick Nadel, "Witchcraft in Four African Societies: An Essay in Comparison," *American Anthropologist* 54 (1952): 18-29.

[47]J. C. Mitchell, "The Meaning of Misfortune for Urban Africans," in *African Systems of Thought,* ed. M. Fortes and G. Dieterlen (London: Oxford University Press,1965), 196.

[48]H. R. Trevor-Roper, *The European Witch-Craze of the Sixteenth and Seventeenth Centuries, and Other Essays* (New York: Harper and Row, 1969), 91.

[49]Keith Thomas, *Religion and the Decline of Magic* (New York: Charles Scribner's Sons, 1971), 650, 663.

[50]H. C. Erik Midelfort, *Witch Hunting in Southwestern Germany* (Stanford: Stanford University Press, 1972), 194.

main, abandoned the idea of personal malice as a cause for misfortune. In contemporary small-scale societies this personal view of misfortune persists, as numerous anthropological studies show.

It is quite clear to anyone who has worked in countries where there is still a general belief in witchcraft that education alone, even at university level, does not destroy the belief. It is quite easy to graft a theory of witchcraft onto a scientific theory of causation such as the germ theory,[51] and thus to assume that even a microorganism can attack one person rather than another because some person used evil magic. Moreover, most rational scientific observers would admit that psychological factors are important in reducing immunity. The reality of psychosomatic afflictions, however, is rather different from imputing each misfortune to the malevolence of one's kin or neighbors. If we look at the history of Europe it is only too evident that education per se was not the major reason for the waning of the craze, indeed, as Joseph Klaits notes, "the educated were in the forefront of the witch hunts."[52] The rebirth of ideas after the medieval period should, one would think, have signalled the end of belief, yet Trevor-Roper observes, "There can be no doubt that the witch-craze grew, and grew terribly, after the Renaissance."[53]

The skeptics who had the courage to challenge the prevailing orthodoxy about witches did not dispute the existence of witchcraft. Not to believe in witches was often seen as tantamount to being an atheist, as Sir Thomas Browne pointed out.[54] What Weyer and Scot in the sixteenth century objected to was the injustice of accusing the wrong people. Bekker in the seventeenth century based his challenge on a fundamentalist piece of theology: if the devil on his fall from heaven was locked up in hell, how then could he be involved with witches here on earth.[55]

Precisely what caused the change from the relatively benign attitude toward witches in the Middle Ages to the hysterical attitude characteristic of the *Malleus Maleficarum*[56] is the subject of an ongoing debate. Cross-cultural study may contribute to our understanding of what caused the end of the witchcraze. One reason may be the only conceivable aspect that our social organization shares with that of the African hunter-gatherers: our mobility.

[51]D. A. Offiong, "Witchcraft among the Ibibio," *African Studies Review* 21 no. 1 (1985): 107-24.

[52]Joseph Klaits, *Servants of Satan* (Bloomington: Indiana University Press, 1985), 1-2.

[53]Trevor-Roper, *European Witch-Craze*, 91.

[54]Thomas Browne, *Religio Medici and Other Works*, ed. L. C. Martin, (Oxford: Clarendon Press, 1964), 29.

[55]Trevor-Roper, *European Witch-Craze*, 174.

[56]See Midelfort, *Witch Hunting in Southwestern Germany*, 193-94.

Humanity is by its nature a mass of contradictions. Impulses for conformity war with those for individualism. Tension develops and somehow has to be resolved. Where it is possible physically to remove oneself from those with whom one is in conflict, the tension disappears. Where this is not possible and where it is socially unacceptable to admit to tension arising from feelings of hate toward close kin, spouses, affines or neighbors, the human imagination seems to build up a whole edifice of fantasy about witches based on childish fears and imaginings. This holds especially true for societies where childrearing practices are harsh. While the details of beliefs may vary according to cultural prescription, the broad outlines are remarkably similar world-wide. They retain their fascination even in our skeptical, secular world, as Bruno Bettelheim has reminded us.[57]

It is Thomas's contention that the surge in witchcraft accusations in the late sixteenth and early seventeenth centuries was not generated by any fundamental change in folk beliefs, but by a change in the structure of society. He speaks of the "increasingly individualistic forms of behavior which accompanied the economic changes."[58] Cross-culturally one might draw a parallel with present-day Africa, where scholars have universally reported the widespread belief that the practice of evil magic has proliferated.[59] In Europe the change was from a feudal society with its well-understood certitudes about class and status; in Africa from a tribal form of social organization in which status was largely ascribed to the emerging societies, in which status can be achieved through education, wage employment, cash-cropping, entrepreneurial, political and religious activities; class divisions have begun to appear and become institutionalized.[60]

During the sixteenth and seventeenth centuries there was enormous social, political, economic, and religious ferment in Europe. This led initially to feelings of deep insecurity in all these arenas of human activity, exacerbated by the Copernican revolution; it also led to unrivaled opportunities for the acquisition of wealth, power, and social status. All this activity generated great divisions in society, as well as powerful emotions such as envy, jealousy, hostility, self-questioning, and guilt. This is entirely consistent with the large number of witchcraft accusations in the Tudor and early Stuart period. A similar phenomenon – though not on quite so lethal a scale – is taking place in Africa today. There appears to be evidence that increasing mobility played a role in bringing an end to European witchcraft beliefs and that it may do so again in Africa.

---

[57]Bruno Bettelheim, *The Uses of Enchantment* (New York: Random House) 1977.

[58]Thomas, *Religion and Decline of Magic,* 561.

[59]John Middleton and E. Winter, eds., *Witchcraft, Sorcery and Magic in East Africa* (London: Routledge and Kegan Paul, 1963), 25.

[60]Max Gluckman, *Politics Law and Ritual in Tribal Society* (Oxford: Blackwell, 1965), 143.

Christopher Hill calls the period 1603-1714 a "Century of Revolution." At the beginning of this period, "heretics were still burnt at the stake, just as suspected traitors were tortured."[61] Both Peter Laslett and Hill speak of the intense mobility of this period,[62] and it is interesting to note that the first mention of the Dick Whittington myth extolling ambition and mobility occurs in 1605,[63] although the Lord Mayor in question actually died almost two hundred years earlier.[64] However, "by 1714 Protestant dissent was legally tolerated, the Church could no longer burn, the state no longer torture."[65] Throughout Hill's century of revolution, intense commercial activity was taking place, activity that was doubtless fostered by the rule of primogeniture. On the one hand, this enhanced stability. On the other hand, it encouraged young men to seek their fortunes in the burgeoning cities and in the colonies overseas. With the coming of the Industrial Revolution and the period of European imperialism, the whole tempo of geographic and social mobility was accelerated. At least spatially, we have achieved – ironically, through the application of a highly complex technology – the same degree of mobility found among the technologically most primitive society – the hunter-gatherers of Africa. There are no doubt many other reasons why the witchcraze waned, but it seems reasonable to suggest that increased mobility – the ability to move away from those one abhors but cannot admit to abhorring – may have been a major contributing factor.

[61]Christopher Hill, *The Century of Revolution 1603-1714* (London: Sphere Books, 1969), 14.

[62] Christopher Hill, *The World Turned Upside Down* (New York: Viking, 1972), 32, 39, 47; Peter Laslett, *The World We Have Lost* (London: Methuen, 1965), 6-8, 154-56.

[63]Ann Jennalie Cook, *The Privileged Playgoers of Shakespeare's London 1576-1642* (Princeton: Princeton University Press, 1981), 36.

[64]Carolyn M. Barron, "Richard Whittington: The Man Behind the Myth," *Studies in London History*, ed. A. E. J. Hollaender and W. Kelloway, (London: Hodder and Stoughton, 1969), 197-248.

[65]Hill, *Century of Revolution,* 14.

Witch Riding Backwards on a Goat (ca. 1500), from *The Intaglio Prints of Albrecht Dürer: Engravings, Etchings & Drypoints,* ed. Walter L. Strauss (New York: Kennedy Galleries and Abaris Books, 1977). Reprinted by permission.

Martin Luther on Witchcraft:
A True Reformer?

Sigrid Brauner

HISTORIANS OF THE EUROPEAN WITCH HUNTS, from the pioneer Gottlieb
Soldan to the present day, have consistently misunderstood, misrepresented
or neglected Martin Luther's views on witchcraft. While Soldan thought
Luther overlooked the importance of the subject, modern historians contend
he was an uncritical believer and said nothing original.[1] This persistent
view is largely based on the analysis of Luther's texts on witchcraft by
Nikolaus Paulus in 1910.[2] Partisan Catholic in tone, the selection of quotations
from Luther's texts on witchcraft presents him in this study as an unoriginal,
credulous believer in witches and their persecution.

My rereading of the Luther texts compiled by Paulus questions this
traditional opinion. Instead, I have found that Luther does present a unique
view of witchcraft, which can only be understood in terms of his discussion
of marriage and the role of women as wives and mothers. For Luther, the
witch, in essence, is the opposite of the pious Christian wife. In what
follows, I will concentrate on Luther's explanation for why the majority
of witches were women. I have chosen this topic for two reasons: around
80 percent of those accused during the height of the witch persecutions
(from 1560 to 1700) were women, and in the theoretical writings on
witchcraft women are commonly described as the prototype of the witch.
My study is limited to the years between 1487 – when the first major
treatise on women and witchcraft appeared – and 1560, the beginning of
the massive witch hunts. Apart from early mass trials at the turn of the
century few witch trials were held during this time. The discussion about
witches, however, did not die down. The first comprehensive work on
what was thought to be a new phenomenon, namely, the sect of witches,
was the *Malleus Maleficarum,* written in 1487 by Heinrich Kramer and

---

[1]Soldan devotes just a few lines to the subject: "Um Luthers Verhältniss zu den Hexenpro-
zessen mit wenigen Worten auszusprechen, so stand er unmittelbar zu dem Gange derselben
in gar keiner Beziehung, mittelbar aber allerdings dadurch, dass er nicht noch weit durchgreifender
reformirte, als er wirklich gethan hat." *Geschichte der Hexenprozesse* (Stuttgart, 1880. 2 vols)
1: 432. H. C. Lea, as many others, portrays Luther as a credulous believer in witches: "His
credulity in the matter of magic knew no bounds; he believed and gravely recited the most
absurd stories of witches and sorcerers." *Materials Toward a History of Witchcraft* (London:
Yoseloff, 1957. 3 vols) 1: 422. H.C. Erik Midelfort, an authority on Early Modern German
witch theories, writes about Luther only in passing: "Luther for one certainly viewed unusual
phenomena as moral messages from God, but he refrained from altering his fairly commonplace
jumble of ideas on witchcraft." "Witchcraft and Religion in Sixteenth-Century Germany:
the Formation and Consequences of Orthodoxy," *Archiv für Reformationsgeschichte* 62 (1971):
270. E. William Monter argues similarly in *Witchcraft in France and Switzerland* (Ithaca: Cornell
University Press, 1976), 30.

[2]Nikolaus Paulus, *Hexenwahn und Hexenprozess* (Freiburg: Herder'sche Verlagsbuchhandlung,
1910), chap. 2: "Luthers Stellung zur Hexenfrage," 20-47.

Jacobus Sprenger, both Dominicans and Papal inquisitors for the German area. The book sums up the traditional theological arguments about witchcraft, but asserts for the first time that it is only women who become witches.[3] The title already indicates that this is the case, for "maleficarum" translates as "female evildoers." A longer section, Part I, Question 6, is devoted to why women rather than men become witches. Here the authors argue that because women are the weaker sex, possess little intelligence, exhibit no self-discipline, and have an animal-like, insatiable sexuality, they are more easily seduced by the Devil than men. The Devil makes women vain promises, often of a monetary nature, forces them into the Devil's pact, and uses them as tools for his malicious crimes: destroying crops, killing cattle, but, above all, causing impotence, infertility, miscarriages and abortions. Next to evil midwives, who procure abortions,[4] lustful women, including those who are married, are Satan's favorite targets, because he enjoys attacking the sacramental institution of marriage.[5] This is made easy for him, since marriage itself is tempting ground for women. Jealous by nature, they fear the competition of unmarried women and therefore might use love magic to ensure their husbands' loyalty. Marital sex, necessary for procreation, will tempt the chastest wife to give into female insatiable lust. The Devil, then, tries to seduce her into adultery by encouraging her sexual fantasies.

Witches, like all women obsessed with the wish to gain power, believe that they actually can practice magic, but this is a mere delusion, evoked again by the Devil. While consistently misogynistic, the authors present a contradictory view of women. On the one hand, they maintain that women, because of their inferior nature, cannot act independently. On the other hand, they credit women with giving into the Devil of their own free will. Women are therefore wholly responsible for their witchcraft, even though their powers are illusionary because they come from the Devil.

---

[3]As Nikolaus Paulus has pointed out, the identification of women with sorcery can be found in texts from the medieval period. There, women's affinity to the magic arts is usually seen as a result of their female nature. A vivid imagination together with spiritual and intellectual weakness make women especially vulnerable to the Devil's temptations. This argument was also taken up in Johann Nider's *Formicarius* (1435). However, Nider did not claim that the practitioners of witchcraft were exclusively women. See Heinrich Kramer, Jakob Sprenger, *Malleus Maleficarum* (Bruxelles: 1969; rept. Lyon 1669); English trans. Montague Summers, (New York: Dover, 1971; rept. 2d ed. London: Rodker, 1948); chap. abbreviations are the same for the Latin ed. and English trans. and refer to both. The *Malleus* is the first to claim that the new kind of witches, whom the authors call "maleficae modernae" [modern witches], are women rather than men (see Part I, Question 6, Question 14).

[4]Supposedly, midwives also kill newborns and offer them to the Devil. The *Malleus* discusses midwives' wickedness in Part I, Question 11.

[5]For the special vulnerability of the sacramental institution of marriage compare Part I, Question 3, Question 6. The Devil attacks marriage through lustful women. He encourages their sexual fantasies so that unmarried women lust for married men, while married women lust for men other than their husbands.

Their offense is their obedience to the Devil and consequent disobedience to God and to the state, a "crimen exceptum" to be punished by death.[6] The authors believe that almost every Christian woman is infected with this heresy; it passes from mother to daughter, but also spreads because every witch has to bring another woman to the Devil. Witches already have seduced many mighty princes and have toppled the world into the horrors of a female era, as described in some versions of the apocalypse.[7] The only remedy for this plague-like growth of witches is extermination.

The *Malleus* is a zealous book. At a time when the Church was confronted with growing religious and social dissent, Sprenger and Kramer present the woman witch as one of the responsible culprits and offer the persecution of witches as a solution to the crisis. Their argument for why women are witches grows out of an elitist, monastic world view with a strong misogynistic component, a world view that emphasizes the righteous spiritual life and debases all carnal existence.[8] Accordingly, the only women

---

[6]During the sixteenth and seventeenth centuries, witchcraft was defined by lawyers as a *crimen exceptum* (exceptional crime). "They meant quite simply that since it was not amenable to the normal principles of proof, normal standards of interrogation and court procedure would not meet the situation. It was necessary to use torture to extract a confession. It was necessary to admit the evidence of those not normally allowed to bear testimony in courts of law; women, children, interested parties and convicted felons." See Christina Larner, "Crimen Exceptum? The Crime of Witchcraft in Europe," in *Crime and the Law*, ed. V.A.C. Gatrell, Bruce Lenman, and Geoffrey Parker, (London: Europe Publications, 1981), 57. The *Malleus* does not use the term *crimen exceptum* but compares witchcraft to another exceptional crime, to the crime of "lese majesty," which also allows anyone to testify and which is punished with death (Part I, Question I). Witchcraft was seen as a crime against the state because of the physical damages it supposedly causes.

[7]"Optimates, praelati & alij diuites saepissime his miseriis inuoluuntur. Et quidem hoc tempus muliebre, de quo Hildegardus (vt Vincen. in spec. histor. refert) praedixit, quod non tandiu durabit, quantum hucvsque perstitit: cum iam mundus plenus sit adulterij, praecipue in optimatibus. Et quid opus scribere de remidiis, qui remedia abhorrent?" (*Malleus*, Lyon, 185). "And when it is found that those of noblest birth, Governors and other rich men, are the most miserably involved in this sin (for this age is dominated by women, and was foretold by S. Hildegard, as Vincent of Beauvais records in the Mirror of History, although he said it would not endure for as long as it already has); and when the world is now full of adultery, especially among the most highly born; when all this is considered, I say, of what use is it to speak of remedies to those who desire no remedy?" (*Malleus*, Summers, 171). Kramer and Sprenger refer to Hildegard of Bingen's (1098-1179) various visions about the end of the world. They were collected in 1220 by Gebeno of Eberbach in *Speculum Futurorum Temporum sive Pentachronon*, were widely distributed and influenced the medieval understanding of the end of the world. Contrary to Sprenger and Kramer, who blame women's carnality for the decadence of the "female era," Hildegard called it "tempus muliebris debilitatis" (era of female weakness) because she saw it as a time when everyone is as vulnerable to sin as women are. She blamed the worldly lifestyle of clerics and princes for it. See Hildegard von Bingen, *Wisse die Wege - Scivias,* trans. Maura Böckeler (Salzburg: Müller, 1954), 330-31.

[8]An excellent analysis of the misogynistic and androcentric view of monasticism, especially from the thirteenth century on, is Eleanor Commo McLaughlin's study "Equality of Souls, Inequality of Sexes: Woman in Medieval Theology," Rosemary Radford Ruether, ed. *Religion and Sexism* (New York, 1974), 213-66. The Dominican order, to which Kramer and Sprenger belonged, has been especially active in producing slanderous texts about women, such as the

the Devil cannot change into witches are nuns and virgins; and the only men not affected by witchcraft are clerics. Not surprisingly, the authors maintain in Part III, Question 9, that next to women, members of the lower classes are the most likely suspects of witchcraft because they associate with criminal elements.[9]

Contrary to the hope of the authors, the *Malleus* did not contribute to an increase of persecutions. The two inquisitors had a hard time starting trials; the resistance by peasants, by clerical and city authorities alike was too strong at that time.[10] But the *Malleus* had success as a book: 13 editions were published before 1520, 16 more between 1574 and 1669. The first edition included a copy of the 1484 bull of Pope Innocence VIII and the 1486 edict of the Holy Roman Emperor Maximilian I – both written in support of Kramer's and Sprenger's witch hunting activities – as well as the approbation of the famous University of Cologne, all of which gave the work an air of highest authority.[11]

Although the authors tried to present the *Malleus* as the official Catholic pronouncement on witchcraft, it neither stood for that nor was it representative of the learned opinions on the topic in the late fifteenth and early sixteenth centuries. Other writers on witchcraft differed on specific details of witch beliefs and practices, or on the remedies for witchcraft, and few if any writers subscribed to the *Malleus'* extreme emphasis on the sexual aspects

---

anti-woman alphabet in the *Summa Theologia* (1477) of the Dominican Antonin of Florence. The twenty four letters of the alphabet constantly describe four main characteristics of women: carnality, wrath, vanity and avarice. Kramer and Sprenger made extensive use of this text in the *Malleus*. See Hjalmar Crohns, "Die Summa Theologica des Antonin von Florenz und die Schätzung des Weibes im Hexenhammer," *Acta Societatis Scientiarum Fennicae* 32, 4 (1906): 1-23.

[9]See *Malleus* Part III, Question 9. Generally, the Devil also prefers to seduce poor women in order to show his contempt for God, i.e. mocking him by getting witches at the cheapest price (Part I, Question 18).

[10]The *Malleus* was partly written in reaction to Kramer's defeat during inquisitorial proceedings in Innsbruck in 1485. The clerical authority for this city, Georg Golser, Bishop of Brixen, banned Kramer from the city after his attempt to try a large number of women had caused an angry and rebellious mood in the town. Neither city officials nor the community believed that witches – as Kramer described them – lived in their midst. See Wolfgang Ziegeler, *Möglichkeiten der Kritik am Hexen- und Zauberwesen im ausgehenden Mittelalter* (Köln: Böhlau, 1973), 82-111. After the publication of the *Malleus* not one successful witch trial conducted by Kramer and Sprenger is documented although both remained papal inquisitors for the German countries. See Joseph Hansen, *Quellen und Untersuchungen zur Geschichte des Hexenwahns* (Hildesheim: Olms, 1963. rpt. Bonn 1901), 393, 506-10, and *Zauberwahn, Inquisition und Hexenprozess* (Aalen: Scientia; 1964. rpt. München 1900), 504, and Richard Kieckhefer, *European Witchtrials. Their Foundations in Popular and Learned Culture, 1300-1500* (Berkeley: University of California Press, 1976), 146.

[11]The approbation of the University of Cologne was – at least partially – a forgery, probably by Kramer. See Joseph Hansen, "Der *Malleus Maleficarum*, seine Druckausgaben und die gefälschte Kölner Approbation vom Jahre 1487," *Westdeutsche Zeitschrift für Geschichte und Kunst* 18 (1898): 119-68.

of witchcraft.[12] But all writers shared the *Malleus'* basic assumption that witchcraft is gender specific and all explained this observation with – albeit brief – references to women's generally inferior nature. Women are seen as the weaker sex and therefore more easily seduced into witchcraft by the Devil.

At first glance, Protestant writers did not develop a discernably new argument on the issue of witchcraft, that is until Martin Luther.[13] He was the first to undertake a longer and partially new explanation of the gender specificity of witchcraft in the sermons that he delivered after his return to Wittenberg from exile in 1522.

In the second group of these sermons, printed in a vernacular edition in 1523, he comments on the first Epistle of Peter. In reference to I Peter 3:1-7, Luther puts forward his ideas on the organization of the Christian family and on the ideal conduct of woman. Since God's law prescribes the submission of woman to man, the wife must be subject to the husband. The woman is not only physically weaker than the man, but also lacks the necessary reason to deal with the adversities of life.[14] The husband therefore must make up for this lack; he has both to think for and educate his wife as if she were a child. Marriage is woman's God-given place, and there she has to fulfill her mission, which is the production of offspring. In addition, wives "should deport themselves in such a way in the matter of gestures

---

[12]Writers such as the nominalist theologian Martin Plantsch (*Opusculum de sagis maleficis* 1505), the abbot and court magician Johann Trithemius (*Antipalus Maleficorum* 1508), the satirist Thomas Murner, (*Tractatus de phitonico contractu* 1499), the court lawyer Ulrich Molitor (*De Laniis et Phytonicis Mulieribus* 1489), the learned magician Agrippa of Nettesheim (*Occulta Philosophia* 1510), to name but a few, had opinions different from the *Malleus* on a number of issues. These included whether witches could really fly, work magic or do harm; whether one should allow witches to repent and live, or whether witchcraft was a dangerous heresy to be uprooted with the sword. For the nominalist critique of the *Malleus'* position by Martin Plantsch, see Heiko Oberman, *Werden und Wertung der Reformation* (Tübingen: Mohr, 1977), 201-37.

[13]That Protestant writers did not develop a specific view of witchcraft in the first part of the sixteenth century has been convincingly documented by H.C. Erik Midelfort in *Witch Hunting in Southwestern Germany, 1562-1684* (Stanford: Stanford University Press, 1972), 64-66. However, as mentioned before, he discarded Luther's ideas as unimportant.

[14]In the same passage Luther advises husbands: "Drumb sihe du drauff, das du eyn man seyest, und deste mehr vernunfft habst, wo sie ym weyb zu wenig ist," D. Martin Luthers Werke. Kritische Gesamtausgabe (Weimar: Böhlau, 1883-) 12:346 (hereafter cited WA) ("Therefore see to it that you are a man and that you have more reason where there is too little in the woman." *Luther's Works* (St. Louis: Concordia Publishing House, 1955-) translates "vernunfft" incorrectly with "thoughtful." I replaced it with the correct "reason." AE 30: 92.). This corresponds to Luther's understanding of Eve – the archetype of all women – as a foolish person, i.e. one who lacks reason and therefore gave in to the Devil. See *Predigten über das erste Buch Mose*, gehalten 1523/24 (WA 14: 131-39) and *In Genesin Mosi librum sanctissimum Declamationes* 1527 (WA 24: 85-91).

English quotations from Luther without AE citations are my translations from the Latin or German. The original text is always given in the note.

and conduct that they entice their husbands to believe."[15] Woman has the power to entice men to righteous behavior by her own pious example: through submissiveness, humility, and the inner beauty of the soul. This moral and spiritual power of the married woman is not only based on her spiritual equality as affirmed by Saint Paul in Galatians, but on Luther's new understanding of the state of matrimony as the primary institution for leading a religious life and one that is superior to the monastic life.

In this sermon, Luther outlines the role of woman in the Christian state of matrimony. Surprisingly, he develops the idea that woman's true spiritual place is marriage in an unusual context; that is, he concludes the section on the Christian woman with an account of female witchcraft. He comments on I Peter, 3:6: "As Sara obeyed Abraham and called him Lord whose daughters you are as long as you do well and not give in to shyness"[16] in the following manner:

> what does he mean by this? This is what he means: It is commonly the nature of women to be timid and to be afraid of everything. This is why they busy themselves so much with witchcraft and superstitions and run hither and thither, uttering a magic formula here and a magic formula there. . . . Whatever happens to her, she should let God rule, and she should remember that she cannot fare badly. For since she knows that her position in life is pleasing to God, why should she fear?[17]

In this passage, Luther comes up with an interesting explanation for the origin of female witchcraft. Women are by nature fearful and practice witchcraft to assuage their fears. But this practice is futile and binds women only more to their fearful nature. They can become free of fear only if they accept their weakness and become obedient, God-trusting wives. The argument of Sprenger and Kramer that an inborn insatiable female lust

[15]AE 30:88. The American Edition incorrectly translates "reytzen" with "induce." I have replaced it with the more appropriate "entice." " . . . so sollen sie sich . . . also halten mit yhrem geperd und wandel, das sie damit die menner zum glawben reytzen . . . " WA 12: 342.

[16]"wie die Sara Abraham gehorsam war/und hies in/Herr/Welcher toechter jr worden seid/so jr wol thut/ und nicht so^b^schuchter seid." (^b^[schuchter] Weiber sind natuerlich schuchter/und erschrecken leicht/Sie sollen aber feste sein/un ob sich ein leiden erhuebe/nicht so weibisch erschrecken.) Martin Luther, *Biblia / das ist / die gantze heilige Schrifft Deudsch* (Leipzig: Reclam, 1983; reprint of Wittenberg 1534) 2 vols. (hereafter cited *Biblia*) 2: CLXI.

[17]AE 30: 91; I have made some changes in the last two sentences given in the American Luther edition for a more appropriate translation. "Was meynet er damit? Das meynet er: Gemeyntlich ist das der weyber natur, das sie sich fur allem ding schewen und furchten, darumb sie so viel zewberey und aberglawbens treyben, da eyne die ander leret, das nicht zu zelen ist, was sie fur gauckelwerck haben. Das soll aber eyn Christlich weyb nicht thun, sondern soll frey sicher daher gehen, nicht also schewslig seyn, und hyn und her lauffen, hie ein segen, dort eyn segen sprechen, wie es yhr begegnet, das sie es lasse Gott walden, und dencke, es kunde yhr nicht ubel gehen. Denn die weyl sie weys, wie es umb sie stehet, das yhr stand Gott gefelt, was will sie denn furchten?" WA 12: 345.

seduces women to witchcraft and makes all women into potential witches is strikingly absent here. In fact, unlike the authors of the *Malleus*, Luther was not very interested in the sexual aspect of witchcraft, and he barely mentions the subject. For Luther sexuality is part of the God-given nature of humans and serves to establish the most important earthly order, the family. Therefore, sexuality in general and even female sexuality in particular cannot be the origin of witchcraft. The redefinition of the function of sexuality also led Luther to a reinterpretation of Genesis 6:2: "The sons of God saw that daughters of men were fair; and they took to wives such of them as they chose."[18] Within orthodox demonology, and especially in the *Malleus* (Part I, Question 3), this verse and the following passages had been used to support the theory that female sexuality is in itself a dangerous force, and that the Devil has sexual contact with witches. This theory was based on interpreting the "sons of God" as fallen angels who were seduced by the beauty of earthly women. Their offspring supposedly were giants, and this sexual union caused the great flood.

Luther rejects the traditional interpretation that the "sons of God" are fallen angels in his sermons of 1527 on Genesis 6:1-4. There he translates "sons of God" with a more general term, namely "kinder Gottes," God's children.[19] He argues that they cannot be fallen angels; they are merely God's children in the sense that we all are, and therefore the sexual contact between God's children and women could not have produced giants:

> Such lack of understanding lead some to dream that this [God's children] means the angels, who are really God's children, as if they had gone to the daughters of men and slept with them and from that the giants were born. But this is foolish.[20]

According to Luther the passage shows that "God's children" had fallen from the path of righteousness, as is evident from their purely lustful selection of women, and that this spiritual degeneration kindled God's wrath and caused the great flood. Thus the cause of the "second fall" was not the alluring power of female sexuality leading to a sexual union

---

[18]Holy Bible, Revised Standard Version, Catholic Edition. The New English Bible and the King James Version also use "sons of God." Luther translates in accordance with his interpretation of the passage: "Da sahen die kinder Gottes nach den toechtern der menschen/wie sie schon waren/ und namen zu weibern welche sie wolten." *Biblia* 1:4.

[19]In Genesin Mosi librum sanctissimum Declamationes: *Über das erste Buch Mose, Predigten sampt einer unterricht, wie Moses zu lehren ist* of 1527, Luther translates Genesis 6:2 as "Da sahen die kinder Gottes nach den toechtern der menschen wie sie schoen waren, und namen zu weibern wilche sie nur wollten." WA 24: 160.

[20]"Aus solchem unverstand trewmen etliche, das die Engel dadurch gemeynet werden, wilche rechte Gottes kinder sind, als seyen sie zu menschen toechtern gangen und sie beschlaffen, daraus denn grosse Rysen odder Giganten sollen geporn sein. Es ist aber narren teyding" WA 24: 162.

between women and demons, but it was the foolish and purely lustful conduct of men who used women. It is this male behavior that Luther objects to.[21] Luther's interpretation of this passage is different from that of the *Malleus* on several levels: he rejects it as a proof for the sexual contact between demons and women, and for the notion of the evil powers of female sexuality. Thus Luther eliminates the very elements that were important for the *Malleus'* definition of female witchcraft.

While his reinterpretation of this passage from Genesis suggests that Luther did not see sexuality *per se* as the cause of morally aberrant behavior, he clearly states in his second lectures on Galatians (1535) that witchcraft itself is not a sin of the flesh. He even corrects Paul's view on the matter: "Among the works of the flesh Paul numbers sorcery, which, as everyone knows, is not a work caused by the desires of the flesh but is an abuse or imitation of idolatry."[22] Therefore, when Luther mentions Eve's fall as one of the explanations for the female practice of witchcraft, one must understand that these comments refer to female foolishness and mental weakness alone, and not to the supposed weakness of the female flesh which was implicit in the orthodox view of witchcraft.[23] When Luther ignores the sexual origin of female witchcraft and stresses innate female fear instead, he does not present an entirely new idea. Female fear born of mental and physical weakness was also one of the explanations for witchcraft put forth in the *Malleus*, but there it was coupled with woman's passion for blind rage and revenge, an aspect of the female character that Luther does not allude to in this context. He instead links fear to foolishness alone, and eliminates women's supposed wish to gain power. The basis for female witchcraft is therefore, according to Luther, mere weakness without a will.

Uncontrollable female passion, mentioned in the *Malleus* as another source of female witchcraft, is also mentioned by Luther, but he understands female passion in a completely different way than the authors of the *Malleus*. It is simply a sort of motherly "loving too much," as he explains in another definition of female witchcraft from his early commentary on the Decalog of 1518:

---

[21]Luther stuck to this explanation – the moral offense of men – in all his commentaries on Genesis 6:2, from his earliest sermons in 1523 to his late lectures on Genesis from 1535-45. See the Latin edition of his earliest sermons on Genesis, *Predigten über das erste Buch Mose* . . . WA 14:184, and his late lectures, *Vorlesungen über I Mose von 1535-45*, WA 42:264.

[22]AE 27:90. "Paulus inter opera carnis enumerat veneficium, quod tamen, ut omnibus constat, non est opus libidinis, sed abusus seu aemulatio idolatriae " WA 40, 1:113.

[23]Luther attributes female witchcraft to women's inheritance of Eve's foolishness in his 1518 commentary on the Decalogue: "Ex prima Heva eis ingenitum est falli et ludibrio haberi" (Since Eve, it is innate for them to be deceived and to be characterized by foolishness), *Decem Praecepta Wittenbergensi praedicata populo*, WA 1:407. And again in 1526 in his sermons on Exodus: "De maga . . . Quare lex plus feminas quam viros hic nominat, quamquam etiam viri in hoc delinquunt? Ut Eva." (On the witches . . . . Why does this law stress women more than men, although men also commit this crime? Because of Eve.), *Predigten über das 2. Buch Mose*. 1524-1527, WA 16:551.

The second age is adulthood and includes those who are already married. During this stage the little wives are easily seduced to sorcery because of their excessive love for their children and their dependence on earthly satisfaction.[24]

Women therefore resort to magical rites; they conjure and they even go so far as to consult witches to cure their children. There is, however, no excuse in Luther's view for these female practices, not even motherly love:

> Here I wish the children possessed reason and could speak so they could punish their mothers for their great foolishness. . . . But they say, "how can we not feel pity for our little children and the fruit of our wombs?" I respond: "Yes, one shall have pity for them, but one shall not overdo it and become a servant of the Devil for it. Both seek natural remedies and pray to God in simple faith and full of creed."[25]

Luther refers to the dangers of "loving too much" also in his commentary on I Peter 3:1-7, where he advises women to overcome their inborn fear and not to give in to witchcraft, but rather to trust the well-being of their children to God: "if your child dies, if you become ill, be of good cheer; commit it to God. You are in a God-pleasing vocation. What better lot can you desire?"[26]

Luther's remedy for the female vulnerability to witchcraft is both simple and original and a logical corollary of his views on marriage: women should accept their God-given place as housewives and use their inherent moral power. Women are still seen in terms of their supposed biological and psychological defectiveness, but their weakness is accounted and compensated for within God's plan. In a way Luther's ideal Christian woman is a nun turned housewife. She is supposed to exercise a form of self-control as severe as any required by monastic discipline. She must be a mother, but she is not allowed to love too much. She can overcome the fear that breeds witchcraft, but only at the high cost of self-denial: she must accept herself as an inferior creature and give over her will to husband and God. While this ideal is as lonely and as hard to attain as that of the Virgin Mary, Luther makes even more demands on women by emphasizing that

---

[24]"Secunda est iuventus et eorum qui coniugio iam sunt astricti, ubi affectus prolis et rerum mulierculas mire seductiles reddit in hoc opere diaboli." *Decem Praecepta*. . . , WA 1:402.

[25]"Hic ego vellem pueros intelligere et loqui, ut matres suas tam insignis stultitiae arguerent. . . . Dicunt autem 'Quis non misereatur infanti et filio utri suo'? Respondeo: Miserendum, sed non usque ad servitutem diaboli: vel naturalem quaere medicinam, vel deum exora in simplici fide." *Decem Praecepta* . . . , WA 1:402.

[26]AE 30:91. "Styrbt dyr deyn kind, wirstu kranck, wol dyr, befihls Gott, du bist ynn dem stand der Gott gefelt, was kanstu bessers begeren?" WA 12:345.

the choice between being a good Christian woman or a prey to the Devil is entirely up to the woman herself:

> But if she does not let herself be enticed by this [her place as housewife], she will not be helped in any other way. For you will accomplish nothing with blows; they will not make a woman pious and submissive. If you beat one Devil out of her, you will beat two into her.[27]

For Luther, the bad woman is not bad because of her nature; she becomes bad because of her misuse of her own free will and her refusal to become a good housewife. The bad woman who turns into a witch therefore is the woman who refuses her prescribed social and religious role and negates the divine and secular order. Thus Luther juxtaposes the deviant behavior of the witch to the ideal behavior of the housewife, and not to that of a virginal nun as Sprenger and Kramer did in the *Malleus*. Luther's explanation for the female practice of witchcraft is therefore based on his new ideas on the theological function of the family. This is Luther's new and unique contribution to the definition of the witch.[28]

Furthermore, Luther was probably the first to introduce the issue of female witchcraft into the sixteenth-century discourse on women's nature and women's roles. According to Ian MacLean's study, *The Renaissance Notion of Woman*, the discussion of female sorcery was curiously absent in treatises on women and was reserved for technical treatises on witchcraft.[29] He points out that Lutherans usually interpreted I Peter 3 as a proof of women's dependence on men, but he was not aware of the 1523 sermon on this passage by Luther, who used it to discuss women's marital role and female witchcraft. MacLean's observation is therefore not true for writings in the German area from 1523 on.

Luther might have been the first, but he was not the only one to discuss the female witch in the context of women's roles within the family, or to use the witch as a negative role model for women, as he did in the sermon

---

[27]AE 30: 88. Again, AE incorrectly translates "reytzen" with "induce." I replaced this verb with the more appropriate "entice." "Wilche sich aber das nicht lesst reytzen, da wirt sonst nichts helffen. Denn mit schlagen wirstu nichts ausrichten, das du eyn weyb frum und bendig machst, Sclechstu eyn teuffel herauss, so schlechstu yhr zween hyneyn." WA 12: 342-43.

[28]In other respects, Luther's general opinion on witchcraft, expressed in bits and pieces in some twenty different sermons, letters, his Bible translation and the *Table Talks,* can largely be identified as belonging to what Midelfort, *Witch Hunting in Southwestern Germany,* 64, has called the "Episcopi tradition." Protestants as well as orthodox writers subscribed to this tradition. They considered witchcraft a form of idolatry, viewed the effects attributed to witchcraft as providential and the result of divine punishment, and counseled the afflicted to seek remedy in prayer and pious living. Luther's adds to this the family angle.

[29]Ian Maclean, *The Renaissance Notion of Woman* (Cambridge: Cambridge University Press, 1980), 88.

analyzed above. Two other Protestant German writers, both strongly influenced by Luther's theology, used the witch similarly in didactical plays on marriage written after 1523. The shoemaker-poet Hans Sachs was the first to write a play in which the main characters were a witch, a housewife, and the Devil, in *Der Teufel mit dem alten Weib* (*The Devil and the Hag*) in 1524. Here, a perfectly content marriage is torn apart by the machinations of the Devil and his helper, an old, greedy witch. With lies and other tricks she seduces a pious wife into disobedience towards her husband: she becomes an enraged shrew and beats her husband. In many other poems and farces, Sachs equates "das böse wib" (the unruly wife) – a standard figure in farces and tales since the Middle Ages – with the witch.[30] In his play, *Die Hochzeit zu Cana* (*The Marriage of Cana*) of 1546, the pastor and playwright Paul Rebhuhn similarly juxtaposes a shrewish witch, plus a figure he calls "Eheteufel" (Marriage Devil), against an ideal housewife.

Although both authors were Lutherans, it is unknown whether they were familiar with Luther's definition of female witchcraft as it appeared in the 1523 sermon. It seems that both authors conceived of their witch figures independently of each other and of Luther's definition of witchcraft, by following Luther's theology of marriage and using traditional farces that center on gender roles in marriage. Both plays are didactic in intent and follow the traditional medieval formula of teaching by negative example. From the *Malleus* on, the witch became the embodiment of female evil and therefore the logical counterpart to the ideal woman. Accordingly, both writers use the combination of Devil and witch as a dramatic and didactic tool: Devil and witch create a crisis in the everyday life of a pious marriage. The playwrights then demonstrate how this crisis can be resolved by acting according to moral reason and social convention. The figure of the witch, an old, destitute hag, who gives in to the Devil for a pair of shoes, is clearly used as a deterrent: it teaches women, and especially young wives, what can happen to them unless they cultivate their talents as good housewives and are willing to obey and learn from their husbands and to realize their true potential in becoming excellent household managers.

As in Luther's sermon, these plays emphasize the education of women as wives as the most effective means to combat witchcraft. They clearly show a change in the description of the witch. The *Malleus*, the only earlier treatise that discussed the issue of female witchcraft more fully, contended that the institution of matrimony itself led women to become witches, and that only the woman who chose a religious life was saved from witchcraft. Such arguments were obviously unattractive to Protestants who were interested in promoting and defending the married state.

[30]I discuss Sachs's plays in depth in "Hexenjagd in Gelehrtenköpfen", *Women in German Yearbook* 4 (Boston: University Press of America, 1987), 187-215.

Renaissance Humanists and scientists drew a similar connection between bad wives and witches. In Erasmus's colloquy *Marriage* of 1523, the ideal housewife, Eulalia, advises the typical shrew, Xanthippe: "You don't need sorcery or charms. No charm is more effective than good behavior joined with good humor".[31] The physician Paracelsus discusses witches in such a way as to equate them with bad wives. In his fragmentary essay *De Sagis et earum operibus* (*Of Witches and Their Works*) of 1537, he analyzes the genesis of witches; they are born during mismatched marriages of the heavens, i.e. under bad astrological signs. Paracelsus believed that the only way to deal with such witches was to reeducate them during childhood. If left alone, they would inevitably develop a certain pathology which he describes as follows: (1) they hide from men; (2) they want to be alone; (3) they associate with artists; (4) they visit sorceresses and follow the Devil's teachings; (5) they don't look at men; (6) they do not cook; (7) they do not wash themselves; (8) they love to be lazy.[32] When one reads this list in the reverse, one discerns the qualities attributed to Christian housewives: (1) they seek men; (2) they are fearful alone; (3) they never associate with artists, nor with sorceresses; (4) they never follow the Devil's teachings; (5) they look to men; (6) they cook; (7) they wash; (8) they love to be busy.

During the first half of the sixteenth century the concept of the witch was introduced into the discourse about the ideal behavior of married women. Luther was one of the first authors to do this. In his 1523 sermon, he juxtaposed the witch to the ideal wife within the context of his theology of marriage. In the following years, other Protestant and Humanist writers, who had ideas similar to Luther's, and who began to see the family as the foremost social and religious institution, defined the witch as the unruly wife. Protestants and Humanists rejected the argument put forth in the *Malleus* that women are witches because of their sexual nature; nevertheless they created a far more threatening image of the witch. Because obedience within the family is seen by Protestant authors as the basis for social and

[31]*The Colloquies of Erasmus*, trans. Craig R. Thompson (Chicago: University of Chicago Press, 1965), 124. "Nihil opus venificiis aut incantamentis. Nullum incantamentum efficacius, quam morum probitas cum suavitate conjuncta" Desiderii Erasmi Roterodami. *Opera Omnia.* 10 vols. (Hildesheim: Olms, 1961; rpt. Leiden, 1703). 1:706.

[32]This is an abbreviated list. Paracelsus also mentions that witches can be recognized by their obsessive piety, by their facing backwards during certain rituals of the mass in order not to be affected by their imagined power, and by physical disfigurations, which they transfer to their children: "1. mann fliehen,/2. feirtag eben observirem,/3. zeichnet an inen selbs./4. zeichnete kinder,/5. ceremonien gebrauchen,/6.verbergen, allein sein, mann nicht fahen,/7. knstlern nachfragen,/8. an sich hengen zeuberin und lernen, darzu sie der geist treibt,/9. kein mann ansehen,/10. selten kochen, haar, stirn nicht waschen, das fleisch,/11. hinder sich in kirchen umbkehren,/12.wol liegen, allein sich versperren. das sind die hauptzeichen, die die hexen an inen haben, so sie der geist ascendens berwunden hat und wil sie zu meistern machen." Theophrast von Hohenheim, genannt Paracelsus, *Sämtliche Werke*, ed. Karl Sudhoff, 14. vols. (Berlin, 1922-1933), 14:12-13.

spiritual life, the unruly wife opposes not only the God-given order within the family but threatens the very foundation of order in state and church. The *Malleus'* authors also had portrayed witches as attacking marriage, but according to Kramer's and Sprenger's world view this meant that witches attacked an inferior social institution; they could not attack members of the more important monastic orders.

Furthermore, the Protestant and Humanist redefinition of the witch was revolutionary in that it steered away from attacking magical practices and instead criticized female behavior. The choice women made of whether or not to become a witch receives more emphasis than it did in the *Malleus*. There witches are women who fall prey to their own sexual nature; but a life-long vow of virginity as a nun could save a woman from witchcraft. In Protestant thought, women must fight the Devil every day through the exercise of their own free will. The power of free will in women, however, remains as ambiguous as in orthodox Catholic thought. While women, like men, possess free will, they possess less reason; they are therefore more liable to sin than men. From this emerges a dangerous double image of woman, namely that the pious housewife, who behaves submissively, might only be disguising her true nature as a passionate witch. And, furthermore, the witch, now defined as the unruly wife, becomes a potential member of every Christian family.

The new definition of the witch invaded private households, at least those of educated city burghers and artisans. Unlike the theological treatises on witchcraft written in Latin, such as the *Malleus*, the texts mentioned above (with the omission of Paracelsus's) were printed in the vernacular and were intended for a lay audience. These didactic texts served to establish new moral values and boundaries, especially for the daughters and wives of city burghers and artisans. Like Luther's sermon on Peter, they were intended to inspire men and women with pride in their roles as husbands and wives. But they also demonized unruly female behavior by equating it with that of the witch. We must look at this demonization of unruly female behavior in order to understand the impact of the "reformed" concept of the witch on the mass persecutions that started some decades later. We know that the majority of the accused women in the mass trials of the late sixteenth and seventeenth century were poor, single or widowed women.[33] Why such women were singled out has been commonly explained in terms of their deprived economic status, which left them vulnerable as scapegoats for community tensions.[34] My findings on the new conception of the witch in the writings of Luther and other Protestants and Humanists

[33]See Brian P. Levack, *The Witch-Hunt in Early Modern Europe* (London: Longman, 1987), 131-34.

[34]See Keith V. Thomas, *Religion and the Decline of Magic* (London: Weidenfeld, 1970), 546-68.

confirms speculations that changes in family values made those women additionally vulnerable to suspicions of witchcraft because, as unmarried women, they were masterless, i.e. potentially unruly.[35]

The period, during which Humanists and Protestants created the image of the witch as an unruly wife has usually been seen as one of respite, when few persecutions took place and when the question of the existence of witches was still open to debate.[36] However, if we want to understand how this seemingly dormant period is related to the persecutions at the end of the century, it is important to consider the ways in which the concept of the witch was used to demonize deviant female behavior. It will remain a task for future research to find out whether or not and in what way the reformed concept of the witch influenced witch persecutions after 1560.

[35]See Midelfort, *Witch Hunting in Southwestern Germany,* 164-93.

[36]Sachs and Erasmus, for example, are usually cited as authors who had liberal views regarding witches. Cf. Hansen, *Zauberwahn,* 515-16.

Witchcraft and Domestic Tragedy in
The Witch of Edmonton

Viviana Comensoli

*T*HE WITCH OF EDMONTON (1621) DRAMATIZES the historical execution of
Elizabeth Sawyer for witchcraft on April 19, 1621. The play's immediate
source is *The Wonderfull Discouerie of Elizabeth Savvyer a witch,* a pamphlet
written by Henry Goodcole, chaplain of Newgate prison, and entered in
the Stationers' Register on April 27 of the same year. The pamphlet records
Goodcole's "interviews" with Elizabeth Sawyer shortly before her execution.
Goodcole's question-and-answer scheme is essentially a tract against the
dangers traditionally associated with witchcraft. Elizabeth's answers form
a conventional catalogue of descriptions about the causes and effects of
demonology, revealing little about the personality of the woman or the
social roots of witchcraft. In the account of Elizabeth's covenant with the
Devil, for example, Elizabeth's replies, like Goodcole's questions, are mechanical
and predictable, their sole function being to underscore her guilt:

> *Question.* What sayd you to the Diuell, when hee came vnto you
> and spake vnto you, were you not afraide of him? if you did feare
> him, what sayd the Diuell then vnto you? *Answere.* I was in a very
> greate feare, when I saw the Diuell, but hee did bid me not to
> feare him at all, for hee would do me no hurt at all, but would
> do for mee whatsoeuer I should require of him . . . .[1]

Dekker, Ford, and Rowley, on the other hand, initially portray Mother
Sawyer as knowing nothing about witchcraft. Unlike Goodcole's compliant
prisoner, she forcefully insists on her innocence. In addition, she is endowed
with a powerful eloquence that deflects the accusations of her enemies.
During her first appearance on stage, Mother Sawyer's soliloquy reveals a
bold and agile mind:

> And why on me? why should the envious world
> Throw all their scandalous malice upon me?
> 'Cause I am poor, deform'd and ignorant,
> And like a Bow buckl'd and bent together,
> By some more strong in mischiefs then my self?
> Must I for that be made a common sink,

---

[1]*The Wonderful Discouerie of Elizabeth Savvyer a witch,* C1v-C2; quoted in Cyrus Hoy,
Introductions, Notes, and Commentaries to Texts in "The Dramatic Works of Thomas Dekker" Edited
by Fredson Bowers, 4 vols. (Cambridge: Cambridge University Press, 1980), 3: 248-49.

> For all the filth and rubbish of Men's tongues
> To fall and run into?
>
> (II.i.1-8)[2]

In breaking with theatrical decorum by having a poor, uneducated female describe with considerable rhetorical acumen her status as a social outcast, the dramatists elevate and dignify the character, enhancing the audience's sympathy for her.

Unlike the other domestic "witch plays" of the period,[3] namely the anonymous *Merry Devil of Edmonton* (c. 1599-1604), *The Wise Woman of Hogsdon* (c. 1604), and Heywood and Brome's *The Late Lancashire Witches* (c. 1612-1634), in which the magical roots of witchcraft are treated as unproblematic, *The Witch of Edmonton*, with its undertone of pain and bewilderment, makes a bold statement about demonology: Mother Sawyer is not an agent of supernatural powers but a victim of an entrenched social code that relegates old and poverty-ridden spinsters to the Devil's company. A handful of commentators have noted the non-magical treatment of witchcraft in the play,[4] although its scrutiny of the social dynamics of the witch phenomenon has been more fully appreciated by those who have

---

[2] *The Witch of Edmonton*, in *The Dramatic Works of Thomas Dekker*, ed. Fredson Bowers, 4 vols. (Cambridge: Cambridge University Press, 1953-1961): 3. Subsequent references to the play will be to this edition.

[3] The play has been classified as a domestic or homiletic drama because it includes four major components of the genre: it treats a topical event; it concerns the tragedy of common people; like many domestic plays, it deals with the subject of witchcraft, combining popular beliefs in sorcery and its influence on family affairs; and it incorporates (at least ostensibly) what Henry Adams, *English Domestic or, Homiletic Tragedy 1575-1642* (New York: Columbia University Press, 1943), 141, has defined as the genre's major scheme, that is, a pattern of "sin, discovery, repentance, punishment." For Adams "the most noteworthy characteristic of *The Witch of Edmonton* is its careful adherence to the customary practices of homiletic drama." A qualified view is offered by Andrew Clark, in *Domestic Drama: A Survey of the Origins, Antecedents and Nature of the Domestic Play in England, 1500-1640*, 2 vols. (Salzburg: Universität Salzburg, 1975), 1: 209, 210, who also notes the play's homiletic structures but claims that "it would be inaccurate to suggest that [it] is a dramatized homily," in that it "achieves tragic power in its sympathetic insight into human weaknesses and the sufferings of the characters, its sense of irony and the moving pathos of the later scenes."

[4] Katherine M. Briggs, *Pale Hecate's Team: An Examination of the Beliefs on Witchcraft and Magic among Shakespeare's Contemporaries and his Immediate Successors* (London: Routledge & Kegan Paul, 1962), 99, although claiming that "there is little doubt that the witchcraft of which . . . [the play] treats was believed by its authors," proposes that Elizabeth's "complaints are too well imagined to have been written without some sympathy." Etta Soiref Onat, "Introduction," *The Witch of Edmonton: A Critical Edition* (New York and London: Garland, 1980), 72, 73, for whom Mother Sawyer's "pact and the *maleficia* which confirm it" imply that she "is responsible to Heaven," notes that from the outset of the play until Mother Sawyer "goes to the scaffold, surrounded by her malicious and credulous neighbors," the dramatists intend "to place on cruelty and superstition the chief guilt in the process of witch-making." Larry Champion, *Thomas Dekker and the Traditions of English Drama* (New York: Peter Lang, 1985), 119, suggests that Mother Sawyer "exercises free will in choosing evil," but that she is "victimized by external pressures that render her ability to withstand temptation all the more difficult." Similarly, Michael Hattaway, "Women and Witchcraft:

staged the play. "It is Dekker's eternal credit," wrote Edward Sackville-West of the Old Vic Theatre's 1936 production, "that he should have realized . . . the underlying [social] causes of witchdom."[5] More recently, the Royal Shakespeare Company performed the play as "subversively . . . show[ing] [Mother Sawyer] as a wretched old woman shunned by the community who force the role of witch on her before she has done anything more than steal firewood."[6] Mother Sawyer's personal tragedy arises from an inextricable link between her persecution and her internalization of the community's brutality: "Some call me Witch," she declares, "And being ignorant of my self, they go / About to teach me how to be one" (II.i.8-10). Feeling "shunn'd / And hated like a sickness: made a scorn / To all degrees and sexes" (II.i.96-97), she resolves to take revenge against an abusive world since "'Tis all one, / To be a Witch, as to be counted one" (lines 113-14). When Mother Sawyer finally summons the "Familiar" or "devil" her desire for revenge is a coherent response to the violence she can no longer endure.

The subversive structures of the Mother Sawyer plot locate the roots of witchcraft in the external conditions of class, misogyny, and poverty.[7] These structures, moreover, inform the ways in which the play as a whole

---

The Case of *The Witch of Edmonton,*" *Trivium* 20 (May, 1985): 55, argues that unlike *The Masque of Queens,* in which Jonson "accepts the nature of witches as given" (51), *The Witch of Edmonton* makes the devil "responsible for the acts of will that lead to sin, for turning intent into effect," thereby "arous[ing] compassion for his victims." Jonathan Dollimore, *Radical Tragedy: Religion, Ideology and Power in the Drama of Shakespeare and his Contemporaries* (Chicago: University of Chicago Press, 1984), 176, commenting on Mother Sawyer's madness, writes that the play is "remarkable for the way it depicts how habit, socially coerced, becomes another – or rather 'anti' – nature."

[5]Edward Sackville-West, "The Significance of *The Witch of Edmonton,*" *The Criterion* 17 (1937): 24.

[6]Irving Wardle, "*The Witch of Edmonton*: Other Place," *The Times,* 17 September 1981, 9.

[7]In this context, *The Witch of Edmonton* corroborates recent historical and sociological accounts of the witch phenomenon of the sixteenth and seventeenth centuries. Keith Thomas, for one, in *Religion and the Decline of Magic* (New York: Scribner's, 1971), 520, writes that "the judicial records reveal two essential facts about accused witches: they were poor, and they were usually women." In her analysis of the witch craze in Scotland, Christina Larner, *Enemies of God: The Witch-hunt in Scotland* (Baltimore: The Johns Hopkins University, 1981), 91, notes that "Suspects were . . . from the settled rather than the vagabond or outcast poor," and, as in the rest of Europe, "they were predominantly women." Yet the "stereotype" of the woman as witch, notes Larner, was prevalent "long before there was a witch-hunt. The stereotype rests on the twin pillars of the Aristotelian view of women as imperfectly human . . . and the Judaeo-Christian view of women as the source of sin and the Fall of Man" (92). For further discussions of the link between witchcraft and misogyny see Joseph Klaits, *Servants of Satan: The Age of the Witch Hunts* (Bloomington: Indiana University Press, 1985), ch. 3; Ben Barker-Benfield, "Anne Hutchinson and the Puritan Attitude Toward Women," *Feminist Studies* 1 (1972): 65-96; and E. William Monter, "The Pedestal and the Stake: Courtly Love and Witchcraft," in *Becoming Visible: Women in European History,* ed. Renate Bridenthal and Claudia Koonz (Boston: Houghton Mifflin, 1977), 119-36.

displaces conventional schemes of domestic or homiletic tragedy. While the Mother Sawyer plot debunks popular notions of witchcraft, the marriage plot involving Frank Thorney and his wife, Susan, identifies the witch phenomenon as part of the broader cultural need to punish those who transgress social boundaries. The two plots are loosely integrated by the influence of the supernatural on the protagonists. The marriage plot combines domestic tragedy with the supposed effects of black magic. Although already secretly married, Frank Thorney yields to familial and social demands and marries Susan, the daughter of a rich yeoman. Frank consoles himself with the thought that a wise woman, "Known and approv'd in Palmestry," (II.ii.116) has foretold he would have two wives. But as the result of a sudden demonic impulse, attributed by society to the evil influences of the "Witch" Sawyer (V.iii.21-27), Frank ruthlessly kills Susan. The link between the two plots through Mother Sawyer and her supposed witchcraft has been consistently viewed as a melodramatic device which undermines the tragic potential of the events dramatized. George Rao, for one, writes that "the popular belief in witchcraft is made one of the chief reasons for the domestic crime," Mother Sawyer being "the source of mischief."[8] A close analysis of the action, however, reveals considerable complexity in the portrayal of the connection between witchcraft and domestic crime. The popular explanation for Susan's demise, namely Frank's bewitchment, is undermined by a number of complications, foremost of which is Frank's admission that he is defeated primarily from within. Moreover, we shall see that Susan, the paragon of wifely patience and humility, dies, like Mother Sawyer, at the moment when she is most assertive. The link between witchcraft and assertive women was frequently drawn by Protestant commentators. As Allison Coudert observes, witches were frequently "women who rebelled," and in Puritan circles in particular "rebellion was routinely equated with witchcraft and rebellious wives with witches."[9] That Mother Sawyer and Susan meet similar ends underscores the general fear of female behavior that threatened patriarchal authority.

In locating the witch craze within this larger framework, the play's treatment of witchcraft claims a unique position in English Renaissance drama. In addition, the dramatists go well beyond not only the play's analogues but also the pious indictments of both continental and English skeptics. The play's rational perspective had been current in a number of

---

[8]George Rao, *The Domestic Drama* (Tirupati: Sri Venkateswara University Press, 1978), 187. George Herndl, *The High Design: English Renaissance Tragedy and the Natural Law* (Lexington: University Press of Kentucky, 1970), 272, complains that in the Frank Thorney plot "the action is so presented that the motive of the 'sin' is hardly felt to lie within the will of the sinner, which is paralyzed by the power of evil," while in the Mother Sawyer plot "tragic emotions dwindle into sentimentality."

[9]Allison Coudert, "The Myth of the Improved Status of Protestant Women: The Case of the Witchcraze," in this volume.

discourses on demonology since the latter half of the sixteenth century. This perspective was most forcefully articulated by the physician Johann Wier, whose *De praestigiis daemonum* (1563) was published at the time when witch prosecutions in Germany were entering their most intense phase. While not rejecting the reality of witchcraft, Wier claimed that the confessions for which women were being executed were illusions incited either by devils or by melancholia. Wier's misogynist bias, however, is evident in his proposal that women are easier prey than men to the sleights of demons because women are inherently prone to delusion.[10] Since the Middle Ages, the notion of women's credulity had been current in European writings about women as the "weaker" sex. In witchcraft treatises it appears as early as the *Malleus Maleficarum* (1487), the first printed encyclopedia of demonology, whose authors Heinrich Kramer and Jacob Sprenger described women as "more credulous" than men, "naturally more impressionable, and more ready to receive the influence of a disembodied spirit."[11] Critiques similar to Wier's were later put forth by Neoplatonists, Hermeticists, Paracelsians, and even a few Aristotelian commentators, all of whom claimed that sorcery was founded upon illusion and was therefore harmless.[12] In England, Wier's arguments were refined in 1584 by Reginald Scot, who cast doubt on the prevalent belief in *maleficium* by offering non-magical theories of its causes. Dekker, Ford, and Rowley's sympathetic portrayal of Mother Sawyer suggests their possible debt to Scot's *The Discovery of Witchcraft*, an influential treatise which provoked James I in 1597 to write his *Daemonologie*, a tract against witchcraft, denouncing as well those who professed a disbelief in witches.[13] Scot claimed that witchcraft was essentially a myth created

[10]*De praestigiis daemonum*, in *Histoires Disputes et Discours des Illusions et Impostures des Diables*, ed. J. Bourneville (Paris, 1885), 1: 300. The debate on demonology is well documented in D.P. Walker, *Spiritual and Demonic Magic from Ficino to Campanella* (London, 1958); H.R. Trevor-Roper, *The European Witch-Craze of the Sixteenth and Seventeenth Centuries* (New York and Evanston: Harper, 1967); and Sydney Anglo, "Melancholia and Witchcraft: The Debate Between Wier, Bodin, and Scot," in *Folie et déraison à la Renaissance* (Brussels: University of Brussels, 1976), 209-28. A useful survey of the play's intellectual background is found in Etta Soiref Onat, "Introduction," *The Witch of Edmonton*, 1-23.

[11]Henricus Kramer and Jacobus Sprenger, *Malleus Maleficarum*, trans. Montague Summers (London: Pushkin Press, 1928), 43-44.

[12]Trevor-Roper, *The European Witch-Craze*, 132-34. Thomas, in *Religion and the Decline of Magic*, 579, claims that it was easier for Neoplatonists "to advance a 'natural' explanation for the witches' *maleficium* than it was for those who had been educated in the tradition of scholastic Aristotelianism" which frequently supported diabolical explanations.

[13]Stuart Clark, "King James's *Daemonologie*: Witchcraft and Kingship," in *The Damned Art: Essays in the Literature of Witchcraft*, ed. Sydney Anglo (London, Henley, and Boston: Routledge & Kegan Paul, 1977), 164-65, notes that before coming to England, James I dealt cautiously and even skeptically with accusations of witchcraft; however, he later "became a witch-hunter and demonologist" apparently "to satisfy political and religious pretensions at a time when they could be expressed in few other ways." He "found in the theory and practice of witch persecution a perfect vehicle for his nascent ideals of kingship," among which was the duty of the king to be "the people's teacher and patriarch." Elsewhere, "Inversion, Misrule

by the faithless: "The fables of Witchcraft have taken so . . . deepe root in the heart of man, that fewe or none can (nowadaies) with patience indure the hand and correction of God. For if any adversitie, greefe, sicknesse, loss of children, corne, cattell, or libertie happen unto them . . . they exclaime uppon witches."[14] For Scot, the persecutions of those believed to be witches conflicted with the Protestant idea of Providence whereby neither good nor evil could occur without God's will: "certeine old women heere on earth, called witches, must needs be the contrivers of all mens calamities, and as though they themselves were innocents, and had deserved no such punishments."[15] Scot considered Wier's assertion that melancholia induced women to confess to impossible acts as only one naturalistic cause among others. Many aged women, he pointed out, were physically ill and in urgent need of medical and financial assistance, their vulnerability making them easy targets. *The Witch of Edmonton* echoes Scot's critique of witch persecutions as a denial of divine providence. The play also upholds the skepticism of George Gifford, who in 1593 wrote that legal convictions were founded on doubtful evidence and conjecture, and that the more gruesome the punishments the more people were wont "to thirst even in rage after innocent blood."[16]

By 1621 skepticism had gained widespread acceptance, as is evident from the growing number of accusations both of imposture on the part of those claiming demonic possession and of judicial fraud.[17] However, the link which Dekker, Ford, and Rowley draw between witchcraft, domestic crime and the threat to the established order represents a radical point of departure from the skeptical tradition. Whereas Reginald Scot had dismissed witchcraft primarily on theological grounds, *The Witch of Edmonton* forces the audience to confront the destructive effects of marginality and patriarchal claims on the individual.

---

and the Meaning of Witchcraft," *Past and Present* 87 (May, 1980): 117, Clark suggests that James's "attempt in 1590-91 to write into the confessions of the North Berwick witches a special antipathy between demonic magic and godly magistry had been a way of authenticating his own, as yet rather tentative initiatives as ruler of Scotland."

[14]Reginald Scot, "The Fables of Witchcraft," in *The Witchcraft Papers: Contemporary Records of the Witchcraft Hysteria in Essex 1560-1700,* ed. Peter Haining (Secaucus, N.J.: University Books, 1974), 67. Four years prior to the publication of Scot's treatise, Bishop Thomas Cooper, *Certaine Sermons* (1580), 176, had warned that "Whensoever misery or a plague happeneth to a man, it cometh not by chance or fortune, or by a course of nature, as vain worldly men imagine, but by the assured providence of God."

[15]Scot, "Fables of Witchcraft," 67.

[16]*A Dialogue concerning Witches and Witchcraft* (1593); quoted in Katherine M. Briggs, *Pale Hecate's Team,* 34.

[17]Wallace Notestein, *A History of Witchcraft in England from 1558 to 1718* (1909; rpt. New York: Crowell, 1968), 143.

A number of modern historians have pointed out that the witch beliefs of early modern Europe were generated not by aged women practicing sorcery in different villages (they had more or less always been tolerated) but by inassimilable women – old or diseased spinsters, widows, prostitutes, obstreperous wives, healers, and midwives.[18] As *The Witch of Edmonton* makes clear, the marginality and rebelliousness of such women posed a problem for those intent on preserving the patriarchal structure of the family and society. In addition, because these women were essentially powerless they easily became scapegoats. From the outset the play discredits supernatural causation. Long before Mother Sawyer's pact with the "Familiar" or "devil," she is accused of "Forespeak[ing]" her community's cattle and of "bewitch[ing] their Corn" and "their Babes at nurse" (II.i.12-13). Demonology is thus used to explain away both the community's economic hardship and behavior which poses a disturbing challenge to moral and cultural codes. It is essentially through desperation that Mother Sawyer conforms to society's expectations to the point where she becomes consumed by "madness" (IV.i.152). Her madness attests to what E. William Monter claims witchcraft itself had become, that is, "a *magical* form of violent revenge, practiced by exactly those persons who could not employ physical violence."[19] Marginalized women suited this description especially well: "They had many grievances; they wanted revenge; yet recourse to the law often was beyond their economic power, and successful physical violence was beyond their physical power."[20] They gained revenge by arousing their accusers' fear of magic.

Just as medieval and Renaissance demonologists depicted witches "as usually poor, old, solitary, and female,"[21] the social stigma which branded Mother Sawyer as an outcast are her age, her gender, her physical deformity, and her poverty. Mother Sawyer's demise epitomizes what awaits those in her world who "feel / The misery and beggary of want; / Two Devils that are occasions to enforce / a shameful end" (I.i.17-20). Her strategy of survival shares with certain revenge plays of the sixteenth and seventeenth

[18]Midwives, notes Mary Nelson, "Why Witches Were Women," *Women: A Feminist Perspective,* ed. Jo Freeman (Palo Alto, California: Mayfield, 1975), 346, 347, were "expert in methods of birth control, and most likely cooperated in abortions and infanticides" with families who were either too poor to sustain many children, or who "did not wish to jeopardize their new prosperity." Allison Coudert, "Witchcraft Studies to Date," unpublished MS, 21, suggests that the "early association of the term *maleficium* with abortofacients and sterilizing potions, together with the almost universal assumption that the users of such potions would be women, helped to feminize the crime of witchcraft and to associate it with the women healers and midwives."

[19]Monter, "Pedestal and Stake," 134.

[20]Ibid. Cf. Thomas, *Religion and Decline of Magic,* 522, "Although the witch might expect to gain some material benefits from her diabolical compact, these were subordinate to her main desire, to avenge herself upon her neighbors. Such a desire was to be found at all levels in society, but it was usually only the poor and helpless who hoped to attain it by witchcraft, because for them the normal channels of legal action or physical force were not available."

[21]Ibid., 21.

centuries a definition of revenge as a response to social dislocation. In his study of the radical Elizabethan and Jacobean revenge play, Jonathan Dollimore notes that the protagonists, once alienated from society, become "bereaved, dispossessed, and in peril of their lives, . . . suffer[ing] extreme disorientation" as they "are pushed to the very edge of mental collapse."[22] The dark side of seventeenth-century England is represented by the villagers of Edmonton, including prominent citizens, all of whom exploit Mother Sawyer's deprivation. The dramatists' portrayal of the overlap between the upper and lower classes' attitude toward witchcraft foregrounds the historical paradox that "in the witch trials, members of the elites and ordinary folk found a common cause."[23]

The accusations against Mother Sawyer are initiated by her landlord, Old Banks, who calls her "Witch" (II.i.17) and "Hag" (line 17) and beats her when she refuses to return the "few rotten sticks" (line 21) she has gathered from his property. (The incident is not recorded in Goodcole.) It is significant that the spectator first sees Mother Sawyer collecting bits of firewood from her landlord's property. In England, witchcraft trials coincided with the enclosure laws, which "broke up many of the old co-operative village communities,"[24] increasing the numbers of poor people, many of them widowed and elderly, and depriving them of any means of subsistence. The enclosure movement further coincided with "the bureaucratization of poor relief under the Elizabethan Poor Laws" which "divested the individual of responsibility for charity."[25] Although the clergy insisted on the ethical imperative of Christian charity, many townships now strictly prohibited alms-giving.[26] The poor and elderly women indicted for witchcraft were usually those whose names were listed as having been dependent upon the old custom of parochial charity.[27]

The play stresses the absence of neighborly support. Mother Sawyer is repeatedly rebuked as a burden to Edmonton and a threat to the community's well-being. That she first invokes the Familiar during the beating by her landlord – "What spells, what charms, or invocations, / May the thing call'd Familiar be purchased?" (II.i.35-36) – challenges the conventional notion requiring the witch's private pact with the devil to stem from arcane practices. Instead the pact is rooted, as it was for many of those accused

---

[22]Dollimore, *Radical Tragedy,* 40.

[23]Klaits, *Servants of Satan,* 51.

[24]Thomas, *Religion and Decline of Magic,* 562.

[25]Larner, *Enemies of God,* 61.

[26]Thomas, *Religion and Decline of Magic,* 563.

[27]J.F. Pound, "An Elizabethan Census of the Poor," *University of Birmingham Historical Journal* VIII (1961-62): 138, 141.

of witchcraft, in the need for security and self-esteem.[28] The Familiar's shape immediately underscores the play's concern with madness as a response to dispossession. Once Mother Sawyer resolves to "Abjure all goodness" (II.i.107) the Familiar manifests itself as a black dog, directly corresponding to her mental image of Banks as a "black Cur" (line 111). The Familiar promises to take "just revenge" against Mother Sawyer's enemies (line 124). He also does to her precisely what she has accused Banks of doing, that is, "suck" her "very blood" (line 112) but with a startling result: the Familiar's drawing of her blood is a gratifying experience. The creature's appearance in the likeness of Mother Sawyer's image of Banks demystifies the supernatural, maintaining the spectator's interest in Mother Sawyer as an isolated human being desiring her community's approval. As a mental image of Banks, the Familiar is clearly a wish-fulfillment of material comfort and social status. The dog is also a projection of a profound desire for one who loves her and who soothes her suffering and anger:

> *Sawy.* My dear *Tom*-boy welcome.
> I am torn in pieces by a pack of Curs
> Clap'd all upon me, and for want of thee:
> Comfort me: thou shalt have the Teat anon.
>
> (IV.i.148-51)

The emotive component of Mother Sawyer's relationship with the Familiar substantiates the role of the dog as a demon lover emphasized in the 1962 production of the play (by the Mermaid Theatre in London), in which Mother Sawyer was depicted as "a pitiable old woman who turns to the Devil because no one else will have her, and whose contract is undisguisedly a love relationship."[29] The pathos surrounding the fantasy, however, challenges the myth of the sexually potent and threatening witch figure encountered in Renaissance treatises on witchcraft. Since the Middle Ages, women had been considered naturally disposed toward lust, which made them easy prey for the devil. In the *Malleus Maleficarum* we read, "All witchcraft comes from carnal lust, which is in women insatiable . . . Wherefore for the sake of fulfilling their lusts they consort even with devils."[30] While in medieval demonology lust was only one among many causes leading women to worship demons, in the sixteenth and

---

[28]"Seventeenth-century English women at the margins of society," writes Larner, *Enemies of God,* 95, "did not expect that their soul would qualify them for silk and riches. Instead they said that the Devil promised them mere freedom from the extremes of poverty and starvation." Thomas, *Religion and Decline of Magic,* 520, writes: "The Devil promised that they should never want; he offered meat, clothes and money, and was ready to pay their debts."

[29]"Fascinating Rag-Bag of Dramatic Idioms," *The Times,* Thursday 22 November 1962, 15.

[30]Summers, ed., *Malleus Maleficarum,* 47.

seventeenth centuries "sexual overtones became the leading theme of demon-
ological imagery," as witch hunters emphasized the sabbat as the expression
of perverse sexual practices.[31] However, the witches' sabbat, wherein the
devils' worshippers "blasphem[ed] against God, copulat[ed] with their master,
and indulg[ed] in orgies of sexual promiscuity,"[32] is never mentioned in
the play. Rather than exploit a popular motif for its sensational appeal, the
playwrights depict the relationship between Mother Sawyer and the Familiar
in terms of its psychological interest: in reality Mother Sawyer's physical
needs are thwarted by her age, deformity, and poverty; in the sexual fantasy,
however, she exerts a form of power over the source of her degradation.
The fantasy, moreover, corroborates historical evidence indicating in both
Scotland and England that "the fear of witchcraft bestowed power on the
powerless,"[33] relieving their feelings of "impotence and desperation."[34]

The scenes which follow stress Mother Sawyer's persecution rather
than her sorcery. After summoning the dog, she orders him to carry out
a series of vengeful tricks which provoke the villagers to burn her thatch,
a common ritual designed to prove witchcraft. According to Goodcole, the
thatch "being so burned, the author of . . . mischiefe should presently
then come."[35] Even Goodcole recognizes that the custom is irrational,
although he does not go as far as to disparage it. On the one hand, he
describes it as "old" and "ridiculous," and the community's suspicions as
"great presumptions"; on the other hand, he writes that the court learned
the custom worked because Elizabeth came "without any sending for." In
the pamphlet the thatch is burned after the sudden death of infants and
cattle. In the play Mother Sawyer's power to influence nature and human
behavior is portrayed in such a way as to undermine conventional ideas
about witchcraft through parody and farce. The first set of reasons given
for the thatch-burning climaxes in a theatrical *reductio ad absurdum*: 1) a
villager has caught his wife and a servant with stolen corn, a theft readily
attributed by the wife to her bewitchment by Mother Sawyer (IV.i.5-9);
2) Old Banks' horse has contracted a fatal disease, which Banks blames on
"this Jadish Witch, Mother *Sawyer*" (line 4); 3) Banks has been plagued
by an uncontrollable urge to raise his cow's tail and kiss its behind, a habit
which has made the community of Edmonton "ready to be-piss themselves
with laughing" him "to scorn" (lines 57-58). The broad comedy elicited
by the rich landowner's predicament exposes not only the folly of the
villagers' vindictiveness against Mother Sawyer, but also the social tensions
at the heart of the community between elite and popular culture. At the

---

[31]Klaits, *Servants of Satan*, 53.

[32]Ibid., 2.

[33]Larner, *Enemies of God*, 95.

[34]Thomas, *Religion and Decline of Magic*, 520.

[35]Goodcole, A4-A4v; quoted in Hoy, *Introduction, Notes, and Commentaries*, 3: 258.

same time, the epithets hurled at Mother Sawyer, in particular "Hag" (II.i.27) and "hot Whore" (IV.i.24), together with the villagers' frenzied ritual in carrying out the thatch-burning amid the chant "Burn the Witch, the Witch, the Witch, the Witch" (IV.i.15) and the chilling refrain "Hang her, beat her, kill her" (line 29), sustain the focus on the social causes of her dislocation.

A more serious charge concerns Mother Sawyer's apparent hand in the madness and death of Old Ratcliff's wife, Anne. The Anne Ratcliff episode takes place moments after the villagers have burned Mother Sawyer's thatch. Exasperated and "dri'd up / With cursing and with madness" (IV.i.152-53), Mother Sawyer reminds the Familiar about Anne Ratcliff, "Who for a little soap lick'd by . . . [Mother Sawyer's] Sow, / Struck, and almost had lam'd it" (lines 169-70). This incident further explores a classic precondition of sixteenth- and seventeenth-century witch trials, namely village quarrels, usually involving household disputes, which would give rise to accusations of witchcraft. In England the targets of these accusations were frequently elderly women who sought charity.[36] Having been refused charity by Anne Ratcliff, Mother Sawyer wonders whether the Familiar has "pinch[ed] that Quean to th' heart" (line 171). Her comment is followed by the stage direction, *"Enter Anne Ratcliff mad."* A number of critics have commented on the ambiguity surrounding Anne's madness, although the episode has not been explored in detail. David Atkinson observes that "the play does not make it entirely clear whether or not the witch really is responsible for the death of Anne Ratcliff," and suggests that "the episode was probably imperfectly assimilated from the source."[37] Etta Soiref Onat, on the other hand, points out that Mother Sawyer's Familiar rubs Anne Ratcliff after she has gone mad, and proposes that "her suicide might very well have been caused by nothing more than a coincidental madness, not the result of demonic possession at all."[38] Michael Hattaway also offers an insightful, although cursory, reading: "the text makes it legitimate to conjecture that [Anne's] madness arose independently of the devil's action," the "motives for action aris[ing] out of social transactions" while the "chains of causation are left incomplete."[39] The structural indeterminacy, I believe, crystallizes the interplay between the social and psychological construction of both Mother Sawyer's and Anne Ratcliff's madness. Beneath the surface conflict, the dramatists create a number of structural links between the two characters. To begin with, economic destitution is a source of mental anguish for both women. Just as Mother Sawyer's indigence is

[36]Klaits, *Servants of Satan,* 86-88.

[37]David Atkinson, "Moral Knowledge and the Double Action in *The Witch of Edmonton,*" *Studies in English Literature* 25, no. 8 (Spring, 1985): 431.

[38]Onat, "Introduction," *The Witch of Edmonton,* 94.

[39]Hattaway, "Women and Witchcraft," 53.

of mental anguish for both women. Just as Mother Sawyer's indigence is responsible for the trespass of her sow, poverty has led Anne to injure the animal. Although the two women are enemies,[40] Anne's jabber about privation echoes the cynical perspective which Mother Sawyer has maintained, namely that there is no justice for the dispossessed:

> *Ratc.* Hoyda! a-pox of the Devil's false Hopper!
>   all the golden Meal runs into the rich Knaves
>   purses, and the poor have nothing but Bran. Hey
>   derry down! Are not you Mother *Sawyer*?
> *Sawy.* No, I am a Lawyer.
> *Ratc.* Art thou? I prithee let me scratch thy Face;
>   for thy Pen has flea'd off a great many mens skins.
>   . . . I'll sue Mother *Sawyer,* and her own Sow
>   shall give in evidence against her.
> *Sawy.* Touch her.   [Dog *rubs her.*]
>
>   (IV.i.176-82)

Significantly, the Familiar "rubs" Anne when, like Mother Sawyer, she is emotionally vulnerable and railing against the disparity between the rich and the poor. The verbal exchange between the two women highlights their mutual estrangement. Although the dog touches Anne during her delirium, Mother Sawyer believes she has induced Anne's madness. The old woman delights in inverting the power structure of her world by fancifully assuming the role of "Lawyer." As she rails at Anne for being uncharitable – "That Jade, that foul-tongu'd whore, *Nan Ratcliff*" (IV.i.168) – Mother Sawyer ironically denounces her enemy with epithets identical to those which the community had formerly levelled at her, namely "Jadish" and "whore" (IV.i.4; 24). Eager to take credit for Anne's social and mental disorientation, Mother Sawyer strips the married woman of her socially sanctioned identity, taking revenge upon the community that has been responsible for her own suffering. However, that Anne's derangement has also stemmed from social coercion is suggested by the sudden and unsettling interpolation of society's need to link women and madness:

> *O. Bank.* Catch her [Anne] fast, and have her into
>   some close Chamber: do, for she's as many Wives are,
>   stark mad.
>
>   (IV.i.193-94)

[40]Thomas, *Religion and Decline of Magic,* 561, observes the striking irony that "Essentially the witch and her victim were two persons who ought to have been friendly towards each other, but were not. They existed in a state of concealed hostility for which society provided no legitimate outlet. They could not take each other to law; neither could they have recourse to open violence."

[*Countryman*] 2. Rid the Town of her, else all
    our Wives will do nothing else but dance about . . .
    Country May-poles.
[*Countryman*] 3. Our Cattel fall, our Wives fall,
    our Daughters fall, and Maid-servants fall . . . .
                    (IV.i.10-14)

Anne's nameless anxiety, which she and the community can attribute only to supernatural causes, is thus fundamentally related to a type of "madness" experienced not only by Mother Sawyer but also by many women in Edmonton.

Following Anne Ratcliff's suicide Old Banks spearheads the move "to burn . . . [Mother Sawyer] for a Witch" (IV.i.215). During the arraignment scene, Mother Sawyer is momentarily spared by the intervention of a Justice and Sir Arthur Clarington. In a significant addition to Goodcole's description of this event, the episode initially stresses the Justice's wisdom and compassion in reprehending the villagers for their violent actions, which he labels "ridiculous" (IV.i.40) and "against Law" (line 51). "Instead of turning [Mother Sawyer] into a Witch," he warns, "you'll prove your selves starke Fools" (line 42). The villagers' fury subsides when the Justice insists on treating the old woman with mildness. Mother Sawyer, however, continues to vilify her detractors. When Sir Arthur, a libertine and a schemer, joins the interrogation, she exposes his false rectitude and denounces a concept of honor based on class and privilege: "Men in gay clothes, whose Backs are laden with Titles and Honors, are within far more crooked than I am; and if I be a Witch, more Witch-like" (IV.i.86-88). Her boldest denunciation is reserved for the court where, she claims, are found "painted things . . . / Upon whose Eye-lids Lust sits blowing fires / Upon whose naked Paps, a Leachers thought / Acts Sin in fouler shapes than can be wrought" (lines 103-107). Henceforth, the accusations against Mother Sawyer abruptly shift from conspiracy with the devil to insubordination. Ironically, her spirited and vituperative self-defense, which the Justice calls her "sawcie[ness]" and "bitter[ness]," (IV.i.81) rather than her alleged crimes, secures her imprisonment.

Although virtually the entire community shares in the responsibility for Mother Sawyer's death, and although most of the prominent citizens are themselves guilty of moral backsliding, none of the villagers is punished through any real or symbolic intervention of Divine Providence, as would be expected in homiletic tragedy. And while in the denouement Mother Sawyer utters the conventional public-repentance speech of the genre (V.iii.50-51), the implication is that in the world of the play she has been condemned irrevocably. Henry Adams writes that the Mother Sawyer plot "is unusual" in its treatment of the redemption scene, and that Mother Sawyer's "well-chosen words against the court anticipate a development many generations in the future."[41] David Atkinson, on the other hand, while noting "some doubt as to Mother Sawyer's ultimate fate," nonetheless argues for homiletic closure: "As she goes to her execution" no one "expresses the conviction that she will achieve salvation. But the onlookers are deeply prejudiced against her . . . ," so that "it is perhaps just to believe that she can still benefit from the mercy of God."[42] From the outset, however, the Mother Sawyer plot has been moving toward an indeterminate ending. Mother Sawyer's fate cannot be accommodated to the typical conclusion of homiletic tragedy because only Mother Sawyer is tried and executed for her transgressions, suggesting the universe has become indifferent to human action. The complication forestalls the melodramatic effect of Mother Sawyer's pitiable death, attesting to authorial doubt about the genre's ability to provide solutions for human conflict.

*   *   *

The dramatists' uneasiness with homiletic schemes connects the Mother Sawyer action and the marriage plot, where the relationship between power and gender, as it bears upon the witch phenomenon and on domestic conduct in general, is further explored. Under profound emotional strain, Frank Thorney commits bigamy rather than defy his father's and the community's wishes that he marry Susan, whose wealthy family makes her a respectable catch. Rather than confess his clandestine marriage with another woman, Frank submits to a series of inescapable compromises, indulging in a painful web of lies in order to retain his father's and the world's approval until, in a sudden demonic rage, he kills Susan. Frank's inability to reconcile personal and social claims underlies Susan's murder, which thematically unifies the two plots. The cruelty to which Susan is subjected directly parallels that experienced by Mother Sawyer and, by implication, Anne Ratcliff. Like the conventional patient wife, Susan enters marriage believing that a wife's duty is to be passive and solicitous, and above all to yield to her husband's will (II.ii.79-88). Susan's notions of wifely perfection lead her to blame herself for Frank's discontent, a reaction based on a set of conventional moral prescriptions governing conjugal behavior.[43] When Susan finally thwarts convention by passionately asserting

---

[41]Adams, *English Domestic*, 141.

[42]Atkinson, "Moral Knowledge," 432-33.

[43]Contemporary literature providing instruction on marital relations was extensive. While the general consensus was that harmony should serve as the natural solution for all marital disputes, wives were admonished to practice absolute patience and self-abnegation, and husbands to exert their authority courageously but firmly. See Ian Maclean, *The Renaissance Notion of Woman: A Study in the Fortunes of Scholasticism and Medical Science in European Intellectual Life* (Cambridge: Cambridge University Press, 1980), 55ff. For an overview of how Elizabethan and Jacobean domestic drama absorbed these prescriptions, see Andrew Clark, *Domestic Drama*, 1: 27-99; and George Rao, *The Domestic Drama*, passim.

her sexual desire, Frank reproaches her for undermining her role as a "perfect Embleme of . . . modesty" (II.ii.104). Her ardent speech on Frank's "power / To make me passionate as an *April*-day" (II.ii.89) elicits a startling reply:

> *Frank.* Change thy conceit, I prithee:
>   Thou art all perfection: *Diana* her self
>   Swells in thy thoughts, and moderates thy beauty.
>
>   . . . .
>
>   . . . still as wanton *Cupid* blows Love-fires,
>   *Adonis* quenches out unchaste desires.
>   (II.ii.94-106)

Susan's passion shocks and confuses Frank, whose response embodies two cardinal contemporary notions of ideal male and female behavior: he denies Susan's sexuality by viewing her as an emblem of chastity, and he upholds the husband's duty to command by instructing his wife on how to be decorous. Before Susan reveals her passion, Frank cannot even contemplate her death:

>   . . . thou art so rare a goodness,
>   As Death would rather put it self to death,
>   Then murther thee. But we, as all things else,
>   Are mutable and changing.
>   (II.ii.138-41)

As a paragon of modesty, Susan is exempt from mutability; as a flesh-and-blood woman, Susan, like Mother Sawyer and Anne Ratcliff, pays dearly for her humanity.

Ignoring her husband's command to be silent, Susan persists in her importunities (lines 107-110), her romantic notions making her an easy victim: "till this minute," Frank charges, "You might have safe returned; now you cannot: / You have dogg'd your own death" (III.iii.37-39). In Frank's claim that Susan has "dogg'd" her own death, there is an inescapable association between Susan and carnality as represented by the dog who courts Mother Sawyer and who independently paws Frank prior to Susan's murder (III.iii.15). In making the association, Frank instinctively articulates the widespread suspicion about female sexuality challenged in the Mother Sawyer plot, namely that women are inherently disposed toward lust. Woman "is more carnal than a man," write the authors of the *Malleus Maleficarum*, "as is clear from many carnal abominations" for which "there are more women than men found infected with the heresy of witchcraft."[44]

---

[44]Summers, ed., *Malleus Maleficarum*, 44-47.

Susan dies because she fails to fulfill Frank's expectation that chastity is an essential aspect of female virtue, as defined by contemporary culture. The conclusion of the marriage plot is notable for its resistance to homiletic closure. Lying seriously ill as a result of a self-inflicted wound designed to make others believe he was attacked by Susan's murderers, Frank is overcome with remorse and guilt. He sleeps badly, eats little, and hallucinates about death, for which he longs. Unable to envision a better life, he muses on the possibility of suicide (IV.ii.20-27). In prison, he is forced to realize that he cannot escape divine justice, and his repentance speech (lines 134-42), which brings about society's forgiveness, conforms with the stock scaffold speeches of domestic tragedy, sharing with them the recognition of "the justice of earthly punishment."[45] Frank's speech also includes the conventional didactic address to the audience, but his advice to the world to marry for love and not for material gain (V.iii.107-10) has a hollow ring when juxtaposed with Susan's murder. Frank's repentance is further qualified by his spiritual malaise, for only the certainty of death gives him the inner strength to face his punishment.[46]

The final scenes, moreover, do not end in praise of the mysterious workings of Providence as do typical domestic tragedies. Instead, the play foregrounds society's role in the tragic events we have been witnessing. On his way to Frank's hanging, Susan's grief-stricken father meets Mother Sawyer, who is being executed simultaneously for witchcraft. Without cause, Old Carter blindly accuses her of having been the "instrument" (V.iii.21) of Frank's murder of Susan. A few moments later, however, when face to face with Frank, Old Carter acknowledges that social claims are the root cause of his daughter's demise: "if thou had'st not had ill counsel, thou would'st not have done as thou didst" (lines 116-18). Ironically, the "ill counsel" to which Old Carter refers is neither palmistry nor witchcraft but his and Old Thorney's enforcement of Frank's marriage to Susan.

In different but related ways, then, the deaths of Frank, Susan, Anne Ratcliff, and Mother Sawyer are brought about by the characters' psychological fragmentation, which is portrayed as a direct response to social barriers created by class, poverty and misogyny. By locating the witch phenomenon

---

[45]Adams, *English Domestic*, 136.

[46]Leonora Leet Brodwin, "The Domestic Tragedy of Frank Thorney in *The Witch of Edmonton*," *Studies in English Literature* 7 (1967): 322. Elsewhere Brodwin, *Elizabethan Love Tragedy 1587-1625* (New York and London: the University Presses, 1971), 174, contends that Frank's "final desire is that death may extinguish the despair which [his] ultimate self-recognition has brought." Etta S. Onat, "Introduction," *The Witch of Edmonton*, 86, while conceding that Frank's repentance is "not the mere stock convention of homiletic drama," claims that it is "dramatically credible" because "Frank has been characterized as a man of some conscience and feeling."

in the complex dynamics of social and domestic life, the two plots of *The Witch of Edmonton* inscribe a subversive discourse about witchcraft which exposes the limits of tidy homiletic conclusions in mitigating tragic events.

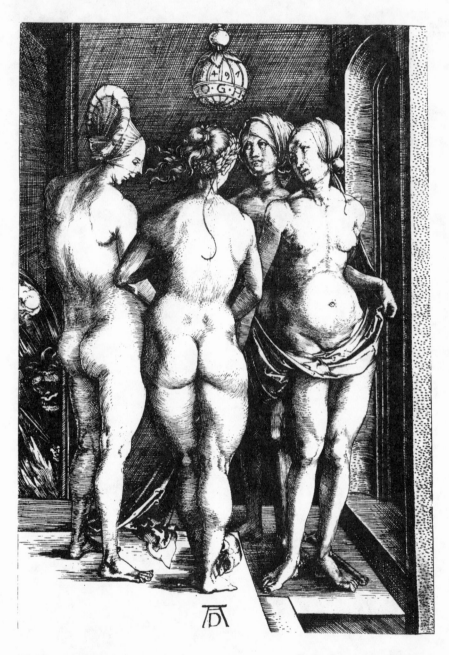

The Four Witches, (ca. 1597), from *The Intaglio Prints of Albrecht Dürer:
Engravings, Etchings & Drypoints,* ed. Walter L. Strauss (New York:
Kennedy Galleries and Abaris Books, 1977). Reprinted by permission.

The Myth of the Improved Status of Protestant Women: The Case of the Witchcraze

Allison P. Coudert

BELIEF IN WITCHES AND WITCHCRAFT has existed in just about every society and every part of the world.[1] But only in Christian Europe and Christian America, where witchcraft was characterized as heresy, did witch beliefs lead to a "witchcraze" responsible for the death of between 60,000 and 200,000 people.[2]

The witchcraze was not the product of ignorance and superstition. It occurred during the period described as the scientific revolution and age of triumphant rationalism. During the same years that Kepler discovered the elliptical orbits of the planets and Galileo formulated the law of inertia, while Montaigne wrote his skeptical essays and Descartes forever changed the way men perceived the world, unrecorded numbers of women (including Kepler's mother) were accused of witchcraft, pricked, racked, and stappadoed until they confessed they were indeed the Devil's disciples, at which point they were burned at the stake or hanged. In 1602 the witch hunter Henri Boguet announced that a vast host of 1,800,000 witches threatened Europe, a more formidable army than any Europe had ever experienced in its long history of warfare.[3]

Boguet was a lesser light among a galaxy of geniuses who believed in witchcraft and actively supported witch hunts. That the witch hunters and witch theorists were for the most part educated, intelligent men proves that the witchcraze was not an aberrant event or throwback to outmoded occult beliefs, but integral to the scientific revolution. The evolution of

---

[1]Jeffrey B. Russell, *Witchcraft in the Middle Ages* (Ithaca: Cornell University Press, 1972), 13ff.; Max Marwick, ed., *Witchcraft and Sorcery* (London: Penguin Books, 1970); Gustav Henningsen, *The Witches' Advocate: Basque Witchcraft and the Spanish Inquisition* (Reno: The University of Nevada Press, 1980), 12.

[2]Brian P. Levack, *The Witch-Hunt in Early Modern Europe* (New York: Longmans, 1987), 19, estimates that 100,000 were officially tried and 50,000 executed. E. William Monter, "The Pedestal and the Stake: Courtly Love and the Witchcraze," in *Becoming Visible*, ed. R. Bridenthal & C. Koonz (Boston: Houghton Mifflin, 1977), 130 estimates 100,000. Rossell H. Robbins, *The Encyclopedia of Witchcraft and Demonology* (New York: Crown Publishers, 1959), 180, and G. R. Quaife, *Godly Zeal and Furious Rage: The Witch in Early Modern Europe* (New York: St. Martin's Press, 1987), 79, suggest 200,000. Even the conservative estimate of 50,000 is large, considering how much smaller European population and how uneven the effects of the witchcraze were. In the aftermath of the witch trials in 1585, for example, two villages in the Bishopric of Triers were left with one female inhabitant apiece. See Charles Henry Lea, *Materials Towards a History of Witchcraft*, arranged and ed. Arthur C. Howland, 3 vols. (New York: Thomas Joseloff, 1939), 1188-89.

[3]Henri Boguet, *An Examen of Witches*, ed. Montague Summers, tr. E. A. Ashwin (London: Rodker, 1929; originally published 1602), xxxii. He also writes, ". . . there are witches by the thousand everywhere, multiplying upon the earth even as worms in a garden," xxxiv.

modern concepts of science was in fact encouraged by the scientific debate prompted by the investigation of witchcraft allegations.[4] Since the witchcraze cannot be dismissed as an anachronism in an age otherwise remembered for its scientific discoveries, we must ponder what made intelligent, educated men view witches as so terrifyingly real during this relatively brief period in Western history. This is a crucial issue, for while witchcraft beliefs were prevalent in Europe among Christians (who had inherited them from the ancient world), the full-blown stereotype of the witch as a poor, old, disruptive, and sexually threatening woman did not appear until the late fifteenth century.[5] Before then, witches could be either male or female, and they were often well-born, if not noble.[6] But by the sixteenth century, when the witchcraze begins, the witch appears as an old, wizened crone.[7] During the period of the witchcraze (roughly between 1570 and 1700) witch hunting became more gender specific than ever before: between 71 and 92 percent of those accused, tried, and executed were women.[8] We are therefore faced with the problem of trying to understand why poor, old women became suddenly threatening.

Historical explanations of the witchcraze reveal much about the biases of historians. Eighteenth-century philosophers, for example, blamed superstitious peasants. Protestants blamed Catholics and Catholics Protestants. The polemical and tendentious nature of most studies of witchcraft led Erik Midelfort to protest in 1968 that "more pure bunk" had been written about witchcraft than about any other field in history.[9] But in the last twenty years a reverse of Gresham's law has taken effect: the good scholarship has edged out the bad. The recent emphasis on the newer fields of social history, popular history, family history, women's history, the history of childhood, and psychohistory has thrown new light on the dark episode of the witchcraze.

---

[4]Irving Kirsch, "Demonology and Science during the Scientific Revolution," *Journal of the History of Behavioral Sciences* 8 (1980): 359-68; Stuart Clark, "The Scientific Status of Demonology," in *Occult and Scientific Mentalities in the Renaissance,* ed. Brian Vickers (Cambridge: Cambridge University Press, 1984), 351-74. and Allison Coudert, "Henry More and Witchcraft," forthcoming in *Of Mysticism and Mechanism: Tercentenary Studies of Henry More,* ed. Sarah Hutton (Dordrecht: Kluwer Academic Publishers).

[5]H. C. Erik Midelfort, "Heartland of the Witchcraze: Central and Northern Europe," *History Today* 21 (Feb. 1981): 27-31, and Dale Hoak, "Witchcraft and Women in the Art of the Renaissance," *History Today* 21 (1981): 22-26.

[6]Peter Brown, "Sorcery, Demons, and the Rise of Christianity from Late Antiquity into the Middle Ages," in *Witchcraft Confessions and Accusations,* ed. Mary Douglas (London: Tavistock Publications, 1970), 17-45.

[7]See, for example, Dale Hoak, "Art, Culture, and Mentality in Renaissance Society: the Meaning of Hans Baldung Grien's 'Bewitched Groom' (1544)," *Renaissance Quarterly* 38 (1985): 488-510.

[8]Monter, "Pedestal and Stake," 132.

[9]H. C. Erik Midelfort, "Recent Witch-Hunting Research, or Where Do We Go From Here," *Papers of the Bibliographical Society of America* 62 (1968).

With all the new material available it may seem perverse that this paper resurrects the old thesis that the witchcraze was more severe in Protestant than Catholic countries. But it is precisely because of this new wealth of scholarly material that I wish to do so. I do not propose, however, to resuscitate the old partisan debate between Catholic and Protestant scholars. My intention is rather to enumerate specific aspects of the Reformation period in general and of Protestant ideology in particular that made the image of the female witch more threatening than ever before. I add the proviso that, while I will be emphasizing what seems to me to be the intensified misogyny accompanying the period of the witchcraze, I do not believe that misogyny by itself explains the witchcraze. Misogyny was not a new phenomenon, but large numbers of women were not always burned at the stake. The politics, economics, and intense religious conflicts of the Reformation period, together with changes in the law, combined to focus misogyny in the image of the witch in this one relatively short period. In this discussion, I will not distinguish among the various denominations of Protestants. When it came to women, there was a remarkable (in every other respect unheard of) consensus.

To understand the fear and dread aroused by witches, we need to identify who they were. The most conspicuous attribute of witches was their gender. In her study of American witchcraft, Carol Karlsen has found that men who confessed to the crime of witchcraft were often rebuked as liars, while women were taken at their word and executed.[10] Erik Midelfort has noted a similar tendency of males to believe and convict females.[11] Another salient characteristic of the witch was her age. Women over forty were more likely to be accused of witchcraft and, after being accused, to be executed.[12] In short, the stereotype of the witch as an old, querulous crone is remarkably accurate, but the women who were the most likely candidates for witchcraft accusations were also women who did not fit masculine stereotypes of the good woman as the obedient, silent, and submissive wife and mother, dependent on male kin. The majority of witches were past child-bearing age and a good percentage were unmarried,

---

[10]Carol Karlsen, *The Devil in the Shape of a Woman. Women and Witchcraft in Colonial New England* (New York: W. W. Norton & Co., 1987), 51-52.

[11]H. C. Erik Midelfort, *Witch-hunting in South Western Germany, 1562-1684: The Social and Intellectual Foundations* (Stanford: Stanford University Press, 1972), ch. 6, attributes the decline of witch panics in southwest Germany to the disinclination of male jurors and male judges to convict male suspects. A similar situation occurred at Salem. Once men were accused in significant numbers, the ludicrousness of the charges dawned on judge and jury alike. See Paul Boyer and Stephen Nissenbaum, *Salem Possessed: The Social Origins of Witchcraft* (Cambridge, Mass.: Harvard University Press, 1974), 32-33 and passim.

[12]Karlsen, *Devil in the Shape of a Woman*; John P. Demos, *Entertaining Satan: Witchcraft and the Culture of Early New England* (New York: Oxford University Press, 1982), 64-70; and idem, "Underlying Themes in the Witchcraft of Colonial New England," *American Historical Review* 75 (June, 1970): 1311-26.

widowed, or living alone.[13] Among the younger witch suspects, a significant number were charged with sexual crimes–fornication, adultery, abortion, or infanticide–or had given birth to illegitimate children.[14]

This profile of the witch holds true for both Catholic and Protestant countries, yet witches were treated far more leniently in those areas in which the Catholic Inquisition was firmly entrenched, Spain, Italy, Portugal, than in Protestant and Catholic countries beyond the jurisdiction of the Inquisition. In his study of the Basque witchcraft trials, Gustav Henningsen describes the scrupulous care and leniency with which the Spanish Inquisition handled most cases involving witchcraft accusations. In a later study Conteras and Henningsen contend that the Spanish Inquisition did not authorize the burning of a single witch after 1610, even though the number of cases involving magicians and witches increased after that date.[15] These findings are further corroborated by William Monter and John Tedeschi's study of the Italian Inquisitions. While they have discovered that Italian Inquisitors became increasingly preoccupied with superstition, magic, and witchcraft in the 1570s through the 1600s, these crimes were treated with surprising leniency: witchcraft was rarely punished with death, and first offenders who repented were not turned over to civil authorities.[16] Carlo Ginzburg's study of the Benandanti documents the quite extraordinary patience and leniency with which Italian Inquisitors treated this sect of self-proclaimed witches.[17]

What factors combined, then, to make the figure of the witch especially menacing to Protestants? First, the devil and his servants, the witches, were more conspicuous and menacing figures for Protestants than for Catholics. Second, there was an ambiguity and tension in Protestant ideology about

---

[13]Karlsen, *Devil in the Shape of a Woman*, 73 ff., 295 n. 93; Midelfort, *Witch-hunting in South Western Germany,* 184ff.

[14]For a discussion of intolerance of sexual deviancy in relation to the witchcraze, see Joseph Klaits, *Servants of Satan,* (Bloomington: Indiana University Press, 1985), 21; G. R. Quaife, *Wanton Wenches and Wayward Wifes: Peasants and Illicit Sex in Early Seventeenth-Century England* (New Brunswick, N.J.: Rutgers University Press, 1979); and J. A. Sharpe, "The History of Crime in Late Medieval and Early Modern England: A Review of the Field," *Social History* 7 (1982): 200ff.

[15]Gustav Henningsen, *The Witches' Advocate: Basque Witchcraft and the Spanish Inquisition* (Reno: The University of Nevada Press, 1980) and Jaime Contreras & G. Henningsen, "Forty-four Thousand Cases of the Spanish Inquisition (1540-1700): Analysis of a Historical Data Bank," in *The Inquisition in Early Modern Europe,* ed. G. Henningsen & J. Tedeschi (DeKalb, Ill: Northern Illinois University Press, 1986), 100-29, esp. 122.

[16]E. William Monter & John Tedeschi, "The Dispersed Archives of the Roman Inquisition," *The Inquisition in Early Modern Europe: Studies on Sources and Methods,* ed. Gustav Henningsen & John Tedeschi in Association with Charles Amiel (DeKalb, Ill.: Northern Illinois University Press, 1986), 130-57. See also E. William Monter, "Women and the Italian Inquisition," in *Women in the Middle Ages and the Renaissance,* ed. Mary Beth Rose (Syracuse: Syracuse University Press, 1986), 82.

[17]Carlo Ginzburg, *I Benandanti: Stregonerie e culti agrari tra Cinquecento e Seicento* (Rome: Giulio Einaudi editore, 1966; English translation 1983).

women that made Protestant women appear more threatening than their Catholic counterparts. Third, the lack of a centralized institution, such as the Inquisition or Parlement of Paris, to handle witchcraft cases in many Protestant countries meant that witchcraft trials were more subject to the views of individual magistrates and consequently more susceptible to the local hysteria generated by witch panics.

*   *   *

To establish the context for the witchcraze, it is important to recognize that the Reformation and Counter-Reformation periods witnessed a new and unparalleled, concern with order and orthodoxy. The breakdown of social, political, and religious consensus was paralleled by the collapse of traditional intellectual and scientific systems. Fascination with monsters, amazons, hermaphrodites, prodigies, apparitions, comets, and, witches, in short with everything "unnatural," was indicative of the profound anxiety awakened by the destruction of existing categories. New categories without ambiguity had to be imposed or created.[18] Questions of identity and especially of gender identity were involved in these larger issues. As Stephen Greenblatt and others have demonstrated, anxiety about precisely what constituted "the self" increased during the Renaissance as power and class relationships were redefined. Dichotomies such as active versus passive, dominant versus subordinate, reason versus sense, and public versus private had to be reformulated for an increasingly centralized, commercialized urban society. Since these categories were themselves subsumed under the broader antithesis between masculine and feminine, the issue of what it was to be male and female assumed fundamental importance. The differentiation of roles by gender is emphasized in the conduct books of the period. In his handbook for the instruction of young boys, Erasmus advises young males as follows:

> Attention must be paid to the care of the teeth, but to whiten them with fine powder is for girls. . . . It is boorish to go about with one's hair uncombed: it should be neat, but not as elaborate as a girl's coiffure. . . The hair should neither cover the brow nor flow down over the shoulders. To be constantly tossing the hair with a flick of the head is for frolicsome horses. The gait should be neither mincing nor headlong, the former being a sign of effeminacy, the latter of rage.[19]

---

[18]Katharine Park & Lorraine J. Daston, "Unnatural Conceptions: The Study of Monsters in Sixteenth- and Seventeenth-Century France and England," *Past and Present* 92 (1981): 20-54.

[19]Desiderius Erasmus, *On Good Manners for Boys/ De Civilitate Morum puerlium,* (1530), trans. and annotated Brian McGregor, *Collected Works of Erasmus* (Toronto: University of Toronto Press, 1985), 25: 269-89, esp. 276-78.

Erasmus emphasizes what not to do, differentiating male behavior from that of women and animals. Calling attention to this essentially negative self definition, Greenblatt inventively explores distinctions introduced in Simone de Beauvoir's *The Second Sex* and emphasizes the importance of "the other" in male "self-fashioning":

> Self-fashioning is achieved in relation to something perceived as alien, strange, or hostile. This threatening other – heretic, savage, witch, adulteress, traitor, Antichrist – must be discovered or invented in order to be attacked and destroyed.[20]

While problems of order and disorder and the issue of identity affected both Catholics and Protestants, I would argue that Protestants were affected disproportionately. For Protestants were instrumental in the dissolution of the old order, as Catholics never tired of reminding them. They had rejected one authority, that of the Church, and one father, the Pope. They were therefore constrained to establish a new order and authority and to construct a new identity that would justify their rebellion. Both activities involved rejection and reconstruction. The avenue that this took was twofold, an excoriation of the Catholic Church as the embodiment of all that was corrupt, evil, and sinful, and the imposition of a new order based on rigid notions of patriarchal authority and obedience. The violence of the Protestant rejection of the Catholic Church in terms of both verbal invective and the physical destruction of Church property helped to create the sense of identity that Protestants were seeking. As I will argue in this paper, the Protestant construction of a new order and belief system had a profound and, in the short term, detrimental effect on women. For women in general and the witch in particular were at the core of the "other" against which Protestant males defined themselves. Just as a humanist like Erasmus delineated the proper behavior of young males as a mean between two poles, effeminacy on the one hand and bestiality on the other, so too did Protestants. But for Protestants there was a tendency for this polarity to collapse into the single figure of the unruly witch, who was both female and bestial.

The polarization of the sexes was symptomatic of the kind of dualism characterizing early modern thought as a whole and religious thought in particular. The tendency to see things in the black and white terms of good or bad, for or against, orthodox or heretical, lawful or illegal was further encouraged by millenarian and apocalyptic thought.[21] In the two generations preceding the Reformation, apocalypticism spread, contributing to the sense of doom and expectation that set the stage for the Reformation

---

[20]Stephen J. Greenblatt, *Renaissance Self-fashioning: From More to Shakespeare* (Chicago: University of Chicago Press, 1980), 9.

[21]R. W. Scribner, *For the Sake of Simple Folk: Popular Propaganda for the German Reformation* (Cambridge: Cambridge University Press, 1981), 247.

proper.[22] Although millenarianism transcended denominational boundaries, it flourished with particular intensity among Protestants, contributing to and confirming their preoccupation with sin and the devil.[23] Believing that they were living in the last dark days before the defeat of the Antichrist and arrival of the Messiah, Protestant millenarians were anxious to do all they could to hurry the process along by helping to institute God's kingdom on earth. Before the "godly" could rule, however, the "ungodly" had to be instructed, disciplined, and, if all else failed, exterminated. The complacency and downright pleasure with which religious people accepted the misfortunes and even the deaths of those with whom they disagreed can only be understood in the context of the religious fanaticism and millenarianism promoted by the Reformation and subsequent wars of religion. As Lamont has succinctly put it, witch hunts are "the other side of the 'Godly Rule' coin, an expression of the same messianic conviction of the need to purify."[24] A. H. Williamson has described the "massive religio-legislative enactments" undertaken by the Scottish parliament with the goal of instituting Christ's Kingdom on earth.[25] In Scotland millenarianism and witch hunting combined to generate some of the heoprest episodes of the witchcraze.[26]

The devil assumed a centrality in Protestant thought that he never achieved in Catholic dogma. Luther, Calvin, and their followers emphasized that the life of a true Christian was one of perpetual struggle against a demonic "other," and, at the same time, they removed the supports of priests and saints.[27] The devil's ascendancy in Protestant thought is reflected in the immense popularity of a new genre of popular literature, the devil book. In its most common form the devil book singled out a particular vice, smoking, drinking, dancing, swearing, or gambling, and showed how

---

[22]Marjorie Reeves, *The Influence of Prophecy in the Later Middle Ages: A Study in Joachimism* (Oxford: Oxford University Press, 1969); Hans Preuss, *Die Vorstellung vom Antichrist im späteren Mittelalter, bei Luther und in der konfessionellen Polemik* (Leipzig: J. C. Heinrichs, 1906).

[23]Robin Barnes, *Prophecy and Gnosis: Apocalypticism in the Wake of the Lutheran Reformation* (Stanford: Stanford University Press, 1988), 3 and passim, argues that apocalyptic thinking was far more prevalent among Lutherans than Catholics. As early as A.D. 431, the belief in the millennium had been condemned as superstitious by the Council of Ephesus. Catholic theologians followed Augustine in rejecting the idea of an earthly paradise, preferring to interpret the book of Revelation as a description of a heavenly city in the world to come. The Church recognized that messianic speculation was potentially revolutionary and inimical to the interests of the Chrch as an institution.

[24]William M. Lamont, *Godly Rule: Politics and Religion, 1603-60* (New York: St. Martin's Press, 1969), 98.

[25]A. H. Williamson, "The Jewish Dimension of the Scottish Apocalypse: Climate, Covenant and World Renewal," paper delivered at the International Workshop on Menasseh Ben Israel and His World, Hebrew University, Jerusalem, 1985.

[26]See Christina Larner, *Enemies of God: The Witch-Hunt in Scotland* (Baltimore: The Johns Hopkins University Press, 1981).

[27]Keith Thomas, *Religion and the Decline of Magic* (New York: Charles Scribner's Sons, 1971), ch. 3-6.

devilish it was; other strategies involved exposing how powerful and ubiquitous the devil and his followers were. By conservative estimate, there were some 100,000 individual copies of devil books on the German market in the 1560s, an enormous number considering the low level of literacy.[28] The sale of devil books was forbidden in Catholic countries, and although they were smuggled in and read by Catholics, devil books were a characteristically Protestant form of literature.

The difference between the Protestant and Catholic attitude toward the ancient idea of a demonic pact provides another indication of the heightened fear of the devil in Protestant thought. The prominence of covenant theology in Protestantism had its dark side. If a covenant was possible between man and God, a diabolical one was equally possible. Such a pact did not even require a formal declaration, simply the intention to sin or indulgence in vice. A comparison of stories involving diabolical pacts, that of Theophilius, a monk, and Dr. Faustus, illustrates how much harder it was for Protestants to renounce a pact once made. The Catholic church told men exactly how to cheat the devil by calling on the Virgin or the saints. Theophilius followed instructions and was saved; Faustus, for whom recourse to the Virgin was out of the question, suffered a horrible death and went to Hell.[29]

The debate over magic that began with the rediscovery of Neoplatonic, Hermetic, and Kabbalistic texts in the Renaissance also had repercussions affecting subsequent Protestant attitudes towards witchcraft. Many Protestants identified Hermetic and esoteric natural magic with the magical aspects of Catholic sacraments and ritual. Their wholesale rejection of magic, together with a providential view of natural events, had important implications for the conception of the witch; for these ideas predisposed many Protestants to accept the "new" definition of a witch as an essentially powerless creature controlled by the devil. The definition of a witch as powerless, first set forth by the Catholic authors of the notorious *Malleus Maleficarum*, became the hallmark of Protestant beliefs about witches.[30] Unlike the medieval stereotype of the witch – the stereotype which continued to serve the Catholic Inquisition – the "new" witch possessed no potions, unguents,

---

[28]Heinrich Grimm, "Die deutschen 'Teufelbucher' des 16 Jahrhunderts: ihre rolle im Buchwesen u. ihre Bedeutung," *Archiv für Geschichte des Buchwesens* 16 (1959): 513-70; Max Osborn, *Die Teufelliteratur des XVI Jahrhunderts,* rpt. (Hildesheim: Georg Olms, 1965), and Keith L. Roos, *The Devil in Sixteenth-Century German Literature: The Teufelsbücher* (Bern: Peter Lang, 1972). Roos gives the much higher estimate of 240,000 but this includes the tracts which were bound together in the three editions of Sigmund Feyerabend's *Theatrum Diabolorum* (1569, 1575, 1587-8), which, if individually counted would, by Roos's estimate, come to over 100,000.

[29]See Roos, *Devil in German Literature,* 48.

[30]See Midelfort, *Witch-hunting in South Western Germany,* 52-53, and Levack *Witch-Hunt in Early Modern Europe,* 8.

books, or spells. Her powers were strictly unnatural and diabolical.[31] Not only did the idea that witches were the unwitting dupes of the devil accord with the Protestant emphasis on the power of God and impotence of man, but it also implied that even evil, threatening, and castrating women, were ultimately controlled by men, something that many Protestant men were desperately eager to hear for reasons explained below. It is tempting to suggest that Protestant insistence on the witch's utter subservience to the devil and denial that she possessed any independent power indicates on a subconscious level a heightened fear of women in general. This brings me to my second point, the attitude toward women in Protestant ideology.

It used to be the accepted view that Protestantism offered women an important step toward liberation. Protestant theologians encouraged women to become literate. They emphasized the importance of women as spiritual leaders in the home, and they encouraged women to free themselves from the intellectual and spiritual domination of priests. By rejecting celibacy and virginity as signs of a more perfect spiritual state and advocating the holiness of married life, Protestantism ennobled the one career open to the vast majority of women.[32] While these positions undoubtedly attracted women to Protestantism, recent scholarship has pointed to aspects of Protestant ideology having less positive implications for women.[33] For one thing, Protestant writers inherited the scholarship and attitudes of Renaissance Humanists, and although there are those who argue that Humanists had an enlightened attitude towards women,[34] qualifications are necessary.

Humanists were first and foremost classicists who had read their Aristotle and knew that women were imperfect males with less of a sense of justice (something Freud would rediscover some twenty-three centuries later). Aristotle's philosophy put the inferiority of women on a scientific basis,

[31]Edward Peters, *The Magician, the Witch and the Law* (Philadelphia: University of Pennsylvania Press, 1978).

[32]W. Kawerau, "Lob und Schimpf des Ehestandes in der Litteratur des 16. Jahrhunderts," *Preussische Jahrbücher* 69 (1892): 760-81; James T. Johnson, *A Society Ordained by God: English Puritan Marriage Doctrine in the First Half of the Seventeenth Century* (Nashville: Abingdon Press, 1970); idem, "The Covenant Idea and the Puritan View of Marriage," *Journal of the History of Ideas* 32 (1971): 107-18; James D. Douglas, "Women and the Continental Reformation," in *Religion and Sexism,* ed. R.R. Ruether (New York: Simon and Schuster, 1974); Margo Todd, "Humanists, Puritans and the Spiritualized Household," *Church History* 49 (1980): 18-34; and Edmund Leites, "The Duty to Desire: Love, Friendship, and Sexuality in Some Puritan Theories of Marriage," *Journal of Social History* 15 (1982): 383-408.

[33]This does not mean that Protestant ideology did not contribute to women's eventual liberation, simply that was not its original intention. The message given by males was not necessarily the one women received. For a provocative discussion of this discrepancy, see Margaret Miles, *Image as Insight: Visual Understanding in Western Christianity and Secular Culture* (Boston: Beacon Press, 1985).

[34]Kathleen M. Davies, "The Sacred Condition of Equality – How Original were Puritan Doctrines of Marriage?" *Social History* 5 (1977): 567ff.; Todd, *Humanists, Puritans, and Household."*

which suggests that science is not value free and never was.[35] Women were wet and cold, men were hot and dry. The coldness of women dictated their intellectual inferiority as well as their physical shape – fat hips, narrow shoulders, small brains – for being cold, women lacked sufficient energy to drive matter upward. What might have been female brains remained, alas, below the waist. That women rarely become bald was, remarkably, a further sign of their inferiority. Men grow bald because of their internal heat, which literally burns the hair off their heads. Besides Aristotle, there was Xenephon to show both Humanists and Protestants that women's place was in the home. There was Ovid to provide remedies for love-sick males and Juvenal (in his Sixth Satire) to point out how mercenary, repellant, and ridiculous women essentially are.

Protestant ideas about women must be interpreted within the context of this inherited misogyny. In fact, the supposed Protestant emphasis on the worth and dignity of women is only understandable in terms of increased stress on the family as the basic unit of society and on the husband and father in his role as the God, priest, and ruler of his "little commonwealth." By entrusting husbands with functions which had previously been divided among husbands, rulers, and priests, Protestantism reinforced patriarchy.[36] Catholic women could at least go to a priest if things got tough at home; but for Protestant women, the priest in a very real sense lived at home. William Gouge makes it perfectly clear that whatever the actual character of a particular husband might be, his position in the family must not be challenged: "Tho an husband in regard of evil qualities may carry the image of the devil, yet in regard of his place and office, he beareth the image of God."[37] Gouge's insistence that a husband retains his privileged position regardless of his moral state rests on an argument specifically rejected by Protestants in the case of Catholic priests, namely that the office takes precedence over the individual. Consistency was not the hobgoblin of this Protestant male mind.

[35]Maryanne C. Horowitz, "Aristotle and Women," *Journal of the History of Biology* 9 (1976): 183-213.

[36]Gordon J. Schochet, *Patriarchialism in Political Thought: The Authoritarian Family and Political Speculation and Attitudes, Especially in Seventeenth-Century England* (New York: Basic Books, Inc, 1975); Retha M. Warnicke, *Women of the English Renaissance and Reformation* (Westport, Conn.: Greenwood Press, 1983), 85-86 and passim; Roberta Hamilton, *The Liberation of Women: A Study of Patriarchy and Capitalism* (London: Allen & Unwin, 1978), 68; Keith Thomas, "Women and the Civil War Sects," *Crisis in Europe, 1560-1660*, ed. Trevor Aston (New York: Basic Books, 1965), 317-40; and Levin L. Schücking, *The Puritan Family: A Social Study from the Literary Sources,* trans. Brian Battershaw (New York: Schocken Books, 1979; first published 1929).

[37]William Gouge, *Of Domesticall Duties: Eight Treatises* (London: Bladen/Haviland, 1622), 275.

During the sixteenth and seventeenth centuries patriarchy also received support from rulers intent on consolidating their political power. Robert Filmer, whose *Patriarcha* argued for the divine right of kings, parallels patriarchy in the family and government, both of which reflect patriarchy in the heavens: "We find in the Decalogue that the law which enjoins obedience to Kings is delivered in terms of: Honour thy Father."[38] Filmer simply leaves out the rest of the commandment, "and thy mother." He was not alone. Hobbes excludes the mother from his definition of the family: ". . . a great Family if it be not part of some Common-wealth, is of it self, as to the Rights of Soveraignty, a little Monarchy; whether that Family consist of a man and his children; or of a man and his servants; or of a man, and his children, and servants together; wherein the Father or Master is the Sovereign"[39]

Literary scholars have recently called attention to how often mothers were left out in the seventeenth century. Louis Montrose has commented on the significant lack of mothers in Shakespeare.[40] Mothers are significantly absent from male autobiographies as well. One would hardly know from reading the autobiographies of Baxter and Locke, for example, that they had been "of woman born."[41] Jonathan Goldberg notes the same omission of mother in Stuart family portraits.[42] Political imagery shows male rulers taking over female roles. King James I of England envisioned himself as the single parent of his realm, as "a loving nourish-father" who provided his subject with "their own nourish-milk."[43] Scientists were so entranced by this patriarchal rhetoric that they claimed to have made microscopic observations of spermatozoa containing perfect little embryos. In this sort

[38]Robert Filmer, *Patriarcha and Other Political Works of Sir Robert Filmer,* ed. Peter Laslett (Oxford: Basil Blackwell, 1949), 188.

[39]Thomas Hobbes, *Leviathan, or the Matter, Form, and Power of a Commonwealth, Ecclesiastical and Civil* (1651), ch. 20, par. 15.

[40]Louis Montrose, "A Midsummer Night's Dream and the Shaping Fantasies of Elizabethan Culture: Gender, Power, Form" in *Rewriting the Renaissance: The Discourse of Sexual Difference in Early Modern Europe,* ed. Margaret W. Ferguson, Maureen Quilligan & Nancy J. Vickers (Chicago: University of Chicago Press, 1986).

[41]See Schücking, *The Puritan Family,* 85 ff.

[42]Jonathan Goldberg, "Fatherly Authority: The Politics of Stuart Family Images," in *Rewriting the Renaissance: The Discourses of Sexual Difference in Early Modern Europe,* ed. Margaret W. Ferguson, Maureen Quilligan & Nancy J. Vickers (Chicago: University of Chicago Press, 1986), 85ff.

[43]Stephen Orgel, "Prospero's Wife," *Rewriting the Renaissance: The Discourse of Sexual Difference in Early Modern Europe,* ed. Margaret W. Ferguson, Maureen Quilligan, & Nancy J. Vickers (Chicago: University of Chicago Press, 1986), 59.

of macho science, the female role in generation was reduced to that of a nest or warming oven in which the male-engendered embryo hatched.[44]

The androcentrism in Protestant ideology conflicted with the very real power that women had as mothers, wives, and mistresses. The view of women as feeble minded, physically weak, and in need of male domination simply did not fit the facts, as Margaret Ezell has made abundantly clear in her book *The Patriarch's Wife*.[45]I would argue that this discrepancy fostered a collective anxiety about women and about their potentially destructive power that betrays itself quite openly in the cultural fantasies surrounding the witch.

The sixteenth century has been described as one of the most bitterly misogynist periods in Western history.[46] By rejecting celibacy as an inherently more desirable spiritual state and by making marriage the rule for priest and layman alike, Luther unwittingly contributed to an upsurge in misogynist literature. In their initial stages both Lutheranism and Calvinism attempted to eliminate the double standard by making men adhere to the same ideal of chastity before marriage and fidelity during marriage prescribed for women.[47] Such an ideal made illicit sexual activity seem even worse and, with the abolition of the confessional, male guilt over sexual transgressions intensified. Guilt leads to projection, to the transfer of responsibility to the other party, in this case women. The polemical debates among Protestants about the pros and cons of marriage reveals considerable projection, which expresses itself in explicit discussions of the repellent, untrustworthy, and downright dangerous nature of women.

[44]Joseph Needham, *A History of Embryology* 2d ed., rev. (New York: Abelard-Schuman, 1959). This stunning devaluation of the female role in reproduction goes back to Aristotle's theory that the female provides the matter of the embryo, while the male provides the vital seed or life force – later called the souls, which molds the matter into predictable human form. In Aeschylus's *Eumenides* Apollo defends Orestes against the charge of parricide on the grounds that Clytaemnestra was not his parent, only his father could rightfully be called that. In Shakespeare's *Midsummer Night's Dream* this way of thinking provides the argument as Theseus explains to Hermia why her father has the right to dispose of her as he will: "To you your father should be as a God: / One that compos'd your beauties, yea, and one / To whom you are but as a form in wax / By him imprinted, and within his power / To leave the figure or disfigure it. (I.1.47-51).

[45]Margaret J. M. Ezell, *The Patriarch's Wife: Literary Evidence and the History of the Family* (Chapel Hill: University of North Carolina Press, 1987).

[46]Ruth Kelso, *Doctrine for the Lady of the Renaissance* (Urbana, Ill.: University of Illinois Press, 1956), 6, 10-13; H. C. Erik Midelfort, "Heartland of the Witchcraze: Central and Northern Europe," *History Today* 21 (Feb. 1981): 27-31; David Kunzle, *The Early Comic Strip* (Berkeley: University of California Press, 1973), 222-57; Klaits, *Servants of Satan*, 52.

[47]Keith Thomas, "The Double Standard," *The Journal of the History of Ideas* 20 (1959): 195-216; Keith Thomas, "Puritans and Adultery: The Act of 1650 Reconsidered," in *Puritans and Revolutionaries: Essays in Seventeenth-Century History. Presented to Christopher Hill*, ed. Keith Thomas & D. Pennington (Oxford: Clarendon Press, 1978); Robert V. Schnucker, "La position puritaine l'gard de l'adultre," *Annales: Économies, Sociètès, Civilisations* 27 (1972): 1379-88; and E. William Monter, "Women in Calvinist Geneva (1550-1800)," *Signs* 6 (1980): 189-209.

Clearly misogynist satire was not an exclusively Protestant genre. One has only to read medieval fabliaux or Renaissance texts devoted to the "*querelle des femmes*" to realize that misogyny transcends religious and national barriers. But the sheer quantity and viciousness of Protestant misogynist satire available is second to none.[48] Moreover, the epicenter of this misogyny was Germany, where Lutheranism began, the witchcraft panics were most intense, books about the devil most popular, and executions for witchcraft most numerous. Probably more witches were executed within the boundaries of present-day Germany than in the rest of Europe put together.[49] Sixteenth- and seventeenth-century German broadsheets are filled with descriptions of the marital woes of model husbands. Disorderly women beat and trick their husbands, drink excessively, feast extravagantly, ignore housework, take lovers, and consult witches. The image of the woman on top and wearing men's breeches was as common as it was cautionary; and it was universally agreed that women were sexually rapacious. Engravings and woodcuts of Adam and Eve, Samson and Delilah, Hercules and Omphale, David and Bathsheba, Solomon and his wives, and Aristotle and Phyllis emphasized the dangers of female sexuality, as did the disquieting image of Virgil left dangling in a basket outside the window of a spiteful woman with whom he thought he had an assignation.[50] One broadsheet presents a sardonic "summary of how every woman with a wretched, dissolute husband shall lick him with sticks until his ass-hole is roaring."[51] Such images of treacherous women originated long before the Reformation, but with printing they were more widely disseminated than ever before.

Husband-beating was obviously a hot topic, even though it was far more likely to be the other way around. The prerogatives allowed to husbands in the early modern period advocated a remarkable degree of sheer brutality.[52] Sixteenth-century broadsheets contain fulsome advice about how husbands should deal with obstreperous wives, and this advice invariably includes cudgeling. In one, "Furst's well-tested recipe to cure the evil

---

[48]The *querelle des femmes* reached new heights in both volume and invective during the sixteenth century. The *querelle* has been dismissed as a literary genre with no intrinsic consequences for women on the grounds that the same authors wrote both for and against women. But, as we have learned from Freud, jokes are not all fun. At their best jokes are still camouflaged acts of aggression. In any case, both the attacks and the defenses of women offered the same basic message that a good woman, however rare, was silent, submissive, and obedient.

[49]Midelfort, *Heartland of the Witchcraze*, 21; Monter, "Pedestal and Stake," 130; Levack, *Witch-Hunt in Early Modern Europe*, 19.

[50]Jane C. Hutchinson, "The Housebook Master and the Folly of the Wise Man," *Art Bulletin* 48 (1966): 73-78; George Sarton, "Aristotle and Phyllis," *Isis* 14 (1930): 8-19; and Kunzle, *Early Comic Strip*, 224.

[51]Kunzle, *Early Comic Strip*, 226.

[52]Michael MacDonald, *Mystical Bedlam: Madness, Anxiety, and Healing in Seventeenth-century England* (Cambridge: Cambridge University Press, 1981), 98-105.

disease of disobedient wives," the husband solves his marital problems by beating his wife to death. His solution is not seen as excessive. Indeed, it appears to be fully sanctioned, for in the last scene he is celebrating in a tavern as his wife's funeral cortege files by the open door.[53] Beating was so routinely recommended to husbands as the solution for their marital troubles that satirists personified the concept in the allegorical figure of Dr. Kolbmann. The following ditty about wife-beating cut across national boundaries and became something of an international conceit:

Hastu ein boses Weib am Sontag.
So fahr ins Holt am Montag.
Und haw Bengel am Dinstag.
Schlag dapfer drauf am Mitwoch.
So wird sie kranck am Donnerstag.
Und legt sich gewiss am Freytag.
Stirbt sie dann am Samstag.
So begrebst du sie am Sontag.
Und darauf machst ein guten Montag[54]

This light-hearted bit of male folk wisdom fits in well with the sixteenth-century commonplace that a married man has only two days of happiness: the day he is married and the day he buries his wife.[55]

It still might be objected that all of this is simply in jest. Unfortunately it was not, as is evident from the laws condoning wife-beating, promulgated in the Middle Ages, but still on the books during the period of the witchcraze. The common law of Beauvais, for example, allowed a man to beat his wife "when she refuses her husband anything." A law of Bergerac permitted a husband to draw blood as long as he did so with "bono zelo." Customary law in Bordeaux went so far as to exonerate a husband who had killed his wife in a fit of rage, but only if he confessed under oath that he was repentant.[56] English law on wife-beating was more subtle. It was legal for a husband to beat his wife unconscious, but not to the point at which her inert body farted, a sign that she was in shock and possibly dying.[57] Wife-beating was so common in sixteenth-century London that civic regulations forbade it after nine in the evening because of the noise.[58]

---

[53]Kunzle, *Early Comic Strip*, 229.

[54]William A. Coupe, *The German Illustrated Broadsheet in the Seventeenth Century*, 2 vols., Historical and Iconographical Studies. Bibliotheca Bibliographica Aureliana 17 (Baden-Baden: Verlag Librarie Heitz GMBH, 1966), 51.

[55]Kawerau, "Lob und Schimpf," 42ff.

[56]Jean-Louis Flandrin, *Families in Former Times: Kinship, Household and Sexuality* (New York: Cambridge University Press, 1976).

[57]John Gardner, *The Life and Times of Chaucer* (New York: Knopf, 1977), 53.

[58]Warnicke, *Women of Renaissance and Reformation*, 156.

Protestants took it for granted that if wives failed to be duly submissive, they should be chastised by their husbands. Even in cases of extreme battering, Protestant authorities were reluctant to sanction a wife's request for divorce or separation.[59]

Since wives were so in need of correction, it is not surprising that the figures Bigorne and Chichevache enjoyed renewed popularity in the sixteenth century. Chichevache first appears in an anonymous French poem early in the fourteenth century and is mentioned by Chaucer as well.[60] Bigorne appeared about the same time. Both sum up marriage from a male point of view. Bigorne, or Fillgut, waxed monstrously fat on a diet of obedient husbands; while Chichevache, or Pinch Belly, starved on a diet of virtuous wives. In the sixteenth-century Chichevache becomes an eater of virgins, which explains his even greater emaciation. What had been a medieval satire on shrewish women becomes a Reformation satire on the unchastity of women, a shift of emphasis which reflects increased concern in sixteenth-century Protestant thought with the uncontrollable nature of female sexuality.

This review of attitudes toward women makes it clear that the notion that wives were devious and dangerous was not a Protestant invention, but a commonplace throughout Europe before the Reformation. Nevertheless, the fact that the theme of female subservience becomes a central topic in the many treatises written by Protestants on "domestical duties" suggests that the image of the overbearing wife was especially troublesome for Protestant men. It was troublesome, I would suggest, because of the inherent contradiction in the Protestant attitude toward women. While women were admitted to be men's spiritual equals (on the basis of Gal. 3:28) and worthy of love, they were declared men's inferiors in every other respect. Consider, for example, the contradictory statements in the following passages written by the Protestant William Tyndale:

> Ye must understand that there be two states or degrees in this world: the kingdom of heaven, which is the regiment of the gospel, and the kingdom of this world, which is the temporal regiment. In the first state there is neither father, mother, son, daughter; neither master, mistress, maid, man-servant, nor husband, nor wife, nor lord, nor subject, nor man, nor woman: but Christ is all . . . .
> In the temporal regiment, thou art a person in respect of others; thou art an husband, father, mother, master, mistress, lord, ruler, or wife, son, daughter, servant, subject, etc. And there thou must do according to thine office. If thou be a father, thou must do the

---

[59]Susan C. Karant-Nunn, "Continuity and Change: Some Effects of the Reformation on the Women of Zwickau," *Sixteenth Century Journal* 12 (1982): 32-33; Monter, "Women in Geneva."

[60]Coupe, *German Broadsheet*, 2: 145ff.; Geoffrey Chaucer, "The Merchant's Tale," in *The Works of Geoffrey Chaucer*, ed. F. N. Robinson (Boston: Houghton Mifflin, 1957), 114.

office of a father, and rule, or else thou damnest thyself. Thou must bring all under obedience, whether by fair means or foul. Thou must have obedience of thy wife, of thy servants, and of thy subjects; and the other must obey. If they will not obey with love, thou must chide and fight, as far as the law of God and the law of the land will suffer thee. And when thou canst not rule them, thou art bound in many cases to deliver them unto the higher officer, of whom thou didst take the charge over them.[61]

Protestant thinkers clearly had a problem explaining precisely why the spiritual and temporal status of women were so different; but they never gave up trying. To quote William Whately: "[e]very good woman must suffer herselfe to be convinced in judgement, that she is not her husbands equall. Out of place, out of peace; and woe to those miserable aspiring shoulders, which will not content themselves to take their room below the head."[62] William Gouge admitted that whenever he preached the doctrine of female submission and inferiority, there was a certain amount of "squirming" and "murmuring" on the part of the women in the audience. This simply convinced him that more preaching was necessary. The writings and preaching of theologians and ministers (as well as statements by women themselves), together with the popular broadsheets of the period, suggest that Protestant women had taken the teaching on the spiritual equality of the sexes to heart, while conveniently forgetting that they were at the same time domestically subordinate and intrinsically inferior. In *A Looking-Glasse for Good Women* (1645), the preacher John Brinsley vented his spleen against the women in his congregation who had "such high and imperious spirits . . . as if they were made only to Rule, not at all to obey." What really annoyed Brinsley was that these women had voted with their feet, deserting his congregation. If they could do that to him, he warns, just think what they might do to their husbands: "[such women] will not stoop to any kinde of subiection, specially to their Husbands. . . . If their Husbands weare the Crown, yet they will sway the Scepter. If their Husbands be in places of Authority, they will Rule with them, if not over them."[63]

Brinsley had sufficient cause for alarm. Examples of strong, independently minded Protestant women abound. Catherine Schültz, the wife of the Strasbourg reformer Matthew Zell, had the temerity to quote Scripture in support of sexual equality to the very Bishop who had excommunicated her husband:

---

[61]William Tyndale, "Exposition of Matthew V, VI, VII," in *The Work of William Tyndale*, ed. G. E. Duffield. (Philadelphia: Fortress Press, 1965), 238-39.

[62]William Haller & Malleville Haller, "The Puritan Art of Love," *Huntington Library Quarterly* (1942): 235-72, esp. 249.

[63]John Brinsley, *A Looking-Glasse for Good Women*, (London, 1645), 39.

You remind me that the Apostle Paul told women to be silent in church. I would remind you of the word of this same apostle that in Christ there is no longer male nor female [Gal. 3:28] and of the prophecy of Joel [2:28-9]: "I will pour forth my spirit upon all flesh and your sons and your daughters will prophesy."[64]

Argula von Grumbach was another Protestant women who dared to defy the male establishment.[65] David Underdown has argued that English women working in better-paying trades were becoming increasingly independent economically at the very time they were granted more spiritual authority in the home. These developments undermined the authority of husbands. Restoring this authority obsessed magistrates, increasing substantially the numbers of women prosecuted as scolds by the ecclesiastical courts.[66] Hugh Peters' condemnation of Anne Hutchinson provides a further illustration of how Protestant magistrates reacted to women who ventured beyond their allotted sphere. He was more troubled by her masculine behavior than by her antinomian opinions. Such behavior threatened the natural superiority of the husband in the family unit. As Peters said, "You have stept out of your place. You have rather been a husband than a wife; and a preacher than a hearer; and a magistrate than a subject; and so you have thought to carry all things in church and commonwealth as you would and have not been humble for this."[67] Anne Hutchinson was brought to trial for her insubordination.[68]

The two prevailing images of women in Protestant writings suggest that husbands were not as secure as they might have wished. The first, the good woman who cheerfully accepts her role as submissive wife illustrates the way men would had liked things to be. The second, the "man-kinde woman" or "masterly wife," a monster of perversion, who must be broken

[64]Douglas, "Women and Continental Reformation," 307.

[65]See Albrecht Classen, "Footnotes to the Canon: Geman Women Writers and Patrons in the Fifteenth and Sixteenth Centuries," in Part 2, below.

[66]David Underdown, "The Taming of the Scold: The Enforcement of Patriarchal Authority in Early Modern England," in *Order and Disorder in Early Modern England*, ed. A. Fletcher & J. Stevenson (Cambridge: Cambridge University Press, 1985); S. D. Amussen, "Gender, Family and the Social Order, 1560-1725," in *Order and Disorder in Early Modern England*, ed. A. Fletcher & J. Stevenson. (Cambridge: Cambridge University Press, 1985),

[67]C. F. Adams, ed., *Three Episodes of Massachusetts History: The Settlement of Boston Bay, the Antinomian Controversy, A Study of Church and Town Government*. (New York: Russell & Russell, 1892; rpt. 1965).

[68]Ben Barker-Benfield, "Anne Hutchinson and the Puritan Attitude Toward Women," *Feminist Studies* 1 (1972): 65-96.

like horses,[69] indicates how many men really viewed the situation. One of the most common symbols for virtuous Protestant wives was a snail. To quote Luther:

> Just as the snail carries its house with it, so the wife should stay at home and look after the affairs of the household, as one who has been deprived of the ability of administering those affairs that are outside and that concern the state. She does not go beyond her most personal duties.[70]

As Sigrid Brauner has argued above, the antithesis of Luther's ideal wife is the witch who upsets the natural order in the family by being verbally aggressive when she should be silent, promiscuous when she should be chaste, domineering when she should be obedient, and out and about when she should stay at home. In short, witches were women who rejected the private world of female domesticity for the public world of men. They were women who rebelled and in Puritan circles rebellion was routinely equated with witchcraft and rebellious wives with witches. To quote Cotton Mather, who is quoting 1 Sam. 15:23, "Rebellion is as the sin of witchcraft."[71] In 1692 William Good told one of the Salem judges that "he was afraid that [his wife Sarah] either was a witch or would be one very quickly" because of "her bad carriage to him."[72] The figure of the witch was held up to women in sermons, devil books, and plays as a deterrent to untractable behavior, but the antithesis between the good wife and the witch masked the very real masculine fear that deep down all wives are potential witches. They are potential witches precisely because of their subservient position. Thomas Cooper makes exactly this point in his treatise *The Mystery of Witchcraft*. Women are, he says, "usually more ambitious and desirous of Soveraignety the rather because they are bound to subiection."[73] Copper recognizes what Freud did not, that because women are disenfranchised in a patriarchal system, they are bound to work against it.

[69]Hoak, "Art, Culture, and Mentality," points out the link in sixteenth-century thought between wild horses and demonic women and argues that the strange iconography in Baldung's "Bewitched Groom" is derived from the German folktale, "die Hexe als Pferd." In this tale, a witch, who temporarily assumed the shape of a black horse, awakes to find herself with horse shoes nailed to her hands and feet. The implication is that men tame women just as they do horses.

[70]Martin Luther, *Luther's Works* general ed. Jaroslav Pelican (vols. 1-30, St. Louis: Concordia, 1955-) & Helmut T. Lehmann (vols. 31-55, Philadelphia: Fortress Press, 1955-), 1:202-3. Hereafter cited AE (American Edition), followed by volume and page numbers.

[71]Cotton Mather, *On Witchcraft: Being the Wonders of the Invisible World,* first published at Boston in Octr. 1692 and now reprinted (New York: Bell Publishing Co, n.d.), 157.

[72]Karlsen, *Devil in the Shape of a Woman,* 149.

[73]Thomas Cooper, *The Mystery of Witchcraft* (London, 1617), 206.

Even more interestingly, the very behavior demanded of women by patriarchal society encouraged traits that belong more properly to a witch than to a good wife. Wives were expected to "cajole," "charm," and "entice" their husbands away from evil thoughts and deeds. As Luther says, wives "should deport themselves in such a way in the matter of gestures and conduct that they entice [reytzen] their husbands to believe."[74] While the ends of a wife might be different from that of a witch, their means are surprisingly, indeed, uncannily alike.

Historians of witchcraft have long noted that the witches' sabbath was a late development, appearing after the publication of the classic Catholic treatise on witchcraft, the *Malleus Maleficarum*. While the horrendous, yet titillating spectacle of witches congregating in wild, mountainous lairs, where they indulged in obscene sexual acts, danced riotously, and feasted on loathsome foods, was sufficient to send chills down most male spines, the new group identity and group activity of the witch was especially threatening to Protestant males because it corroborated their deepest fears about Protestant women. Protestant women played an active and noticeable role in the early years of the Reformation, and while their participation was initially encouraged, it was discouraged once Protestantism was established. At that point, Protestant males were eager to reassert their authority, but they did not find women as eager to accept it.[75] The reaction of the Protestant male hierarchy to the women who continued to teach, preach, and even lead sectarian groups makes it clear that in their opinion these women were no better than witches, precisely because they rebelled against male authority. The intemperate language with which the Puritan minister John Cotton denounces Anne Hutchinson for daring to hold religious meetings reveals that in his mind these meetings are nothing short of a witches' sabbath and Anne's behavior that of a witch:

> You cannot evade the Argument. . . that filthie Sinne of the Communuitie of Woemen; and all promiscuous and filthie comings togeather of men and Woemen without Distinction or Relation of Marriage, will necessarily follow . . . . Though I have not herd,

---

74See Sigrid Brauner, *Luther on Witchcraft: A True Reformer?* above.

75See Thomas, "Women and the Civil War Sects"; Claire Cross, "Great Reasoners in Scripture: The Activities of Women Lollards, 1380-1530," *Medieval Women*, ed. Derek Baker (Oxford: Oxford University Press, 1978); Jerome Nadelhaft, "The Englishwoman's Sexual Civil War: Feminist Attitudes Towards Men, Women, and Marriage, 1650-1740," *Journal of the History of Ideas* 43 (1982): 555-79; Robert Stupperich, "Die Frau in der Publizistik der Reformation" *Archiv für Kulturgeschichte* 37 (1955): 204-33; Paul A. Russell, *Lay Theology in the Reformation: Popular Pamphleteers in Southwest Germany, 1521-1525* (Cambridge: Cambridge University Press, 1986); and Susan C. Karant-Nunn, "Continuity and Change: Some Effects of the Reformation on the Women of Zwickau," *Sixteenth Century Journal* 12 (1982): 32-33.

nayther do I thinke you have been unfaythfull to your Husband
in his Marriage Covenant, yet that will follow upon it.[76]

The witch was the antithesis of the virtuous, chaste, and silent Protestant
wife in one other extremely important way. The witch was stereotypically
barren. Not only was she barren, she took positive delight in producing
barrenness in others, either through malicious witchcraft or by turning
innocent young girls away from holy, heterosexual matrimony. The barrenness
of the witch and her apparent wish to spread barrenness about her would
have been especially upsetting to Protestants for whom virginity, except
prior to marriage, had no positive associations. Basing his view on Saint
Paul's first epistle to Timothy (2:14-15),[77] Luther argued that women's
justification and salvation lay in her womb:

> *She will be saved.* That subjection of woman and domination of
> men have not been taken away, have they? No. The penalty
> remains. The blame passed over. The pain and tribulation of childbear-
> ing continue. Those penalties will continue until judgment. So
> also the dominion of men and the subjection of women continue.
> You must endure them. You will also be saved if you have also
> subjected yourselves and bear your children with pain. *Through
> bearing children.* It is a very great comfort that a woman can be
> saved by bearing children, etc. That is, she has an honorable and
> salutary status in life if she keeps busy having children. We ought
> to recommend this passage to them, etc. She is described as "saved"
> not for freedom, for license, but for bearing and rearing children.[78]

In Luther's opinion the ability to give birth enabled women to atone for
their responsibility for the Fall. The womb was therefore woman's true
calling.[79] Within this context the barren yet sexually insatiable witch was
especially repellent.

Many historians have commented on the apparent increase in sexual
anxiety during the early-modern period.[80] The introduction of syphilis into
the Old World contributed to sexual anxiety as well as to an upsurge in

---

[76]Emery Battis, *Saints and Sectarians: Anne Hutchinson and the Antinomian Controversy in
the Massachusetts Bay Colony* (Chapel Hill: University of North Carolina Press, 1962), 242.

[77]"And Adam was not deceived, but the woman being deceived was in the transgression.
Notwithstanding she shall be saved in childbearing, if they continue in faith and charity and
holiness with sobriety."

[78]AE 28:279.

[79]Robert V. Schnucker, "Elizabethan Birth Control and Puritan Attitudes," *Journal of
Interdisciplinary History* 4 (1975): 655-67.

[80]See, for example, William J. Bouwsma, "Anxiety and the Formation of Early Modern
Culture," in *After the Reformation. Essays in Honor of J. H. Hexter,* ed. Barbara C. Malament.
(Philadelphia: University of Pennsylvania Press, 1980).

misogyny.[81] But sexual anxiety was more than a response to a physical disease. It was symptomatic of basic changes in social and religious attitudes, which, I would argue, were intensified by the Protestant Reformation. The disparagement of the body was by no means a Protestant invention, but it did become particularly characteristic of Protestants, for whom the senses and the imagination had few positive associations. While the Catholic Church sanctioned the use of statues, music, incense, vestments, and elaborate pageantry, these appeals to the senses were violently rejected by Protestants, who tended to identify the senses not simply as the enemies of reason but as peculiarly wily and "feminine" enemies of reason. Protestants routinely employed male/female imagery to describe their own psychology. The masculine will had to keep in check the feminine "heart," which included all the physical aspects of being. Greenblatt points out that the poet Wyatt dubs the senses "mermaids" within, who have "usurp[ed] a power in all excess. They must be constrained to obey the rule that reason shall express."[82] To take another random example of this kind of sexist imagery so prevalent in Protestant writings, Gerrard Winstanley describes the sins of his contemporaries in terms of the usurpation of the feminine flesh over the masculine spirit: "They have been led by the powers of the curse in flesh, which is the Feminine part; not by the power of the righteous Spirit which is Christ, the Masculine power."[83] Luther drew a similar comparison between the flesh and women, on the one hand, and the spirit and men, on the other:

> . . . therefore we are the woman because of the flesh, that is, we are carnal, and we are the man because of the spirit which yields to the flesh, we are at the same time both dead and set free.[84]

Because of their identification with the body, the senses (and, by association, women) become the almost exclusive locus of temptation in Protestant polemical writing. That there should be such an emphasis on the senses and sensuality as the principle cause of sin in Protestant thought is understandable when one considers the inherent contradiction between Protestant marriage doctrine and the Protestant emphasis on justification.

In a provocative rereading of Milton's *Samson Agonistes,* John Guillory sets out "to show that Samson Agonistes is a prototype of the bourgeois career drama, which conventionally sets the vocation of the husband against

---

[81]One commentator, Stanislas Andreski, has gone as far as to suggest syphilis as the precipitating cause of the witchcraze. See his "The Syphilitic Shock: A New Explanation of the 'Great Witch Craze' of the Sixteenth and Seventeenth Centuries in Light of Medicine and Psychiatry," *Encounter* (1985): 7-26.

[82]Greenblatt, *Renaissance Self-fashioning* 122.

[83]Gerrard Winstanley, "The New Law of Righteousness," The Works of Gerrard Winstanley, ed. George H. Sabine (New York: Russell & Russell, Inc., 1965), 157.

[84]AE 25:333.

the demands of the housewife."[85] Milton's Samson is a middle class Protestant husband (though admittedly not wholly typical!), and the underlying conflict in the poem is between Samson's vocation and his marriage, or, more simply, a conflict between work and sex. As Guillory points out, the conflict between the two was exacerbated by Protestant marriage doctrine. By confining sex within marriage more strictly than ever before, while at the same time suggesting that sexual satisfaction was a legitimate expectation for both partners, Protestantism intensified the eroticism in the domestic realm.[86] Samson is literally "seduced" by his own wife so that he abandons his true "calling"; and that is the cause of all the trouble.

Before the glorification of romantic love, love was not generally thought of positively.[87] It was an extremely controversial subject for two reasons. First, in as much as it involved physical passion, it could be potentially disruptive; and second, love signified dependency, and dependency was taken as a sign of inferiority. One of Descartes' "proofs" for the inferiority of the body was that it was, in his view, dependent on the mind; by the same token, God's independence was a sign of his perfection. Like every other relationship, a love relationship involved power. Someone had to have the upper hand and be on top. Thomas Gataker makes this point in his marriage manual: "There can bee no ordinary intercourse and commerse or conversing betweene person and person, but that there must be a prededence on the one part, and a yeelding of it on the other."[88] God forbid that the "yeelding" should be that of the man. In his book *The Good Wife, or a Rare One Amongst Women*, Richard Braithwaite warned against precisely this: "Beware (my Sonne), that thou shalt be tide to her/which servitude (though it is too common)/ Disvalues the man that's subject to a woman."[89] Waytt, who clearly failed to take admonitions of this sort seriously enough, exclaims, "I love an other and thus I hate myself." Greenblatt, who quotes this line, comments, "any expression of need or dependence or longing is thus perceived as a significant defeat; the characteristic male as well as national dream is for an unshakable self-sufficiency that would render all relations with others superfluous"[90]

---

[85]John Guillory, "Dalila's House: Samson Agonistes and the Sexual Division of Labor," in *Rewriting the Renaissance: The Discourses of Sexual Difference in Early Modern Europe,* ed. Margaret W. Ferguson, Maureen Quilligan, & Nancy J. Vickers (Chicago: University of Chicago Press, 1986), 110.

[86]Ibid., 116.

[87]J.-L. Flandrin, "Contraception, Marriage, and Sexual Relations in the Christian West," in *Biology of Man in History: Selections from the Annales Économiques, Sociétiés, Civilisations* ed. R. Foster & O. Ranum (Baltimore: The Johns Hopkins University Press, 1975), 23-47.

[88]Thomas Gataker, *Marriage Duties* (London, 1620), 8.

[89]Righard Braithwaite, *The Good Wife, or a Rare One Amongst Women* (London, 1618), sig. B 3r.

[90]Greenblatt, *Renaissance Self-fashioning* 141.

In this kind of social context where hierarchy and dominance are so important, the Protestant emphasis on love in marriage could understandably cause anxiety. Even those Protestant theologians who wrote most about love were not sure exactly how to treat it. William Gouge, for instance, wrote in his *Domesticall Duties* (1622) of "a loving affection" between husband and wife, and yet in another passage he describes fear as an appropriate wifely response: "Love [is] as sugar to sweeten the duties of authoritie, which appertaine to an husband. Feare as salt to season all the duties of subjection which appertaine to a wife"[91]

The choice Samson made of sex over work was not simply a threat to his masculine self-image and identity; it was a threat to his very salvation. For in succumbing to Delilah, Samson was succumbing to the baser side of his own personality, the feminine side, which included the physical delights of sex. Furthermore, the only way anxious Protestants could be certain they were saved was to work hard and succeed. As John Donne put it in his poem "The Break of Day," "the poor, the foul, the false, love can / Admit, but not the busied man." The age-old saw that sex is debilitating for the male, that it literally depletes his vital juices,[92] takes on an even more sinister aspect as sex becomes pitted against work and, via work, salvation. Behind John Winthrop's designation of Anne Hutchinson as the "American Jesabel," lies the conviction that women can "seduce" men mentally and spiritually as well as physically. Sex and heresy are inextricably linked in Winthrop's mind, which explains why he accused Hutchinson of acting just like a witch, who is, of course, both sexually and theologically deviant.

From all the evidence cited, it seems clear that the age-old view that women were intrinsically more evil than men did not disappear with the Protestant emphasis on the spiritual equality of women and on their important role in the family. The old and new view of woman coexisted uneasily, and I am not the first historian to contend that the witchcraze can at least in part be attributed to the inherent tensions in the Protestant view of women. Christina Larner, for example, sees witch hunting in Scotland as an attempt to enforce threatened patriarchal ideals. Carol Karlsen offers a similar interpretation for American witch hunts.[93]

The preoccupation with insubordinate women in Protestant writing makes it all the more interesting that the iconoclasm accompanying the Reformation was especially directed at images of the Virgin Mary and

---

[91]Gouge, *Of Domesticall Duties,* 105, 122.

[92]See James L. Brain, "An Anthropological Perspective on the Witchcraze," in this volume, 15-27.

[93]See Larner, *Enemies of God, 100ff.;* Karlsen, *Devil in the Shape of a Woman,* passim.

female saints, who were compared to "whores" in one Protestant polemic.[94] Smashing "Lady Chapels" and the statues of the Virgin kept in them was commonplace in England and even applauded by Bishop Hugh Latimer on that grounds that men could then turn "from ladyness to Godliness."[95] Clearly, even good women were problematical if they did not keep their place. In Luther's reaction against the Cult of the Virgin, for example, one senses strong resistance to the Virgin's preeminence as a threat to male dominance. In his Personal Prayer Book (*Betbüchlein*) Luther stresses the Virgin's dependence on God, arguing that the Virgin is what she is solely as a result of divine grace, certainly not personal merit:

> Take note of this: no one should put his trust or confidence in the mother of God or her merits, for such trust is worthy of God alone and is the lofty service due only to him. Rather praise and thank God through Mary and the grace given her. Laud and love her simply as the one who, without merit, obtained such blessing from God, sheerly out of his mercy, as she herself testifies in the Magnificat."[96]

Dürer was also appalled by Marian worship. On the back of a woodcut representing the Virgin at Regensburg, he wrote: "This spectre has risen against the Holy Scripture at Regensburg with the permission of the Bishop and has not been abolished because of its worldly usefulness. Lord help us that we should not dishonor the dear Mother by separating her from Jesus Christ. Ahmen."[97]

The limits which Luther and other Protestants placed on Mary's power and independence[98] would have been incomprehensible to the vast majority of Catholics, who considered Mary to be their most valuable intercessor with God and Christ precisely because she was their equal, if not their better. This was apparently the view that Italian peasants took in the mid-sixteenth century, if Paolo Ricci is a credible witness:

> . . . I have heard with my own ears the most of the peasants and all the masses firmly believe that the blessed Mary is equal to Jesus

[94]Phyllis Mack Crewe, *Calvinist Preaching and Iconoclasm in the Netherlands, 1544-1569* (Cambridge: Cambridge University Press, 1978), 23; Emile Màle, "L'Art et le protestantisme," in *L'Art religieux de la fin du XVIe siècle, et du XVIIe siècle* (Paris: Librarie Armand Colin, 1972), 29.

[95]J. Phillips, *The Reformation of Images: Destruction of Art in England, 1535-1660* (Berkeley: University of California Press, 1973), 80.

[96]AE 43:39.

[97]Quoted in Linda C. Hults, Linda C. "Baldung and the Reformation," Hans Baldung Grien: Prints and Drawings Exhibition" organized and catalogue edited by James H. Marrow & Alan Shestack (New Haven: Yale University Art Gallery, 1981), 38-59, esp. 52.

[98]See, for example, William Tyndale, "Obedience of a Christian Man," in *The Work of William Tyndale*, ed. Duffield, 351-52.

Christ in power and in bestowing grace, and some even believe that she is greater. This is the reason that they give: the earthly mother may not only ask but even compel her son to do something; and so the law of motherhood demands that the mother is greater than the son. They say, we believe it is the same in heaven between the blessed Virgin Mary and her son Jesus Christ.[99]

For many Catholics the real Trinity consisted of God, Christ, and Mary. Some went even farther. In the fifteenth century people kept statuettes of the Virgin that opened to reveal the Trinity within. The theologian Jean Gerson, who was, significantly enough, a great promoter of the cult of Saint Joseph, objected strenuously to these statuettes on the grounds that it was heretical to see Mary as the source of the Trinity and not God.[100] Luther's insistence on the Virgin's subordination to Christ reveals the same aversion to powerful, independent women. But while Protestantism swept away images of powerful female saints, these figures continued to provide Catholic men and women with positive images of strong and even eloquent women, who bested the best of men. Saint Catherine, for example, defeated fifty philosophers in debate and converted Saint Anthanasius by her preaching. The place reserved for a powerful woman in Protestant theology was in hell, as a member of that diabolical Trinity of the Pope, Antichrist, and the Whore of Babylon.

The cult of the Virgin Mary has often been described as supremely misogynist because it presented women with a model they could not hope to emulate.[101] I would argue that, on the contrary, the cult of the Virgin was in many respects extremely positive for women. For Mary was considered the second Eve, who repaired the damage done by her predecessor. For Protestants who rejected Mariology, Eve's sin was never balanced or transcended as it was for Catholics. While Eve, and by implication all women, are responsible for man's fall, his sinfulness, and his mortality, there is no female element in the Protestant pantheon to help in man's salvation. The connection between women, sex, sin, and death was consequently reinforced for Protestants in the era of the witchcraze as it was not for Catholics. As we have seen, Catholics considered Mary the equal or superior of Christ, because as a mother she was powerful enough to compel him to do what she wished, even though he was God. Mary's mother, Saint Anne, was another powerful woman and a grandmother to boot. She provided Catholics

---

[99]Carlo Ginzburg, *The Cheese and the Worms* (London: Penguin, 1982), 122.

[100]J. Huizinga, *The Waning of the Middle Ages* (New York: Doubleday Anchor Books, 1954), 156.

[101]Eleanor C. McLaughlin, "Equality of Souls, Inequality of Sexes: Woman in Medieval Theology," in *Religion and Sexism: Images of Woman in the Jewish and Christian Traditions*, ed. Rosemary R. Ruether (New York: Simon & Schuster, 1974), 213-66, esp. 245ff.; Marina Warner, *Alone of Her Sex: The Myth and Cult of the Virgin Mary* (New York: Knopf, 1976).

with a positive image of an old woman to counterbalance the negative image of the evil, old witch.[102] Leonardo's famous picture of the Virgin and Saint Anne with the Christ child is only one of many pictures portraying this basically female and matrilineal Trinity. These positive images of powerful women had been discredited by Protestant theologians and iconoclasts. That they were available to Catholics undoubtedly helped to counteract an idea that becomes something of a leitmotif in Protestant thought, namely that powerful women are by their very nature promiscuous, dangerous, and in the last analysis suspiciously like witches.[103]

This discussion of the implications of Protestant ideology for women suggests that the Protestant emphasis on the spiritual equality of men and women and on marriage and the family as the basic social institutions contributed to the misogynist attitudes and gender conflict that fueled the witchcraze. The emphasis on subordination in marriage also provoked unexpected reactions in women, reactions which also contributed to witch panics.

The seventeenth century has been described as the golden age of demoniacs.[104] Why were so many individuals possessed during the period of the witchcraze? Further, why were women the overwhelming majority of the possessed? This latter question is of great importance in as much as the accusations of possessed women and girls were a significant factor in generating witch persecutions. As historians have discovered, the majority of possessed women were young and unmarried, although a significant percentage of possessed women were also married women approaching or experiencing menopause.[105] The vulnerability of these women to possession may be attributed to a number of specific factors, but their general behavior confirms I. M. Lewis' hypothesis that possession was a strategy used by the weak and oppressed to command attention.[106] In his study of American witchcraft, John Demos documents the marginal position of unmarried girls in New England. In a society that demanded filial obedience and conformity from all its members, but especially from its women, possession

[102]Ton Brandenbarg, "St. Anne and Her Family: The Veneration of St. Anne in Connection with Concepts of Marriage and the Family in the Early-modern Period," in *Saints and She-Devils: Images of Women in the Fifteenth and Sixteenth Centuries,* ed. Lene Dresen-Coenders (London: The Rubicon Press, 1987).

[103]See Carole Levin, "Power, Politics and Sexuality: Images of Elizabeth I," in Part 2 of this volume.

[104]Carlo Ginzburg, *I Benandanti: Stregonerie e culti agrari tra Cinquecento e Seicento* (Rome: Giulio Einaudi editore, 1966; English translation 1983), 115.

[105]John P. Demos, *Entertaining Satan: Witchcraft and the Culture of Early New England* (New York: Oxford University Press, 1982), 97; H. C. Erik Midelfort, "Sin, Melancholy, Obsession: Insanity and Culture in Sixteenth-century Germany," in *Understanding Popular Culture,* ed. Steven L. Kaplan (New York: Mouton, 1985).

[106]I. M. Lewis, *Ecstatic Religion: An Anthropological Study of Spirit Possession and Shamanism* (London: Penguin, 1971).

was the one faultless way for young women to express their rage against the adults and the system which kept them in virtual limbo until marriage. Cotton Mather's description of the behavior of Martha Goodwin, a thirteen-year-old demoniac, is a typical example of what a young girl could never have said or done under normal circumstances: "Her whole carriage to me was with a sauciness that I had not been used to be treated with . . . . She would call me with multiplied impertinences . . . and hector me at a strange rate."[107] In one of her many hysterical fits, Helen Fairfax, the daughter of an English Puritan, was able to speak contemptuously of her father with complete impunity.[108] It is surely significant that the hysterical attacks that touched off the Salem witchcraze began with a seance in which three young women tried to discover the identities of their future husbands. Before Helen Fairfax claimed to have seen a vision of Christ, she had a vision of a handsome young man who asked to marry her. The premium placed on marriage was a source of psychological stress for unmarried girls.

The vulnerability of older women to possession has been attributed to a form of psychological oppression peculiar to them, namely to the premium placed on fecundity as the touchstone of a woman's worth. The value placed on childbearing in Protestant thought, coupled with the incredibly high rates of infant mortality, may have made women especially anxious to find scapegoats in cases of miscarriage and infant death; and menopausal women may have felt the need to blame others for the loss of a highly valued physical capability.[109]

At repeated points in the foregoing discussion I have suggested that while wives, witches, and hysterics existed in both Catholic and Protestant countries, the reaction to them differed. Women, and particularly old querulous women, were far more likely to be convicted of witchcraft in the secular courts of both Protestant and Catholic countries than in the courts of the Catholic Inquisition. Why?

Taking his cue from Claire Guihem's excellent article, "L'Inquisition et la dévaluation du discours féminin," William Monter has gone so far as to attribute the leniency of the Inquisition to its "macho" nature as an institution.[110] Women were simply not considered serious threats, even if they were accused of witchcraft. And possessed women were not accorded as much credibility by the Catholic Inquisitors as they were by Protestant theologians and judges.

[107]Demos, *Entertaining Satan,* 159-60.

[108]Edward Fairfax, *Daemonologia: A Discours on Witchcraft* (London, 1621).

[109]Demos, *Entertaining Satan,* 155ff.

[110]E. William Monter, "Women and the Italian Inquisition," in *Women in the Middle Ages and the Renaissance,* ed. Mary Beth Rose (Syracuse: Syracuse University Press, 1986).

During the sixteenth century the Catholic Church clamped down on female visionaries, probably as a reaction against the swelling tide of female mystics in the late medieval and early modern period.[111] By the seventeenth century mystics were expected to corroborate their visions with tangible evidence. An entire literature grew up on the ways to distinguish true from false revelations. Judith Brown's account of the rise and fall of the lesbian visionary nun, Benedetta Carlini, illustrates the kind of institutional machinery available to help the Catholic theologians distinguish true visions from false, saints from impostors.[112]

The attempts that Protestant theologians made to differentiate true from false visionaries were slipshod and puerile in comparison (for example, Cotton Mather's evaluation of evidence in *The Invisible World*). As Guilhem has shown, the Catholic Church found a way to deal with its female visionaries, hysterics, and demoniacs. When they proved an embarrassment, they were simply declared insane and institutionalized. As mental patients they were robbed of their potential power, even of their identity. As one witness said to the Inquisitors in a case involving a reputed female mystic: "Elle n'existe pas puisqu'elle est folle."[113]

As I said at the beginning of this paper, my intention has been to resurrect the old thesis that the fear of and obsession with witches was greater in Protestant than in Catholic areas and that witch hunts were consequently more severe among Protestants. But the important qualification must be made that these religious distinctions obtain principally for those Catholic countries in which witchcraft trials were conducted under the aegis of the Inquisition or the Parlement of Paris. Centralized legal machinery, together with greater religious stability, kept witch trials in hand and prevented them from developing into full-scale panics and witch hunts.

But even this qualification needs to be examined. The centralization of legal machinery was one consequence of the growing power of centralized political regimes. The centralization that led to adoption of Roman law between the thirteenth and the fifteenth centuries was accompanied by acceptance of inquisitorial procedure and torture. Witch panics were largely generated by the proliferation of accusations obtained under torture. Legal

[111]A. Christian, *Apparitions in Late Medieval and Renaissance Spain* (Princeton: Princeton University Press, 1981); E. W. Kemp, *Canonization and Authority in the Western Church* (New York: AMS Press, 1948).

[112]Judith C. Brown, *Immodest Acts: The Life of a Lesbian Nun in Renaissance Italy* (New York: Oxford University Press, 1986).

[113]Claire Guilhem, "L'Inquisition et la dévaluation du discours féminin," in *L'Inquisition espagnole, xv-xix siècles,* ed. B. Bennasser. (Paris: Hachette, 1979). In England and America charges of insanity and use of mental institutions were not used to control and discipline women until after the witchcraze was over. Cf. Michael Macdonald, *Mystical Bedlam: Madness, Anxiety, and Healing in Seventeenth-Century England* (Cambridge: Cambridge University Press, 1981); Elaine Showalter, *The Female Malady: Women, Madness,and English Culture, 1830-1980* (New York: Pantheon Books, 1985).

reform was therefore the sine qua non of the witchcraze, but if the verdicts of local judges and magistrates were reviewed by superior judges, legal machinery could check the hysteria generated by local panics. This was the case in central France and in those countries under the jurisdiction of the Catholic Inquisition.

Most of Europe's witch trials came from the cultural borderlands, where religious and social diversity were the greatest and where the conflict between Protestants and Catholics was most intense: the Franco-German frontier, southwest Germany and the lower Rhine, the northern alps, and the Franco-Spanish Basque country. In these areas local judges, especially in secular courts, gained greater autonomy 1560. Local magistrates were able to use the full force of the new laws legitimizing inquisitorial procedure and torture against suspect witches; when they did, witch hunts proliferated.[114]

In conclusion, I would argue that while the legal and political situation in sixteenth- and seventeenth-century Europe is too complex to allow for a one-to-one correlation between witch hunts and religious affiliations, the correlation between witch fears and religious affiliation is more straightforward. While the Devil and witches exercised the minds of both Catholics and Protestants, Protestant millenarianism, together with covenant theology, magnified the fear of the Devil at the same time that Protestant theology rejected traditional ways of coping with these fears. Magic and witchcraft were also viewed differently by the Catholic and Protestant intelligentsia who were in a position to intensify or diffuse witch panics. Rejecting all magic as diabolical, many Protestants regarded witches as the devil's disciples; their supernatural crimes could therefore not be proved by ordinary rules of evidence. In the courts of the Inquisition and the Parlement of Paris, older images of the witch as part magician, part sorcerer never entirely disappeared, and consequently more rigorous standards of evidence were demanded. In addition to the new view of the witch, the new ideology about women and marriage in Protestantism contained ambiguities and tensions which made women appear more threatening to men. For Protestant women, the doctrine of spiritual equality coupled with the emphasis on marriage and the inequality of the marriage relationship fostered the insecurity and anger characteristic of those possessed women whose hysterical fits did so much to trigger witch panics. Women, particularly possessed women, posed less of a threat to Catholic Inquisitors. Whatever their crimes and whatever their condition, Catholic women were always subject to male control, whether that of husband, priest, confessor, exorcist, or, if all else failed, Inquisitor.

---

[114]Klaits, *Servants of Satan*, 131ff.; Thomas, *Religion and Decline of Magic*, 245, 438; Levack, *Witch-Hunt in Early Modern Europe*, 80ff., 176ff.

A PURITAN FAMILY
From a print of the sixteenth century.

Part Two:
Marginalized Worthies and Private Letters

Introduction to Part Two

THE SECOND GROUP OF ESSAYS in this collection concerned with the politics of gender continues the familiar process of examining the lives and contributions of individual women. During the early modern period at the same time that economic forces were subtly, if irrevocably, changing the agrarian-based class structure, the consolidation of city states and feudal principalities into nation states ruled by absolute monarchs was affecting concepts of political power. The privileges of class and property were hereditary; so, some women seized power or were thrust into powerful positions. What do these instances in which women gained or received power show us about attitudes toward gender? The following essays show that gender continued to color power relationships. Female power and aspiration continued to be regarded as subversive by both men and women. Powerful queens and religious figures were ignored or flagrantly disparaged.

Carole Levin's essay, "Power, Politics and Sexuality: Images of Elizabeth I," shows how Elizabeth's strategies for self-presentation were undermined by rumors of her unbridled promiscuity and depraved infanticide. Elizabeth fashioned herself as a Protestant parallel to the Virgin Mary, as a beautiful but unattainable Petrarchan mistress, and as the mother of her cherished subjects. Levin's essay illustrates how female power could be denigrated by innuendo and gossip concentrated on female sexuality.

While titillating rumors of sexual excess might tarnish the image of a virgin queen, Marion L. Kuntz shows that established hierarchical religious authority could overlook a woman who earned the epithet the Venetian virgin. In "The Virgin of Venice," Professor Kuntz relates the story of a woman, greatly esteemed in her own time, whose conviction of her own spiritual androgyny and extraordinary practical philanthropy have been ignored. The respect of her contemporaries failed to earn her a position in the mainstream of cultural history as it was later defined.

While public lectures and published treatises about theology have been carefully mined by generations of Reformation scholars, private correspondence, especially of women, affords an important, and too frequently overlooked, source of data. In his essay entitled "Footnotes to the German Canon: Maria von Wolkenstein and Argula von Grumbach," Albrecht Classen sets out to expand the definition of theological debate by arguing that the vigorous correspondence of Maria von Wolkenstein and Argula von Grumbach has received too little attention. Similarly, in "Letters and Literature: Private Correspondence and the French Romance," James B. Fitzmaurice and Martine Rey show how English and French women whose aspirations were confined to a domestic sphere transformed these constraints into an increasingly important locus for literary activity. Adding to the growing literature on the importance of female patrons, this essay describes how as the authors of and audience for familiar letters, women worked underground and on the sidelines to create a literature that contributes to the epistolary tradition that was to nourish the development of the modern novel.

Jean R. Brink
Arizona State University

Power, Politics, and Sexuality: Images of Elizabeth I

Carole Levin

IN A LETTER TO MARY STUART, Elizabeth categorically denied that she favored or practiced deception of any kind: "I love no dissimulation in another, nor do I practice it myself." In spite of this statement, however, Elizabeth I was careful to present herself to her subjects and to the world at large in ways that clearly involved dissimulation. Her self-presentation was calculated, variable, and multifaceted. For example, in a conscious effort to replace the Virgin Mary in the affection of her subjects, she cultivated the image of a royal virgin who was also a mother. Yet she also used courtship as a political tool and made it clear that the romantic adoration of her person provided an avenue of success for upwardly mobile courtiers. She set definite limits to the appreciation of herself as a woman, however. As a queen Elizabeth clearly distinguished herself from other women and behaved in ways that contravened female stereotypes.[1]

Yet despite Elizabeth's brilliance at self-presentation, she was not always able to control the way people responded to her. Together with the love and respect she inspired, she evoked hostile reactions because she was an unmarried female ruler whose position lay outside the traditional role allotted to women in English Renaissance society. Much of the evidence we have for popular reaction to the queen comes from first-hand descriptions of her public ceremonies and progresses, letters, ambassadors' reports, and especially court cases involving people arrested for slandering the queen. While these sources, which abound in rumor and gossip, do not always provide accurate factual information about Elizabeth's life, they tell us a great deal about the social-psychological response to queenship. Jan Vansina comments that "Rumor is the process by which a collective historical consciousness is built. . . . Hence a tradition based on rumor tells more about the mentality of the time of the happening than about the events

[1] This letter is dated June 30, 1568. G.B. Harrison, *The Letters of Queen Elizabeth* (London: Cassell and Co., Ltd., 1935), 53. For the concept of self-fashioning or self-presentation, see Stephen Greenblatt, *Renaissance Self-Fashioning: from More to Shakespeare* (Chicago: University of Chicago Press, 1980); Louis Montrose, "The Elizabethan Subject and the Spenserian Text," in *Literary Theory/Renaissance Texts*, ed. Patricia Parker and David Quilt (Baltimore: Johns Hopkins University Press, 1986), 303-40, and "Shaping Fantasies: Figurations of Gender and Power in Elizabethan Culture," *Representations* 1, no. 2 (1983): 61-94. Research for this essay was completed at the Newberry Library as a Monticello College Foundation Fellow in 1987. I am deeply grateful to the Monticello College Foundation and the Newberry Library for this support and to Constance Jordan, Leah Marcus, Martha Skeeters, Howard Solomon, and Mary Beth Rose for reading early versions of this essay.

themselves."[2] This essay examines Elizabeth I's official and unofficial images to suggest how perceptions of gender focused on sexuality and influenced the complex images associated with the Virgin Queen.[3] The emphasis on Elizabeth's sexuality affected the way she presented herself as well as the way others perceived her. While questions, comments, and gossip about Elizabeth's sexual behavior had begun long before she became queen,[4] attention to her behavior intensified once she gained the throne and continued throughout her reign, even into her sixties. This solicitude over Elizabeth's sexuality allowed the English to voice their insecurity at having a female ruler, while it allowed them to express the hope that she would fulfill her womanly function and have a child – a son who would restore the regular image of monarch, that of king.

For the greater part of the sixteenth century queens ruled in England. The very fact that women ruled created a complex political and social situation with important psychological ramifications. Throughout the Middle Ages, monarchy was, by definition, male. Political theorists perceived a queen as something inherently unacceptable.[5] Queenship called into question the legitimacy of the ruler, a doubt that coincided with the further turmoil

---

[2]Jan Vansina, *Oral Tradition as History* (Madison: University of Wisconsin Press, 1985), 6. For a discussion of the cultural significance of gossip, see Max Gluckman, "Gossip and Scandal," *Current Anthropology* 4, no. 3 (1963): 307-16, Robert Paine, "What is Gossip About? An Alternative Hypothesis," *Man* 2, n.s. (1976): 278-85, and Gluckman's response to Paine, "Psychological, Sociological, and Anthropological Explanations of Witchcraft and Gossip: A Clarification," *Man* 3, n.s. (1968): 20-34; and Patricia Meyer Spacks, *Gossip* (Chicago: University of Chicago Press, 1985).

[3]As Jean Wilson puts it, "The most important fact about Elizabeth I was her sex." *Entertainments for Elizabeth I* (Totowa, New Jersey: Rowman and Littlefield, 1980): 3. Other significant studies on the question of Elizabeth's gender include Leah Marcus, "Shakespeare's Comic Heroines, Elizabeth I, and the Political Uses of Androgyny," in *Women in the Middle Ages and Renaissance: Literary and Historical Perspectives*, ed. Mary Beth Rose (Syracuse, New York: Syracuse University Press, 1986), 135-53; Frances Yates, *Astraea: the Imperial Theme in the Sixteenth Century* (London: Routledge and Kegan Paul, 1975); and Alison Heisch, "Queen Elizabeth I: Parliamentary Rhetoric and the Exercise of Power," *Signs* 1, no.1 (Autumn, 1975): 31-55. Also interesting is Larissa J. Taylor-Smither, "Elizabeth I: A Psychological Profile," *Sixteenth Century Journal* 15, no. 1 (1984): 47-72, which looks at gender issues in terms of Elizabeth's psychological development and how they affected her rule.

[4]Speaking of Elizabeth while a princess, Henry Clifford, *The Life of Jane Dormer, Duchess of Feria*, ed. Joseph Stevenson (London: Burns and Oates, 1887), 86-87, writing early in the next century, says, "In King Edward's time what passed between the Lord Admiral, Sir Thomas Seymour, and her Dr. Latimer preached in a sermon, and was a chief cause that the Parliament condemned the Admiral. There was a bruit of a child born and miserably destroyed, but could not be discovered whose it was; only the report of the midwife, who was brought from her house blindfold thither, and so returned; saw nothing in the house while she was there, but candlelight; only she said, it was the child of a very fair young lady, who was then between fifteen and sixteen years of age. If it were so, it was the judgement of God unto the Admiral; and upon her, to make her ever after incapable of children."

[5]See, for example, the fifteenth-century writings of Sir John Fortescue as quoted in Marc Bloch, *The Royal Touch: Sacred Monarchy and Scrofula in England and France*, trans. by J. E. Anderson (London: Routledge and Kegan Paul, 1973), 130.

brought on by the Reformation. Moreover, Mary I and her sister Elizabeth were both childless, ruining the hope of their subjects that eventually a son would succeed and restore the proper patriarchal order. Mary attempted to follow the traditional path of a woman; she married (although disastrously) and pathetically hoped for a child that did not come, despite a false pregnancy. This marriage to her younger cousin, Philip of Spain, robbed Mary of her power because even though the marriage contract overseen by Parliament attempted to protect Mary's interests, both she and her Councillors deferred to Philip as "king."[6]

Elizabeth, watching from the wings, would hardly be likely to make the same mistake. Courtship was a useful political tool while marriage would have been politically problematic for a woman ruler planning to be anything but a figurehead. In a speech before her first Parliament, Elizabeth declared, "And in the end this shall be for me sufficient, that a marble stone shall declare that a queen having reigned such a time, lived and died a virgin."[7] But by not marrying, Elizabeth rejected the most obvious responsibility of a queen, producing an heir. Elizabeth therefore consciously presented herself to her people as a Virgin Queen who could replace the Virgin Mary and help heal the rupture created by the break with the Catholic Church. She deliberately appropriated the symbolism and prestige of the suppressed Marian cult in order to foster the cult of the Virgin Queen, popularizing a personal mythology that would assist her in dealing with political problems.[8]

The identification of Elizabeth with the Virgin Mary, elaborated largely in the mid 1570s, effectively encouraged loyalty to the queen. Denying her power and prestige, as Protestant reformers did, did not lessen the tremendous appeal the Virgin had on the popular imagination; it simply left a void. The image of Elizabeth, as a Virgin Queen, helped to fill this

[6]According to the marriage treaty, Philip was to receive the title of "king" and be joined with Mary in exercising sovereign power. But he was also bound to uphold the laws of England and he would not possess any executive power in his own right. D. M. Loades, *The Reign of Mary Tudor* (London: Ernest Benn, Limited, 1979), 122. One can see, however, more of the actual power of Philip when one considers his ambassador de Feria's comment at the beginning of Elizabeth's reign. "After all everything depends on the husband she chooses, for the King's wish is paramount here in all things." *Calendar of the Letters and State Papers Relating to English Affairs Preserved in, or originally Belonging to, the Archives of Simancas*, ed. Martin Hume (London: H.M.S.O., 1899), 1: 25. See Constance Jordan's essay, "Woman's Rule in Sixteenth-Century British Political Thought," forthcoming, *Renaissance Quarterly*.

[7]*The Public Speaking of Queen Elizabeth*, ed. George Rice (1951; rpt. New York: AMS Press, 1966), 116.

[8]Particularly useful on this subject are Elkin Calhoun Wilson, *England's Eliza* (Cambridge: Harvard University Press, 1939), and Robin Headlam Wells, *Spenser's Faerie Queen and the Cult of Elizabeth* (Totowa, New Jersey: Barnes and Noble, 1983). Eric W. Ives, *Anne Boleyn* (London: Basil Blackwell, 1986), 283-84, argues that in Anne Boleyn's coronation there was also an identification of the pregnant Virgin Mary with the pregnant Anne Boleyn; John King, "The Godly Woman in Elizabethan Iconography," *Renaissance Quarterly* 38 (1985): 41.

void and to encourage adoration of the monarch. English Protestants came to love and revere Elizabeth as they had previously loved and revered the Virgin. People suggested saying, "Long live Eliza!" instead of "Hail Mary!" John Buxton notes that one of Elizabeth's pictures was carried to Blackfriars in imitation of religious practice relative to the Virgin Mary, "a comparison her subjects did not hesitate to draw."[9] Also a number of the symbols used to represent Elizabeth as Virgin Queen – the Rose, the Star, the Moon, the Phoenix, the Ermine, and the Pearl – were symbols appropriated from the iconography surrounding the Virgin Mary. Roy Strong suggests that although Protestant England banned religious images as idolatrous, images of the monarch were accorded the kind of ceremonial deference reserved for religious icons.[10]

In time, Elizabeth was accepted as a substitute for the Virgin Mary and adulation for the Virgin Queen acquired a religious tinge. For example, many of the members of Elizabeth's court believed that having the queen visit on progress was tantamount to having their house blessed. Lord Burghley wrote about Elizabeth's visit to Theobalds as "consecrating" it; Burghley treated her so splendidly that she visited Theobalds a number of times, a great, if costly, honor.[11] These progresses were critical in systematically promoting the cult of the Virgin Queen for people of all classes and geographical locations.[12]

The celebration of Elizabeth's accession day, November 17, bore the earmarks of a religious festival. The festivities included public thanksgiving for her safety, sermons, and bell-ringing, in addition to more expected and secular contests such as tournaments. After the abortive rebellion in the north in 1569 and the bull of excommunication of 1570, public celebrations marking Elizabeth's accession began spontaneously. The first occurred in Oxford in 1570, but celebrations continued to spread until they were recognized officially as a church holiday in 1576 and given a specific service and liturgy. Part of the service included the entire congregation:

Minister: O Lord, save the Queen.
People: Who putteth her trust in thee.

. . . .

[9]John Buxton, *Elizabethan Taste* (London: Macmillan and Co., l963), 50.

[10]Roy Strong, *Art and Power: Renaissance Festivals, 1450-1650* (Bury St. Edmund's Suffolk: St. Edmundsbury Press, l984), 67.

[11]Cecil identified Elizabeth with his religion in a final letter, *Queen Elizabeth and Her Times,* ed. Thomas Wright, 2 vols. (London: Henry Colburn, 1838), 2: 488, he wrote his son Robert in 1598: "Serve God by serving the Quene, for all other Service is indede bondage to the devill."

[12]John Nichols, *The Progresses and Public Processions of Queen Elizabeth,* 3 vols. (London, 1823; rpt. New York: Burt Franklin, n.d.); J. Neale, *Queen Elizabeth I* (1934; rpt. Garden City, New York: Anchor Books, 1957).

Minister: Let the enemies have none advantage on her.
People: Let not the wicked approach to hurt her.[13]

November 17 became a day of patriotic rejoicing, "in the forme of a Holy Day," as Thomas Holland said in a sermon in 1599 to answer those that "uncharitably traduced the honour of the realm."[14]

Elizabeth's birthday, September 7, was also a day of organized public rejoicing with religious overtones. One prayer asked God to bless Elizabeth and curse her enemies:

to fight against those that fight against her . . . . Bless them that blesse her. Curse them that curse her. . . . Lett her rise. Lett them fall. Lett her flourish. Lett them perish.[15]

In a letter to William Cecil, the Recorder of London, William Fleetwood described how London celebrated this day in the 1580s:

This Weddensday morning all the bells of London do ring for joye, that upon the seven of this monethe, being on this daie . . . her Grace was borne. There will be on this daie but specially great feastings at supper. I have been bidden out this night to supper in six or seven places.[16]

The celebration of Elizabeth's birthday was particularly offensive to English Catholics because September 7 was coincidentally the feast of the nativity of the Blessed Virgin Mary. Catholics such as Nicholas Sanders complained that the English Protestants were ignoring this holy day, and "to the farther contempt of that Blessed Virgine, insteede thereof, most solemnly doe celebrate the birth-day of Q. Elizabeth."[17]

Many of her subjects regarded the fact that Elizabeth shared the nativity of the Virgin Mary as more than simply coincidence; they considered it a divine omen. It was proof that Elizabeth and the Anglican Church were sustained and sanctified by divine providence. This belief was further intensified when the date of Elizabeth's death, March 24, coincided with the eve of the Annunciation of the Virgin Mary. Soon after the queen's death, one anonymous Latin elegy asked, "do you wish to know why it

---

[13]*Liturgies and Occasional Forms of Prayer set forth in the Reign of Queen Elizabeth,* ed. William Keatings Clay (Cambridge: Cambridge University Press, 1847), 554-55.

[14]C.J. Kitching, "'Prayers Fit for the Time': Fasting and Prayer in Response to National Crises in the Reign of Elizabeth I," in *Monks, Hermits and the Ascetic Tradition,* ed. W.J. Sheils (Published for the Ecclesiastical Historical Society by Basil Blackwell, 1985). Thomas Holland, *A Sermon Preached at Paul's in London to 17 of November 1599, the one and fortieth yeare of her Maiestie raigne, and augmented in those places wherein, for the shortnes of the time, it could not be then delivered* (Oxford: Joseph Barnes, 1601), n.p.

[15]Clay, *Liturgies and Occasional Forms of Prayer,* 557 n.

[16]Wright, *Queen Elizabeth,* 2: 309.

[17]Quoted in Holland, *A Sermon's Preached at Paul's,* n.p.

was on the Eve of the Lady that the holy Eliza ascended into heaven?" The answer emphasizes parallels commonly perceived between Elizabeth and the Virgin Mary:

> Being on the point of death she chose that day for herself because in their lives these two were as one. Mary was a Virgin, she, Elizabeth, was also; Mary was blessed; Beta was blessed among the race of women. Mary's heir was her womb, but Elizabeth bore God in her heart. Although in all other respects they are like twins, it is in this latter respect alone thay there are not of equal rank.[18]

An engraving of the queen produced right after her death had as a caption, "She was, She is (What can there more be said?), In earth the first, in heaven the second Maid."[19] In 1607 Christopher Lever helped perpetuate this identification with a long poem about the sufferings Elizabeth endured under her sister Mary's reign. Lever placed Elizabeth among the saints and angels of Heaven, "as one far exceeding all others, the Virgin Mary only except."[20]

People, however, did not solely regard Elizabeth as a Virgin Queen. They were intrigued by her imagined and real sexuality. People talked about her love affairs, speculating on the one hand, about the number of illegitimate children she had borne, and, wondering, on the other, whether she had a physical deformity that kept her from consummating a physical relationship. These rumors served the dual purpose of allowing people to speculate openly about the succession of a male heir, while denigrating Elizabeth in a typically misogynist way – by labelling her a whore.

The interest in Elizabeth's sexuality was undoubtedly heightened by her involvement in many courtships. While Elizabeth proclaimed that she hated these negotiations, many believed otherwise. Sir Henry Sidney thought Elizabeth was "greedy for marriage proposals," a view shared by the Spanish Ambassador, Guzman de Silva: "I do not think anything is more enjoyable to this Queen than treating of marriage, although she assures me herself that nothing annoys her more. She is vain, and would like all the world to be running after her."[21]

---

[18]Quoted in Wilson, *England's Eliza*, 382. When Elizabeth died an engraving was published with the inscription, "This Maiden Queen Elizabeth came into this world the Eve of the Nativity of the Blessed Virgin Mary; and died on the Eve of the Annunciation of the Virgin Mary." Buxton, *Elizabethan Taste*, 51.

[19]Quoted in Yates, *Astraea*, 79.

[20]G.B. Harrison, *A Second Jacobean Journal* (Ann Arbor: the University of Michigan Press, l958), 26.

[21]*Calendar of State Papers (CSP), Spain*, 1:463, 468. Yet while Elizabeth loved proposals, she genuinely hated the the idea of an actual marriage. The thought of it, she once confided, was like having her heart torn out of her body. Elizabeth Jenkins, *Elizabeth the Great* (London: Victor Gollancz, Ltd., l958), 100.

In the first years of her reign, Elizabeth was seen everywhere with Robert Dudley, whom she eventually created Earl of Leicester. Especially after the mysterious death of Dudley's wife, Amy Robsart, many feared she would forget everything in a moment of passion and marry him. Sir Nicholas Throckmorton, the English Ambassador, wrote from Paris that the French gossip about Elizabeth's morals made him wish he were dead: "One laugheth at us, another threateneth, another revileth the Queen. Some let not to say, what religion is this that a subject shall kill his wife, and the Prince not only bear withal but marry with him?" Throckmorton begged William Cecil to discover some method to prevent the marriage. If the queen married Dudley, he predicted, "God and religion will be out of estimation; the Queen discredited, condemned, and neglected; and the country ruined and made prey."[22]

Implicit in these comments and speculations, so carefully gathered by a worried government, is a definite thread of malice – the sense that Elizabeth, this unmarried woman of questionable morals, had no business ruling. In 1560 there were several reports that Elizabeth was pregnant. For instance, Mother Anne Dowe was committed to jail for "openly asserting that the Queen was with child by Robt. Duddeley." Mother Dowe had come in one morning to a tailor's shop, saying that there were things going on that no one should speak about – which she immediately proceeded to do. She told the astonished tailor that Lord Robert had given the queen a child. When the tailor responded, "Why she hath no child yet!" Mother Dowe replied, "He hath put one to the making."[23] Three years later Edmund Baxter openly expressed the not uncommon view that Elizabeth's reputed unchastity disqualified her as a monarch, saying: "that Lord Robert [Dudley] ke   and that she was a naughty woman, and could not rule he   justice was not being administered." His wife added that   e Queen at Ipswich "she looked like one lately come out   Though the ability to administer justice had nothing to   h's sexual behavior, in her subjects' minds, they were inexi   ven the most private sin could have an impact on public   sins carried special weight. Physical corruption of the mo   ct upon the body politic. By labelling Elizabeth unchaste,   ttacking her as a female ruler. Women preserved their hon   gh chastity, but also by maintaining a reputation for chaste   a woman to be thought unchaste, even falsely,

[22]*CSP   e reign of Elizabeth, 1560-1561,* ed. Joseph Stevenson; first published l   ionary Office, London, 1865 (Nendeln, Kiechtenstein: Kraus Reprint, L

[23]*CSl   *; Jenkins, *Elizabeth the Great,* 96; F. G. Emmison, *Elizabethan Life: Disor   *x County Council, 1970), 41.

[24]*CSl   z.,* 11: 534.

jeopardized her honor.[25] The gossip of Mother Anne Dowe and the Baxters was more comprehensible than later rumors because in the 1560s Elizabeth was young, unmarried, and reputed to be indiscreet in her public displays of affection for Robert Dudley.

Elizabeth herself responded to the various rumors surrounding her. In 1564 she told the Spanish Ambassador, de Silva, a man with whom she shared a number of confidences:

> They charge me with a good many things in my own country and elsewhere, and, amongst others, that I show more favour to Robert than is fitting; speaking of me as they might speak of an immodest woman. . . . I have shown favour, although not so much as he deserves, but God knows how great a slander it is, and a time will come when the world will know it. My life is in the open, and I have so many witnesses that I cannot understand how so bad a judgement can have been formed of me.[26]

Yet the gossip about Elizabeth's behavior continued. The Spanish Ambassador heard rumors that Dudley slept with the Queen on New Year's, 1566.[27] In 1570 a man named Marshame was condemned to lose both his ears or else pay a fine of a hundred pounds for saying that Elizabeth had two children by Robert Dudley. The year after, a man named Mather was arrested for saying that "Mr. Hatton had more recourse to Her Majesty in her Privy Chamber than reason would suffer if she were so virtuous and well-inclined as some noiseth her!"[28] The next year Robert Blosse was brought before the Recorder of London, for spreading rumors that Elizabeth

---

[25]Lawrence Stone, *The Family, Sex, and Marriage in England, 1500-1800* (New York: Harper and Row, 1977), 503-504; Spacks, *Gossip*, 32. For a very useful discussion of women's honor and sexuality, particularly as it affected Elizabeth's mother, Anne Boleyn, see Retha Warnicke, "The Fall of Anne Boleyn: A Reassessment," *History* 70, no. 228 (1985): 10-11, and "The Eternal Triangle and Court Politics: Henry VIII, Anne Boleyn, and Sir Thomas Wyatt," *Albion* 18, no. 4 (1986): 565-79. For a discussion of the impact of Protestantism on the concept of honor, see Mervyn Jones, "English Politics and the Conception of Honour, 1485-1642" *Past and Present,* Supplement 3, (1978). It is also useful to look at proverbs about women in the Renaissance to see the linking of sexual misconduct and generally dishonorable behavior. See Morris Palmer Tilley, *A Dictionary of the Proverbs in England in the Sixteenth and Seventeenth Centuries* (Ann Arbor: University of Michigan Press, 1950), 741-49.

[26]*CSP, Spain,* 1: 387. Cecil affirmed the same thing in a letter to Sir Thomas Smith. "Briefly I affirm, that the Quene's Majesty may be, by malicious tongs, not well reported, but in truth she herself is blameless and hath no spot of evill." Wright, *Queen Elizabeth,* 1: 225.

[27]*CSP, Spain,* 1: 520-21.

[28]Jenkins, *Elizabeth the Great,* 166.

had four children by Robert Dudley.[29] That same year Matthew Parker, Archbishop of Canterbury, wrote a very concerned letter to William Cecil about the "most shamefull words against" Elizabeth spoken by a man brought before the mayor of Dover. What the man said about Elizabeth and both Dudley and Sir Christopher Hatton was "a matter so horrible" that Parker would not put it on paper, but instead, wished only to speak of it to Cecil when he had the chance.[30]

In the 1560s and 1570s the rumors of Elizabeth's pregnancies and illegitimate children continued to crop up, especially among hostile foreign Catholics. Writing in 1564, the secretary to the former Spanish Ambassador de Quadra commented on plans for Elizabeth to go to the North of England: "Some say she is pregnant and is going away to lie in."[31] A decade later Antonio de Guaras, acting Spanish agent in London, reported that there would be a marriage between the son of Catherine Grey and "a daughter of Leicester and the Queen . . . who, it is said, is kept hidden, although there are bishops to witness that she is legitimate."[32] In December of 1575 Nicholas Ormanetto, Bishop of Padua and Nuncio in Spain, heard that Elizabeth had a daughter. The pope took the possibility of Elizabeth's having a marriageable daughter seriously and saw it as a way to "bring the realm back to the Catholic faith" without the hazards of war. In 1578 there were rumors on the continent that Alençon would marry, not Elizabeth, but her daughter.[33]

The rumors about Elizabeth's illegitimate children became even more insistent in the last two decades of her reign. By the early 1580s Elizabeth, already in her late forties, was playing out the final marriage negotiations of her reign with the young Duke of Alençon. Critics such as John Stubbs outraged the queen by arguing against the marriage on the grounds that Elizabeth was now too old to bear a child.[34] The rumors about her illegitimate children, often coupled with the suggestion these children had been destroyed, reflect another level of the fear over the succession and the antagonism toward a queen who refused to provide for her people's future.

[29]Wright, *Queen Elizabeth*, 1: 374; John Strype, *Annals of the Reformation*, 2 vols. (Oxford: Clarendon Press, 1824), 2: pt. 2, 503. I am indebted to Dennis Moore for this reference to Blosse. Robert Blosse also spread rumors that Edward VI was still alive, and fifteen years later actually claimed to be Edward VI. For more on this incident, see Carole Levin, "Queens and Claimants: Political Insecurity in Sixteenth Century England," in Janet Sharistanian, *Gender, Ideology, and Action: Women's Public Lives in Historical Perspective* (Westport, CN: Greenwood Press, 1986), 54-55.

[30]Wright, *Queen Elizabeth and Her Times*, 1: 440-41.

[31]*CSP, Spain*, 1: 362.

[32]Ibid. 2: 491.

[33]*CSP, Relating to English Affairs Preserved Principally at Rome, Elizabeth, 1572-78*, ed. J. M. Rigg (London: His Majesty's Stationery Office, 1926), 238, 250.

[34]*John Stubb's Gaping Gulf with Letters and Other Relevant Documents*, ed. Lloyd E. Berry (Charlottesville: University Press of Virginia for the Folger Shakespeare Library, 1968), 51.

In 1580 an Essex laborer, Thomas Playfere, stated that Elizabeth had two children by Lord Robert; he had himself seen them when they had been shipped out at Rye in two of the queen's best ships. The next year Henry Hawkins explained Elizabeth's frequent progresses throughout the countryside as a way for her to leave court and have her illegitimate children by Dudley – five all told. Said Hawkins of the queen, "She never goethe in progress but to be delivered."[35] At the end of the decade, in 1589, Thomas Wendon claimed that "Parson Wylton spake openly in church . . . that the Queen's Majesty was an arrant whore" since "the Queen is a dancer, and Wylton said that all dancers are whores."[36]

The next year a widow named Dionisia Deryck claimed that Elizabeth "hath already had as many children as I, and that two of them were yet alive, one a man child and the other a maiden child, and the others were burned." We do not know exactly how many that was meant to be since the records do not state how many times Deryck herself had given birth. Deryck claimed the father of the queen's children was Dudley, who had "wrapped them up in the embers which was in the chamber where they were born." The same year Robert Gardner told a similar story; Leicester "had four children by the Queen's Majesty, whereof three were daughters alive, and the fourth a son that was burnt."[37]

In 1598 Edward Fraunces, of Melbury Osmond in Dorsetshire, attempted to seduce Elizabeth Baylie by telling her the queen had three bastards by noblemen at court, two sons and a daughter. Why should not Baylie have a sexual relationship without marriage, he asked her, when "the best in England," i.e. the Queen, "had done so." Elizabeth Baylie's refusal made Fraunces angry not only with her, but with the woman he had urged upon her as a model. He called the queen "base born," and he added, "that the land had been happy if Her Majesty had been cut off twenty years since, so that some noble prince might have reigned in her stead." Elizabeth Baylie testified about this conversation before the magistrates, as did others of her neighbors. Fraunces attempted to bribe the witnesses, offering the men twice the money he offered the women. The witnesses, however, were outraged enough by his slander of the queen to refuse. Fraunces amplified his misogyny when he attempted to discredit Baylie's testimony with the statement that "women are base creatures and of no credit."[38]

[35]Montrose, "The Elizabethan Subject and the Spenserian Text," 311; Emmison, *Elizabethan Life,* 42; *CSP, Dom. Eliz.,* 148: 12.

[36]Emmison, *Elizabethan Life,* 42-43.

[37]Ibid., 42

[38]*CSP, Dom. Eliz.,* 269, no. 22, 136-37; G.B. Harrision, *The Elizabethan Journals* (New York: the Macmillan Co., 1939), pt. 2, 51.

As late as 1601 there were still reports of infanticide. The most interesting version came from a man named Hugh Broughton, who again wove together the themes of Elizabeth's lack of chastity, hostility toward her rule, and destruction of the potential heir. According to Broughton, a midwife was taken to a secret chamber where she was told to save the mother (Elizabeth, of course) at whatever cost to the child. The midwife was too skilled; she saved them both:

> And after [delivering] . . . a daughter, [the midwife] was brought to another chamber where there was a very great fire of coals, into which she was commanded to cast the child, and so it was burnt. This midwife was rewarded with a handful of gold, and at her departure, one came to her with a cup of wine, and said, Thou whore, drink before thou goest from hence, and she drank, and was sent back to her house, where within six days after she died of poison, but revealed this before her death.[39]

In Playfere's story of 1580, the children are shipped away. Closer to the end of the reign, in the rumors spread by Deryck, Gardner, and Broughton, the children are actually destroyed. Elizabeth had not only dishonored herself by being a whore, but she had also destroyed, literally burned up, her successors. Gardner, for example, insisted that although Elizabeth's supposed daughters survived, the son, the potential king, died horribly. We cannot interpret these stories of Elizabeth's sexual misconduct as simply proceeding from male discomfort at female rule, since women also participated in this gossip.[40]

At the same time that some people were whispering about just how many illegitimate children Elizabeth had, others were doubting whether she was capable of conceiving a child or of even consummating a sexual relationship. The Scottish Ambassador, James Melville, was convinced that Elizabeth knew "herself incapable of children." The Spanish Ambassador, de Feria, told Philip II, "for a reason they have given me, I understand

---

[39]*CSP, Dom. Eliz.*, 279, no. 48: 24.

[40]Though their style of governing was different, both Mary and Elizabeth had to share the problems of being a female ruler who did not produce an heir. The concern over Elizabeth's potential fertility, which manifested itself in rumors of illegitimate children, has a parallel in Mary's reign as well. Mary was clearly infertile. She married and experienced a false pregnancy that ended in humiliation and despair. Yet in spite of the obvious fact that Mary could not produce a child, a rumor did surface during her reign that she had an illegitimate child by Stephen Gardiner, bishop of Winchester, which was surely an improbable combination. See John Strype, *Memorials of the reverend Father in God, Thomas Cranmer* (Oxford: Oxford University Press, 1840), 456. I think this rumor also represented both denigration of the queen and wish fulfillment. Eventually the rumors about Elizabeth's illegitimate children brought forth an actual imposter, a man calling himself Arthur Dudley, who appeared in Spain in 1587. For more information, see Levin, "Queens and Claimants," 59-60, and *Calendar of the Letters and State Papers Relating to English Affairs Preserved in, or originally Belonging to, the Archives of Simancas,* ed. Martin Hume (London: H.M.S.O., 1899), 4: 101-12.

she will not bear children." Early in her reign, foreign ambassadors bribed the women of Elizabeth's bedchamber for intimate information about her life, and their reports home are filled with such details as Elizabeth's light and irregular periods. The Venetian Ambassador heard that she had been bled in the foot in an attempt to correct this problem. Later, the Nuncio in France heard rumors that Elizabeth flowed from "an issue in one of her legs" since "she has hardly ever had the purgations proper to all women."[41]

There were also rumors that Elizabeth had an impediment that would prohibit regular sexual relations, and thus make conception impossible. Mary Stuart referred to these rumors in a vitriolic letter she wrote to Elizabeth (which William Cecil apparently suppressed). Claiming Bess of Hardwick, the Countess of Shrewsbury, as her source, Mary Stuart wrote, "she says, moreover, that indubitably you are not like other women, and it is folly to advance the notion of your marriage with the duc of [Alençon], seeing that such a conjugal union would never be consummated."[42] This opinion was probably widespread. After Elizabeth's death, Ben Jonson made a similar remark, suggesting that Elizabeth had a membrane that made her incapable of intercourse, though despite that "for her delight she tryed many." At the time of the proposed marriage to Alençon, Jonson claimed, a French surgeon "took in hand to cut it, yett fear stayed her."[43] In 1566, however, the queen's physician assured the French ambassador if Elizabeth married the French king she would have ten children at least, but how much of this was based on any real diagnosis and how much on wishful thinking is another question.[44] William Cecil always assumed that Elizabeth would be able to produce a child.

Doubts about Elizabeth's ability to produce an heir entered into the larger issue of the way the nation perceived its queen. A striking concept in medieval political theory was the belief in the king's two bodies, a body politic and a body natural. Under Elizabeth this concept was reworked with some subtlety. Marie Axton, Louis Montrose, and Leah Marcus have written about some of the political ramifications of the concept of the queen's two bodies. Elizabeth's body politic was seen as pure and virginal, and the incarnation of the sacred principle of male monarchy; but with

[41]Melville's Memoirs; *CSP, Spain,* 1:63; *CSP, Venetian,* 1:105; *CSP, Rome,* 2:363; Jenkins, *Elizabeth the Great,* 77, are very helpful on this topic.

[42]Quoted in Stefan Zweig, *Mary Queen of Scots and the Isles* (New York: the Viking Press, 1935), 299. The original letter appears in French in *A Collection of State Papers Relating to Affairs in the Reign of Queen Elizabeth from 1571 to 1596 left by William Cecil, Lord Burghley,* ed. William Mardin (London: William Bowyer, 1759), 558-59. I have used Zweig's translation.

[43]*Notes of Ben Jonson's Conversations with William Drummond,* ed. David Laing (London: Printed for the Shakespeare Society, 1842), 23.

[44]*CSP, Spain,* 1:569.

the talk of lovers and illegitimate children, people viewed her body natural as potentially corrupt in a manifestly female way.[45]

By being "wed to England," as she so often claimed, Elizabeth could present yet another image to her subjects, that of a mother. The extraordinarily large number of godchildren she sponsored encouraged the concept that all the English were in some sense her children. At the very beginning of her reign, when the House of commons beseeched the queen to marry, Elizabeth responded:

> Yea, to satisfie you, I have already joyned my selfe in Marriage to an husband, namely the Kindome of England. . . . And doe not upbraid me with miserable lacke of children: for everyone of you, and as many as are Englishmen, are children, and kinsmen to me.[46]

John Jewel, bishop of Salisbury, in 1567, referred to Elizabeth as "the only nurse and mother of the church of God."[47] In 1578 a person representing the city of Norwich told Elizabeth in a pageant to celebrate her coming: "Thou art my joy next God, I have no other, My Princesse and my peerlesse Queene, my loving Nurse and Mother." This image was repeated throughout the week of Elizabeth's stay, and when she left she was told, "Farewell,

[45]Ernst Kantorowicz, *The King's Two Bodies: A Study in Mediaeval Political Theology* (Princeton: Princeton University Press, 1957); Marie Axton, *The Queen's Two Bodies* (London: Royal Historical Society, 1977); Montrose, "Shaping Fantasy," and "The Elizabethan Subject and the Spenserian Text," 307-09; Marcus, "The Political Uses of Androgyny," 138; Joel Hurstfield, *The Illusion of Power in Tudor Politics* (London: the Athlone Press, 1979), 22-24. Hurstfield's analysis of the weaknesses of the concept of the king's two bodies in Elizabethan England is extremely useful.

[46]W. Camden, *Annals, or the historie of the most renowned and Victorious Princesse Elizabeth,* 3rd ed. (1635), 16, in Wilson, *England's Eliza,* 6 n. In 1563 she told her Parliament, "I assure you all, that thoughe, after my death, you may have many stepdames yet shall you never [have] a more naturall mother than I meane to be unto you all." *Nugae Antiquae: Being a Miscellaneous Collection of Original Papers . . . by Sir John Harington,* ed. Thomas Park, 2 vols. (London: for Vernor and Hood, 1804), 1: 83. Elizabeth is not the only one to put it in those terms. De Feria wrote to Philip II at the very beginning of her reign that Elizabeth "is very much wedded to the people." *CSP, Spain,* 1: 4. In analyzing Elizabeth's parliamentary rhetoric, Heisch points out that throughout her reign, Elizabeth "pictures and presents herself as a loving and yet virginal mother." *Queen Elizabeth I,* 32.

[47]Ayre, *The Works of John Jewel,* 3: 118. The image of Elizabeth as nurse is a common one. See, for example, a speech in her honor at Cambridge, 1578. She was thanked for what she did "particularly to the two Universities, which were kept by her as by a Nurse in quietness to be nourished in piety, and all other learning." Nichols, *Progresses,* 2: 110. In 1588 Anthony Marten, keeper of the royal library at Westminster, described Elizabeth as "sent from above, to nurse and protect the true Christian commonwealth." "An Exhortation to stirre the Minds of all Her Majesty's faithfull Subjects, to defend their Countrey, in this dangerous Time, from the Invasion of Enemies (London: John Windet, 1588) in *The Harleian Miscellany: A Collection of Scarce, Curious, and Entertaining Pamphlets and Tracts,* ed. by William Olyds and Thomas Parks, 10 vols. (London: John White and John Murray, 1808), 1:174.

oh Queene, farewell, oh Mother dere."[48] At the end of her "Golden Speech" to Parliament in 1601, Elizabeth emphasized the great love she had for her subjects, again a traditionally feminine trait, as opposed to the wisdom or might she described in her presumably male predecessors. "And though you have had, and may have, many mightier and wiser princes in this seat, yet you never had, nor shall have any that will love you better."[49] In a letter to his wife, Sir John Harington referred to Elizabeth when he feared that she was dying as "our deare Queene, my royal godmother, and this state's natural mother."[50] In his ground breaking article on gender and power in Elizabethan England, Louis Montrose argues that "by fashioning herself into a singular combination of Maiden, Matron, and mother, the queen transformed the normal domestic life-cycle of an Elizabethan female into what was at once a social paradox and a religious mystery."[51]

By not marrying, by being both mother of no one and of everyone, and by presenting herself as both a virgin to be revered and a sensuous woman to be adored, Elizabeth exerted a strong psychological hold on her subjects. In 1600 a sailor, Abraham Edwards, was arrested for sending the queen passionate love letters and drawing a dagger in her presence. Officials were convinced that though apparently mad, Edwards had no wish to harm the queen, rather that he was "transported with a humour of love." In the seventeenth century, in his advice to his son about the dangers of passionate attachments, Francis Osborne wrote of the "voluptuous death" of a tailor, who "whined away" for love of Elizabeth.[52]

In 1597 Simon Forman, the astrologer, recounted in his diary a strange sexual dream he had had about the queen. Forman rescued Elizabeth from a man, "distract of his wits" and "frantic" who was trying to kiss the queen, an odd foreshadowing of Edwards. Then he and Elizabeth walked on together, and the queen became "very familiar with me, and me thought she began to love me." Just as the queen began to kiss Forman, he awoke. Montrose analyses the dream in terms of Forman's unconscious linking of Elizabeth, mother of her country, and his own mother. The queen becomes both mother and sex-object.[53]

[48]Quoted in Nichols, *Progresses,* 2:146, 165.

[49]Quoted in *The Harleian Miscellany,* 1:338.

[50]*The Letters and Epigrams of Sir John Harington, together with the Prayse of Private Life,* edited with an introduction by Norman Egbert McClure (Philadelphia: University of Pennsylvania Press, 1930), 96.

[51]Montrose, "Shaping Fantasies," 80.

[52]Osborne, *Works,* 54; *Calendar of the Manuscripts of the Marquis of Salisbury* (London: His Majesty's Stationary Office, 1902), 10: 172-73. One can see how much of a psychological pull a female monarch has even to this day. The incident with Edwards is eerily reminiscent of the case of Michael Fagin, who broke into the second Elizabeth's bedchamber, also professing love. *Time,* August 2, 1982.

[53]Montrose, "Shaping Fantasies," 62-64. Montrose's analysis of the Forman dream is so thorough and convincing I treat it only briefly and refer readers there for more information.

Another man concerned with Elizabeth as a sexual symbol was Richard Topcliffe, one of the most unpleasant characters of Elizabethan England. An occasional Member of Parliament, he was employed by Lord Burghley and described as one of her Majesty's servants. For twenty-five years he zealously hunted and examined recusants, Jesuits, and seminary priests. Topcliffe had a rack of his own design in his house, and was given authority to examine priests there, where he could do what he wished without supervision or being called to account. It was said he would do anything in pursuit of his prey, and even seduced the daughter of a man in whose house Robert Southwell was hiding to gain information. Many Protestants were horrified by his excesses and he was imprisoned briefly several times for exceeding his instructions. Topcliffe gained so much notoriety for his actions that putting someone on the rack became known as a "Topcliffian custom," and in court slang to hunt a recusant was to "topcliffizare."[54] Thomas Portmort, a seminary priest, was one such person hunted. He was arrested in October, 1591, and lodged in Topcliffe's house. Topcliffe pressed Portmort very hard to give information about the Catholic designs on England.

Portmort insisted that during the course of his examinations Topcliffe told him how much, he, Topcliffe, was in the favor of the queen. According to Portmort, Topcliffe proclaimed, "he himself was so familiar with Her Majesty that he hath very secret dealings with her, having not only seen her legs and knees but felt her belly, saying it was the softest belly of any womankind. She had said unto him, 'Be not these the arms, legs and body of King Henry?' to which he answered 'Yea.'" Portmort said Topcliffe boasted that if he wanted her, he could take her away from any company. But she did not save her favors for Topcliffe alone; "she was as pleasant with anyone she loved."[55] Topcliffe, outraged, denied having said any of this. Portmort was executed February 21, 1592 for treason. For two hours before his execution, Portmort was forced to stand in his shirt on a very cold day while Topcliffe harangued at him to deny the story. Portmort refused and went to his death.

The belief in Elizabeth's lovers and in her illegitimate children suggests how significant and complex gender and sexual issues were in the minds of Elizabeth's subjects and how important a part they played shaping the way English men and women regarded their queen. Elizabeth's advisers and Parliament felt a deep need to insure the legitimate succession, to

[54]Augustus Jessopp describes Topcliffe as a "monster," whose "cruelties would fill a volume" in *One Generation of a Norfolk House* (London: Burns and Oates, 1879), 70-71; *Dictionary of National Biography*, s.v. "Topcliffe, Richard." For an example of Topcliffe's dedication to hunting Catholics, see his letter to the Earl of Shrewsbury of August 30, 1578 in Nichols, *Progresses,* 2: 215-19; Thomas Birch, *Memoirs of Queen Elizabeth,* 2 vols. (London: A. Millar, 1754), 1:160.

[55]Harrison, "First Elizabethan Journal," 104.

safeguard the peace of the nation. In the Parliament of 1559, one member maintained that "nothing can be more contrary to the public [interest] than that such a Princess, in whose marriage is comprehended the safety and peace of the Commonwealth, should live unmarried, and as it were a Vestal Virgin."[56] William Cecil, for one, prayed that God "send our mistress a husband and by time a son, that we may hope our posterity shall have a masculine succession."[57] In a letter to his confident, Sir Thomas Smith, he wrote he hoped Elizabeth would marry, "otherwise I assure you, as now thynges hang in desperation, I have no comfort to live."[58]

Elizabeth was queen to a people unused to female rule, a people who were just recovering from the dislocation of the break with the Catholic Church. Elizabeth, unmarried and refusing to name an heir, was both Virgin and Mother. After her death, Robert Cecil described Elizabeth as being both "more than a man, and (in troth) sometyme less than a woman."[59] The very real adoration people felt for Elizabeth made her even more a focus for their distress. Gossip not only serves as "a genre of informal communication," but Robert Paine concludes, "it is a catalyst of social process that can either bring people together or separate them into opposing factions."[60] Elizabeth was not only politically astute but truly loved her subjects and revelled in their love for her. She could not change her sex or the decision she made to not provide England with a king-consort and an heir of her body. The comments about her sexuality were one way for her people to come to express their ambiguous feelings about her position as ruler, and also to come to terms with it.

[56]Quoted in Lacey Baldwin Smith, *Elizabeth Tudor* (Boston: Little Brown and Co., 1975), 122.

[57]Quoted in Smith, *Elizabeth Tudor,* 120.

[58]Wright, *Queen Elizabeth,* 1:188.

[59]Park, *Nugae Antiquae,* 1:345.

[60]Paine, "What is Gossip About?" 278, 285.

The Virgin of Venice and Concepts of the Millenium in Venice

Marion Leathers Kuntz*

A MYSTERIOUS WOMAN WHO LIVED IN VENICE in the sixteenth century provides the modern scholar interested in the history and contributions of women with an amazing array of ideas; some have medieval antecedents, others are surprisingly modern.[1] This woman whose family name is unknown was able to wield influence on wealthy Venetians who aided her financially in support of a hospice which she singlehandedly had established. What is even more surprising is that she became the most enduring voice in the multitudinous writings of one of the most learned Renaissance men, Guillaume Postel. She was known simply as the Venetian Virgin or called by her given name Giovanna or Zuana in Venetian. She did not have support from her family, an order of the Church, or powerful friends. She was not educated in the liberal arts as were some women of her day. She was a simple woman of unknown origin who has been almost overlooked by historians of later centuries.

Her life, however, merges past and present in regard to women's issues.[2] She was a prophetess who refused to be silenced. She forged a career for herself based on spiritual imperatives of her own formulation. She

*I wish to express my thanks to Dottoressa Maria Francesca Tiepolo, Direttore dirigente, Archivio de Stato, Venezia, and her staff for the use of rare materials; to Dottor Gian Albino Ravalli-Modoni, Direttore, Biblioteca Marciana; to Dottoresse Anna Maria Zanotto, Ina Calegari, and Margherita Carboni of the Biblioteca Marciana; to Miss Nancy Romero of the Rare Book and Special Collections Library of the University of Illinois, Urbana, for help in securing photocopies of the 1557 edition of the *Chronicon* of Carion. I am also indebted to Georgia State University and to the Fuller E. Callaway Foundation whose generous support aided my research.

[1]Her life has been documented by Guillaume Postel in three books and numerous manuscripts. See especially his *Les tres merveilleuses victoires des femmes* (Paris, 1553). Also note M.L. Kuntz, *Guillaume Postel. Prophet of the Restitution of All Things . . .* (The Hague: Martinus Nijhoff, 1981), 69-129; "Guglielmo Postello e la 'Vergine Veneziana.'" Appunti storici sulla vita spirituale dell'Ospedaletto nel Cinquecento," *Quaderni* 21 (Venezia: Centro Tedesco di Studi Veneziani, 1981).

[2]Important studies on women in the Middle Ages and Renaissance focus upon various issues which are similar to those faced by the subject of this study. See for example *Medieval Women*, ed. Derek Baker (Oxford: Basil Blackwell, 1978), and especially note in this volume, Stephen Wessley, "The Thirteenth-Century Guglielmites: Salvation through Women," 289-303; Christiane Klapisch-Zuber, *Women, Family, and Ritual in Renaissance Italy*, trans. Lydia G. Cochrane (Chicago: University of Chicago Press, 1985); *Medieval Women Writers*, ed. Katharina M. Wilson (Athens: University of Georgia Press, 1984); Richard Kieckhefer, *Unquiet Souls. Fourteenth-Century Saints and Their Religious Milieu* (Chicago: University of Chicago Press, 1984); Carolyn Walker Bynum, *Holy Feast and Holy Fast. The Religious Significance of Food to Medieval Women* (Berkeley: University of California Press, 1987); *Women in the Middle Ages and the Renaissance . . .*, ed. Mary Beth Rose (Syracuse: Syracuse University Press, 1986); also note Ellen Macek, "The Emergence of a Feminine Spirituality in *The Book of Martyrs*," *Sixteenth Century Journal* 19, no. 1 (1988): 63-80.

proclaimed the need for a universal state and church, predicated upon the principles of universal brotherhood which implies also universal sisterhood. Perhaps most significant for our concerns today is the principle of male-female sexual dualism which she proclaimed as the basis of the new age of restoration. In the Venetian Virgin's teachings gender becomes blurred. For example, she maintained that in the person who has been restored and made complete there must be a union of male-female within the human person.[3] Spiritual androgyny is the basis of her claim that she was the "Papa Reformatore del mondo." She did not timidly ask for equality with men. She claimed a spiritual superiority to men and women, since the male-female nature had found the perfect union in her person through the agency of Christ.[4] In a mystical union with Christ she assumed his higher-paternal nature as He assumed her lower maternal nature.[5]

The union of male and female forms the basis of her call for a universal state and a universal church. In this study we shall trace the development of the Venetian Virgin's thought, its influence on others – especially Guillaume Postel, and the application of her thought to concepts of the millenium in Venice. We shall also look briefly at the teachings of two other Venetian women whose ideas closely resembled those of the Venetian Virgin.

In the formal records of the Ospedaletto the name of the Venetian Virgin does not appear.[6] Rather the names of wealthy Venetian men are listed, since it was not the custom to acknowledge publicly the extraordinary labors of a poor untutored woman who "begged from the rich to give food to the poor" and in so doing established the Ospedaletto, which, even today, is a hospital for the elderly poor in Venice.

The fabulous teachings of the Venetian Virgin and their influence on Postel and others cannot be ignored, and they surely caused consternation

---

[3]On androgyny in the Renaissance see Leah S. Marcus, "Shakespeare's Comic Heroines, Elizabeth I and the Political Uses of Androgyny" in *Women in the Middle Ages and the Renaissance,* 135-53; Natalie Zemon Davis, "Women on Top: Symbolic Sexual Inversion and Political Disorder in Early Modern Europe," in *The Reversible World,* ed. Barbara A. Babcock (Ithaca: Cornell University Press, 1978); Frances A. Yates, *Astraea* (London: Routledge & Kegan Paul, 1975), 42-51; Edgar Wind, *Pagan Mysteries in the Renaissance* (London: Barnes & Noble, 1958), 173-75.

[4]For medieval antecedents of feminine salvation see Carolyn Walker Bynum, *Jesus as Mother. Studies in the Spirituality of the High Middle Ages* (Berkeley: University of California Press, 1982); Wessley, "Guglielmites: salvation through women," 289-303.

[5]Postel often recounts her mystical transformation in 1540. See Kuntz, *Postel: Prophet,* 77-83. On the male-female union in Kabbalistic literature, see Gershom G. Scholem, *Major Trends in Jewish Mysticism* (New York, Schocken Books, 1974), 225-35.

[6]See *Libro di Partte et Determinationi diuerse. Prencipia 1546 finno 1604, Archivio Istituto di Ricovero e Educazione,* Ospedale dei derelitti, Venezia; *L'Archivio IRE Inventari dei fondi antichi degli ospedali e luoghi pii di Venezia,* a cura di Giuseppe Ellero (Venezia, 1987). The name of Giovanna (Zuana) is mentioned, however, in Archivio di Stato, Venezia, Ospedali e luoghi pii, Busta 910.

among the Inquisitors of Venice. Whether this Venetian mystic was called before the Sacred Tribunal has not yet been ascertained. It seems likely, however, that she would have been investigated at the same time as Paola Negri and the *Paolini,* when in 1551 some of the strange teachings circulating at the Ospedaletto of Saints John and Paul had been uncovered.[7]

The name of the Venetian Virgin or Giovanna figured prominently in the trial of Guillaume Postel before the Venetian Inquisition in 1555 because of two books about her life which he had published in Padova in 1555.[8] In addition, the *Chronicon* of Ioannes Carion with the *Appendix* which was written by Guillaume Postel contained a biography of Giovanna Veronese. Two editions of the work had been published in Venice by Vicenzo Valgrisio, had been prohibited by the Inquisitors, and had finally been found in the magazine of Valgrisio located in the Convent of Saints John and Paul.

In 1553 and in 1556 Valgrisio had published the *Chronicon* and the *Appendix* to the *Chronicon* but without the biography of Giovanna Veronese. Since the Inquisitors had become concerned in 1558 about Carion's *Chronicon,* it seems altogether likely that their preoccupation was directed toward the edition of 1557 which contained the biography of Giovanna Veronese, Postel's Venetian Virgin.[9] This edition is probably the one which was found in the magazine of Valgrisio at the Convent of the Church of Saints John and Paul.

Giovanna had long associations with the Church of Saints John and Paul, since around 1528 she founded a soup kitchen in the *campo* adjacent to the Church and eventually secured funds to establish a permanent shelter behind the apse of the great Church.[10] Giovanna's life and work are intimately related to millenarian ideas which were circulating in Venice in the Cinquecento, and it was very likely that her biography, which appeared in the 1557 edition of the *Chronicon,* was one of the reasons for the diligent search and eventual discovery of Valgrisio's magazine in the Convent of Saints John and Paul. We shall return to the role Giovanna, the Virgin of Venice, played in concepts of the millenium in Venice, particularly at her hospice which became known as the Ospedaletto. We must point out, however,

[7]See Consiglio dei Dieci, Segreto, Registro 6, fol. 78^{r-v}, fol. 80^r, Archivio di Stato, Venezia.

[8]See Santo Uffizio, Buste 12 and 159, Archivio di Stato, Venezia.

[9]See above, note 7. The title of the 1557 edition is *Joan. Carionis mathematici Chronicorum libri III. . . . Appendix eorum quae a fine Carionis ad haec usque tempora contingere. Catalogus pontificum, Caesarum, regum, et ducum venetorum. . . .* (Parisiis apud S. Calvarinum, 1557).

[10]See Kuntz, "Guglielmo Postello e la 'Vergine Veneziana'," 3-24; also *Postel: Prophet,* 69-108. William J. Bouwsma, *Concordia Mundi: The Career and Thought of Guillaume Postel* (Cambridge, MA: Harvard University Press, 1957). In addition to the printed texts which Postel wrote about the Virgin of Venice (see above, n. 8), his unpublished texts are filled with accounts of the life and works of the Venetian Virgin. He continued to write of her until the year of his death in 1581.

that this was not the first time that the Inquisition of Venice had directed its attention to the Ospedaletto. The Ospedaletto had come under the watchful eyes of the Venetian Inquisition in 1550-51 when Paola Antonia Negri was questioned along with several monks because of certain prophetic teachings.[11] Paola Negri, a native of Castellanza near Milan, was a woman of very great intelligence who became associated with the group of women in the circle of the noble Milanese Countess Guastalla, Lodovica Torelli.[12] Countess Guastalla was the first woman to ally herself with the Barnabites, a group of priests under the leadership of Giacomo Antonio Morigia of Milan who wanted to reform the laity and the clergy.[13] She was especially devoted to one of the priests, Antonio Zaccaria, who received instructions for the priesthood from Fra Battista da Crema. Fra Antonio was the chaplain of a small group of women whom Countess Guastalla had assembled as associates of the Barnabites. These women, some young, others pious matrons, lived in a palace provided by the Countess. They devoted their lives to good works and pious deeds and to the reform of the monasteries. In 1533 this group of women was granted approval of their own *Istituto*, and in 1535 Pope Paul III issued a bull establishing a feminine religious order under Santo Agostino.[14] Paola Negri joined the group around Countess Guastalla in 1530 and began to teach the novices in the *Istituto*. She remained in Milan until 1536 or 1537, when she was sent to Vicenza to work with Father Bartolomeo Ferrari whose task was to reform two monasteries of the *Convertiti*. Stories of Negri's virtue became well-known in Vicenza, and her reputation for holiness was also circulated in Verona and Padova.[15] Her religious stature was so great that many people including clerics came to consult her as an oracle.[16]

In 1539 a delegation from the Church of Saints John and Paul in Venice requested help from the Barnabites and from the women of the order for the little hospice, known as the Ospedaletto, near the great Dominican Church. Countess Guastalla responded favorably, and among the women chosen to go to Venice to work at the Ospedaletto was Paola Antonia Negri.[17] The mission of feminine Barnabites also known as *Paolini,* had the task of working among the sick, the widows, and orphans who had flocked to this hospice, especially after the plague of 1528. Noble

[11]Archivio di Stato, Venezia, Consiglio dei Dieci, Segreto, Registro 6, fol. 78[r-v]; Santo Uffizio, Busta 159, fol. 21; Consiglio dei Dieci, parti secrete, filza 8, 17 febb. 1551.

[12]See Orazio Premoli, *Storia dei Barnabiti nel Cinquecento* (Roma: Editori Palazzo Doria, 1913); Kuntz, *Postel: Prophet,* 70-73.

[13]Kuntz, *Postel: Prophet,* 71-72.

[14]Ibid.

[15]Ibid., 72, 228 n.

[16]Ibid., 228 n.

[17]Ibid., 72; also Premoli, *Storia dei Barnabiti*, 77-80.

Venetians were supportive of the efforts of these women. Giuseppe Contarini, nephew of the famous Cardinal Gasparo Contarini, was among the first to give aid to this group of feminine Barnabites. In 1545 Pope Paul III issued a formal bull for the Fathers of Saint Barnabas in Venice.[18] This bull also included the women associated with the Barnabites, that is, the *Paolini*.[19]

Paola Antonia Negri demonstrated the same zeal toward the poor and infirm in Venice as she had earlier displayed in Milan and Vicenza. Gasparo Contarini was said to be an admirer of Negri, and her reputation for holiness continued to increase.[20] Paola Antonia Negri claimed that she had received the spirit of God in a mystical transformation; consequently, she had received the Holy Spirit in her person and therefore knew the secrets of the heart. Because of her prophetic utterances and her spiritual claims, her influence among the Barnabites at the Ospedaletto and among certain Venetians was so great that she received the name of "divina Madre," to emphasize her spiritual insight which enabled her to lead souls to God.[21] Although her reputation for virtue was far reaching, she did have her detractors because of her increasingly imperious manner and her harshness toward those whose spirituality she deemed defective.[22] She gained greater control over the Ospedaletto with each passing day, until she appeared to have complete authority not only over the daily operations of the hospice but also of all words and thoughts generated there. She and the Barnabites held public confessions and assigned harsh reprisals to penitents. Priests often were on their knees before "*la detta madre maestra;*" so great was her authority among some priests that she was giving to some and taking away from others the license to celebrate Mass and to dispense the Eucharist.[23] Her usurpation of the office of priests and her other excessive claims about her "divine nature" in time caused the Venetian inquisitors to investigate the commotion she had aroused at the Ospedaletto.[24]

[18]Premoli, 64ff. The group was originally known as the confraternity of Eternal Wisdom; later it used the names Order of Saint Paul Convert, Saint Paul or Paulines, Saints Paul and Barnabas, Saint Barnabas, and finally Barnabites. The formula used as a symbol by the Barnabites was *Jesus Christus Crucifixus amor meus*.

[19]For the history of the Ospedaletto see in addition Achille Bosisio, *L'Ospedaletto e la chiesa di S. Maria dei Derelitti in Venezia* (Venezia: Istituzioni di Ricovero e di Educazione, 1963); Archivio I.R.E., Venezia, *Libro de Partte et Determinationi diverse: Prencipia 1546, finno 1604;* Archivio di Stato, Venezia, Ospedali e luoghi pii, busta 910.

[20]Kuntz, *Postel: Prophet,* 72, 228 n.

[21]Premoli, *Storia dei Barnabiti,* 92.

[22]Ibid., 92-101. As we shall see later, Guillaume Postel refers harshly to the "hypocrite Paulines."

[23]Archivio di Stato, Venezia, Consiglio dei Dieci, Segreto, Registro 6, fol. 78[r-v]. Consiglio dei Dieci, parti secrete, filza 8, 17 febb. 1551; Santo Uffizio, Busta 159, fol. 21. Also see Premoli, *Storia dei Barnabiti,* 101-3.

[24]Ibid.

In 1551 at the time of the investigation of Negri and other Barnabites working at the Ospedaletto Paola Negri was thirty-six or thirty-seven years old. Four years earlier while assigned to the Ospedaletto Negri had written a book of spiritual letters to *angeliche* and notables. This book, entitled *Lettere spirituali de la devota religiosa Angelica Pavla Antonia di Negri, Milanese,* contains letters written between 1547-1549; however, the work did not receive the *imprimatur* until 1563.[25] Her letters are filled with spiritual admonitions to holy poverty, prayer, and good works.[26] Paola writes passionately of wanting to put on the garments and the life of Christ – His poverty, His shame, His suffering, even His temptation.[27] She warns all who attend public festivals but care not for the "festival of heaven" that they will not attain union with God.[28] From accounts of her actions at the Ospedaletto and from her book of spiritual devotions it is clear that Paola Negri felt compelled by God to proclaim the need for universal reform, for universal charity, and for universal brotherhood.

As her fame and authority increased, so also did the consternation of the Inquisitors. Whatever the intentions of Negri may have been, her power and influence over the Barnabites caused many problems, and the Order subsequently was banished in February, 1551.[29] Her imperiousness

---

[25]The copy which I used is in the Biblioteca Apostolica Vaticana, Raccolta teologia IV, 2330. I am indebted to Monsignor José Ruysschaert, Vice-Prefect emeritus of the Biblioteca Vaticana, for providing me with a microfilm of this rare work. No copies exist today in Venice.

It is interesting to note that Father Jacob Lainez, Society of Jesus, noted on the final page that he had read the book, made some corrections, and now found nothing which was contrary to the faith or good morals. Lainez had been a friend of Guillaume Postel during Postel's Jesuit days.

[26]Note *Lettere spirituali . . . ,* 18ᵛ: "ma patiremo noi che a tutti sia nato il Saluatore, et a noi non sia nato? sarà nato il Saluatore, anchora secondo la parola dell'Angelo, se trouaremo esso Saluatore inuolto ne i panni, et reclinato nel presepio, oue ne i panni? cio è, ne i poueri pannicelli, non ricchi ne sontuosi, et reclinato, non nelli alti et belli palazzi, con superbi apparati, ma nel presepio, con la guardia, et custodia, et compagnia de doi animali, lo trouaremo talmente inuolto, et riposto con questi modi poueri, et dentro di noi si sentiremo con desiderio di pouertà, et non solo delle cose esteriori; ma d'ogni desiderio de honore, di esaltatione, et riputatione. . . ."

[27]*Lettere spirituali,* 27, ". . . ma esso solo Christo, si manifestò nel andar in esso deserto, per esser tentato, a darci ad intender, che debbiamo desiderare le tentationi, et conoscer, che le sono il mezzo della corona dell'anima, che non è coronato, se non chi combatte legittimamente, et se egli fu . . . tentato per tutte le cose, come noi debbiamo abhorrire le tentationi, et le contraditioni, et le persecutioni?"

[28]*Letter spirituali,* 61ᵛ, "Ah poueri questi tali che assumono il testamento di Dio per la bocca sua, et predicano le sue giustitie, et essi gettano le discipline della vera charità della fraterna dilettione, della purità della mente, della benignità et mansuetudine, dell'allegrezza che deuono sentire perche Dio sia honorato et seruito in molti, et per molte vie, et per le molte mansioni che sono nella chiesa sua, la gettano dico doppo le spalle, correndo con il ladro demonio a robbar la gloria di Dio. . . ."

[29]Concerning the expulsion order, see Archivio di Stato, Venezia, Consiglio dei Dieci, parti secrete, filza 8. Note also: "Franciscus Donato Dei Dux Venetiarum . . . Per deliberazione del nostro Consiglio dei X con la Zonta vi commettemo che dobbiate intimare alle Donne

bode ill not only for the Barnabites but also for the founder of the little hospice to which Negri had been sent. This woman had been serving the poor, infirm, and orphans in make-shift quarters near the Church of Saints John and Paul for about twenty years before Paola Antonia Negri's arrival.[30] She was called Mother Giovanna and the Venetian Virgin and was lionized by Guillaume Postel as the "Mother of the World and of the New Age." Postel met Mother Giovanna in 1546-47 when he came to perform priestly duties at the Ospedaletto after his separation from the Jesuits in Rome.[31] Postel wrote of the problems at the Ospedaletto which he attributed to the *Paolini*. Although he did not mention Paola Negri by name, his inference is clearly that she, as the most important of the *Paolini*, was the source of Mother Giovanna's troubles at the Ospedaletto.[32] Her harshness was causing Mother Giovanna great anxiety, and it is not surprising. The arrogance of Paola Negri was in sharp contrast to the self-effacing gentleness of Mother Giovanna. Perhaps Paola Negri was jealous of the extravagant praise heaped upon Mother Giovanna by Guillaume Postel. From what we know about Negri she surely wanted no feminine prophetess as rival at the Ospedaletto. Many years before the investigation of Paola Negri the Venetian Virgin had been proclaiming a prophetic message of restitution and reform based on the practice of charity, praise of God, reformation of the clergy, and the "gathering of all sheep into one sheep fold." The prophetic utterances of the Venetian Virgin which were transmitted by Guillaume Postel became for him and others the foundation for the inauguration of a new golden age, which had begun in Venice and soon would envelop the whole world.[33]

The history and the prophecies of the woman called by Postel "*Madre Giovanna*," *Zuana*, *Madre del mondo*, and *Vergine Veneziana*, have been recorded by Postel in numerous texts, unprinted and printed, notably in *Les tres*

---

forestiere della Congregazione di S. Paolo di Milan, che si trovano da li introdotte as governo di alcun luogo Pio et agli Sacerdoti et altri ministri di essa sua Congregazione che debbano in termini di giorni 6, partir da questa Città, et in termini di 15 giorni da tutte le Città, et Terre et Luoghi del dominio nostro astenendosi in fra essi termini dalle solite operationi sue, et che non debbano li medesimi, nè Altri, sì `Donne come Sacerdoti et ministri di detta congregazione, venir et ritornare a questa città di Venezia . . ." Cited by Premoli, *Storia dei Barnabiti*, 97.

[30]Kuntz, *Postel: Prophet*, 86-87.

[31]See Postel's *Le prime nove del altro mondo* (Padova, 1555) sig. Fiv, where he states: ". . . io attendeua a la Spirituale et essa a la corporale cura delli infermi . . ."; also note: "Et la causa della mia faticha fra quasi continui trauagli di confessare, ministrare, et confortare infermi, di celebrare, et di predicare. . . ." sig. Giii.

[32]Postel, *Le prime nove*, wrote: ". . . in quel tempo che gli empii Hippocriti et assassini della povertà, cominciauano gia a dar l'angosciosa morte alla sopradetta Vergine laquale per suo comandamento io chiamo mia madre. . . ."

[33]Kuntz, *Postel: Prophet*, 69-142, and "Guglielmo Postello e la 'Vergine Veneziana'," 3-24.

merveilleuses victoires des femmes, Le prime nove del altro mondo, cioe, l'admirabile Historia . . . intitulata La Vergine Venetiana and in *Il libro della divina ordinatione.*[34] Until quite recently it has been assumed that Postel was the sole biographer of the Venetian Virgin. However, in a recently published article, we have demonstrated that the biography of Giovanna appears also in a work of Lodovico Domenichi entitled *Historia varia* and published in 1558.[35] Domenichi's biography of Giovanna proves that she was esteemed by others in addition to Postel and was considered significant enough to be included in the history of Domenichi, a prolific translator, poet, compiler, and corrector in Venice in mid-sixteenth century.[36]

Giovanna was born in the country between Verona and Padova in 1496 or 1497, but no record of her parents, their religion, their land or age exists. When Postel asked about her parents, she replied: "Nisvno sa donde io sia. . . ."[37] Giovanna could possibly have been from a Marrano family, since she had some knowledge of Hebrew sources. Postel noted that although Giovanna was untutored in ancient languages, she could explain passages in the *Zohar* which had been impossible for him to comprehend.[38] Of course, no certainty can be attached to Giovanna's background, and her interpretations of mystical Hebrew texts could be attributed to her highly

[34]These texts were published in Padova in 1555 and were in large measure responsible for Postel's condemnation by the Venetian Inquisition in 1555.

[35]Kuntz, "Lodovico Domenichi, Guillaume Postel and the Biography of Giovanna Veronese," *Studi Veneziani* n.s. 16 (1988), 33-44.

[36]Giovanna's biography appears in Domenichi's *Historia di Messer Lodovico Domenichi, di detti, e Fatti degni de Memoria di diversi principi, e huomini privati antichi, et moderni* of 1558 and in the edition of 1564, which is entitled *Historia varia . . . nella quale, si contengono molte cose argute, nobili, e degne, di memoria di diversi principi le huomini illustri. . . .* On Domenichi and his other publications see *Annali di Gabriel Giolito De'Ferrari* (Lucca: Tipografia Giusti, 1890), 1: xxv-xxvii; 2:67, 246-49.

[37]Postel, *Le prime nove*, sig. B.; also see *Il Libro dell divina ordinatione* (Padova, 1555).

[38]Postel writes of her profound insights: ". . . et tantam interea Diuinarum literarum cognitionem alias legendi omnino ignara consequuta est, vt in sacris Traditionibus et Libris sacris, nil tam abditum sit, et, quod est summopere mirandum, etiam in secretissimis Hebraeorum, et Vetustissimis priscorum interpretum sententiis, quin clarissime intellegeret, et ita caperet, vt cuiuis explicare posset." Bibliothèque nationale, fonds lat. 3401, fol. 3; Postel, *Le prime nove*, sig. Giii^v, also speaks of the difficulty of translating the *Zohar* and of Giovanna's inspired insight: "Pero io mi misse a cosi difficile et alta impresa dove sono li magiori, et li più alti et profundi et admirandi sensi et piu difficili che siano nel mondo. . . . Onde ogni giorno consolandomi la sacra Madre del mondo, dopo che era si reconciliata, et haueua per Meditatione et Chiarissima visione ragunato le pecore del Signore, essa da sua posta mi mouea certi dubii, li piu alti del mondo, alliquali non sapendo io rispondere, essa mi dicea, o che uoi sapete poco cosi s'intendende. Dopo di questo io trouaua dentro del testo del Zohar, le medesime questioni proposte, ma al costume delli antiqui, cioe con solutione oscurissima. . . . Volendo io far Parafrasi, egli era al tutto impossibile che io l'hauesse dichiarata se primo quella che ha tutte le Dotrine del mondo et ha la chiaue di David, non me l'hauessi esposto et dichiarato. Cosi senza mai monstrarmi saper niente ch'io interpretassi tal cosa ouer hauessi bisogno di simili questioni, essa m'interpretò tutto quanto il detto libro. . . . "

sensitive, mystical nature rather than to any Jewish origin.[39] Be that as it may, when she arrived at the age of discretion, she left her parents' home, determined to serve God in perpetual virginity, in prayer and contemplation and in service to the sick and needy. She worked first in a hospital in Padova, and then in 1520 or 1521 she came to Venice to continue her work among the poor.[40] She worked in different places in Venice in order to serve the destitute.[41] She was convinced that on the day of Judgment God would ask of everyone if he had sought out and given aid to the poor and the helpless.[42]

Giovanna is described by Postel as "la più picciola, bassa, et debile del mondo" who did not cease her efforts until she had secured a company of well-to-do men and women to help her financially in providing a *ridotto* to take in the poor and feed them in a few rooms near the monastery of Saints John and Paul.[43] Little by little Mother Giovanna by good management and hard labor had improved and enlarged her hospice so that orphans and indigent adults were received there. So diligent was Giovanna in her ministry to the poor that she alone cooked for eight hundred people at a time.[44] Many poor, both sick and well, who could not find bread in their own *contrade,* were nourished by the Venetian Virgin in her "open kitchen."[45]

The daily habits of Mother Giovanna, in addition to her constant work for the poor, were equally exemplary. She had lived all her life in perpetual virginity. Although she constantly prepared meat for the hungry, she herself ate no flesh; nor did she consume rich foods but only those seasoned with oil. So abstemious was she that she drank only very small amounts of wine mixed with much water.[46] She slept only a few hours at night because of her constant work at the Ospedaletto. Since her long hours of

---

[39]Postel, *Le prime nove,* sig. Aiv[v], notes: "Et quantunche io essendo gia mosto, et tutto commossso per le stupende cose ch'io in lei di continuo uedeua spesso gli di mandassi, mai mi uolse rispondere a proposito, ma solamente nu diceua La Terra et Il Sangve non hanno parte in Cielo, cercate la generatione uera del Cielo. Nissuno sa donde io sia. . . . Cosi di cosa che hauesse alcuno odore di parenti, sangne, paese, età et altre cose doue si suole attacar il fondamento della fama de mortali, mai ne uolse raggionare." One can point out that after Postel's meeting with Giovanna he became increasingly interested in Hebrew sources.

[40]Ibid., sig. B.

[41]Ibid., sig. B[v]. "Essendo stata parte in Padoua, parte in Venetia, fin al tempo delle pettechie, nelquale guerre per terra et per mare. . . ."

[42]Ibid.

[43]Ibid.

[44]Ibid.

[45]Ibid."Et tal fu la sua diligentia, che lei sola, essendoci qualche uolta fin à ottocento et piu poueri ragunati tanto infermi, come poueri sani, essa sola et cuoceua et ministraua a tutti in tal modo che uedendo la Città come quella era opera divina, in tal sorte che spesso non si potendo per danari in molte contrade trouar pane ne farina, una continua, abondantia iui si ritrouaua. Cosi a poco a poco il luoco fu serrato et acconciato a tal che orfani et infermi dell'uno et dell'altro sesso iui in grandissimo numero se ritrouauano essere benissimo recapitati."

[46]Ibid., sig. Bii.

labor kept her from regular attendance at Mass or public preaching, her usual participation occurred when the Mass was celebrated among the sick along with preaching.[47] Yet after she went to bed she spent the greater part of the night in "contemplating life, death, and the final glory of Christ." Her contemplation filled her with such serenity and such understanding of the Divine Goodness because of her supreme love of God that all, according to Postel, would have been amazed at her profound insights.[48] Postel comments upon her success in securing food for the poor by preaching charity to the rich; he also notes that her labors and unceasing charity had earned her the reputation among the Venetians of an *"opera divina."*[49] Her fame in Venice seems well deserved, and noble Venetians whose names are recorded in the archives of the litte hospital gave her support.[50]

When Postel arrived in Venice in 1546 or 1547, this Venetian mystic had already been director of the Ospedaletto for twenty-six or seven years. Postel records his first meeting with this "little old woman" of about fifty years when she came to him shortly after his arrival and asked him to be her spiritual father and confessor.[51] He writes at length about the remarkable order of her confessions which she had not written down nor had she memorized, since each time her confessions were different. Postel notes that he was very suspicious of her "most ordered discourse" and asked her who had taught her these things.[52] The Venetian Virgin replied: "That one who is and knows all."[53] When Postel asked again who was that person, the Virgin replied: "That one who is alive in me, and I died in him."[54] Fearful lest a bad spirit inhabited this woman, Postel demanded that she tell him who had taught her this most ordered confession. Her response

---

[47]Ibid.

[48]Ibid., sig. Bii^v, ". . . era venuta in tanta consolatione et in tanta conversatione della divina bontà et essentia di Christo Iesu per il supremo amore del quale si sforzaua di responderli, che tutti gli alti misterii et secreti tanto dell cose Divine quanto delle naturali necessarie per conoscere et piu amare IDDIO gli erano talmente riuelate et chiare, che non è intelletto al mondo ilquale udendola non restasse abbagliato."

[49]Kuntz, *Postel: Prophet,* 76 ff.

[50]The records are found in *Libro di Partte et Determinationi diverse, Prencipia 1546 finno 1604,* Ospedale dei Derelitti, Archivio storico di Istituzioni di Ricovero e di Educazione, Venezia. Some of the prominent Venetians who served as deputies during the years in which the Venetian Virgin and Postel worked there were Domingo Loredan, Zuane Basegio, Baldisera Spinelli, Jacomo Foscarini, Lodovico di Viscardi, Jacomo Paralion, Lorenzo Lotto, and Gianmaria Giunta. For additional facts about the Venetian Virgin's life and work at the Ospedaletto, see Bibliothèque nationale, fonds franç., 2115, fol. 105^v.

[51]Postel, *Le prime nove,* sig. Bii^v. Bibliothèque nationale, fonds franç. 2115, fol. 105^v. See also Kuntz, *Postel: Prophet,* 74-76.

[52]Postel, *Le prime nove,* sig. Bii^v.

[53]Ibid. "Quello che è et sa il tutto."

[54]Ibid. "Quello ilquale è uiuo in me, et io morta in lui."

was "none other than my redeemer."[55] Postel's suspicions were not allayed until a Brother from San Francesco della Vigna who had sometimes heard confessions of the sick at the Ospedaletto and also those of the Venetian Virgin, confirmed the same admiration for the order of her confessions and the depth of her thought which Postel had hesitated to believe.[56] After his conversation with the Franciscan, Postel became convinced that this humble Virgin of Venice had power and virtue which were supernatural.

Her previous confessor had been a Brother of the Order of San Francesco della Vigna. This confessor could have been Francesco Giorgio, since she explained to Postel that her confessor had been dead for seven years when Postel arrived in 1547,[57] and Francesco Giorgio had died in 1540. The Venetian Virgin waited seven years before the divinely designated replacement was revealed to her.[58] It is interesting to note that Francesco Giorgio was also influenced by a mystic, the Beata Chiara Bugni of the Convent of San Sepoloro.[59] In a relationship similar to that which developed between Postel and the Venetian Virgin, Giorgio confirmed that the ecstasies of Chiara Bugni had revealed to her the mysterious secrets of divine will and had endowed her with prophetic knowledge which revealed universal salvation granted by God to each individual of faith who participates ecstatically in the divine treasures and in the saving blood of Christ.[60] If Francesco Giorgio had been indeed the previous confessor of the Venetian Virgin, as we have suggested, the similar pronouncements of Chiara and Giovanna may have originally derived from the Franciscan ambience of San Francesco della Vigna. We have recently demonstrated that Giovanna's emphasis upon *povertà, disprezzo,* and *dolore* reflect the teachings of Angela da Foligno, a Franciscan tertiary who died in 1309.[61] Like Bugni the Venetian Virgin had a mystical experience of divine infusion in which the spiritual or

---

[55]Ibid. ". . . nian altro che il mio redentore."

[56]Ibid., sig. Biii.

[57]Kuntz, *Postel: Prophet,* 77-78.

[58]Postel often wrote of this experience: ". . . elle me dist, quelle hauoit expres commande- ment de Dieu de me dire choses de moment, et d'importance pour le bien, paix, et concorde de tout le monde ce que mieuls par apres i'entendroys. Et qu'il y hauoit des-ia long temp quelle en hauoit revelation, de laquelle d'estoit voulu descouurir a ses aultres peres spirituels, mais qu'il luy hauoit este desfendu de par Dieu de leur en parler. Mais au contraire moy arriué la luy hauoit de par Dieu este commandé, de me dire que c'estoit, la somme dequoy c'est, Que Dieu voulait, que toutes les creatures raisonables, fussent vries ensemble en une Bergerie. . . ." Bibliothèque nationale, fonds franç., 2115, fol. 105ᵛ.

[59]See Cesare Vasoli, "Un precedente della 'Vergine Veneziana': Francesco Giorgio Veneto e La Clarissa Chiara Bugni" in *Postello, Venezia e il suo mondo,* a cura di Kuntz (Firenze: Leo S. Olschki, 1987), 203-25.

[60]Ibid., 213.

[61]Marion L. Kuntz, "Angela la Faligno: A Paradigm of Venetian Spirituality in the Sixteenth Century," in *Miscellanea Moreana: Essays for Germain Marc'hadour* vol. 100 of *Moreana* (1988): 449-64.

heavenly body of Christ descended into her person and lived most fully. Postel writes of this miraculous restitution in numerous texts, and he links the salvation of Venice to the extraordinary merits of the Venetian Virgin. In the year 1540, according to Postel, the spiritual or heavenly body of Christ descended into the "most holy virgin Jochanna by name," and she became truly one with the living Christ and carried his substance in her body."[62] The Divine Presence acting within her person revealed to her the mystery of the Restitution of all things.[63] The mysteries revealed to the Venetian Virgin became the foundation for Postel's millenarian ideas which he called the fourth age, or the age of restitution. Postel claimed to be the reed by which the Venetian Virgin's truths of restitution were written.[64] In an interesting passage Postel explains that he called her the "Venetian Virgin" because in Venice she received Christ's Substance and because the name "Venetian" would recall the benefits of Christ which have been conferred "on his spouse whose merits He wished to crown. . . . "[65]

The Venetian Virgin informed the erudite Postel about many mysteries which would bring about universal restitution. In addition, she revealed to her "little son" Postel seven prophecies which are important for us to consider in regard to millenarian ideas which were being circulated in Venice in the Cinquecento as well as for what they reveal about the mysterious Giovanna.

The prophecies of the Venetian Virgin are as follows:[66]

---

[62]Kuntz, *Postel: Prophet,* 77-79. See also the words of Giovanna as recorded by Postel in *Le prime nove,* sig. Biii^v: "Sia in eterno glorificato il mio dolce Sposo Iesu . . . che ui ha voluto dar questa inclinatione, che quello che piu io ho bramato in questa vita mi vogliate concedere, che cosi come io sento et porto di continuo la Sostanza del mio dolce Sposo in me, cosi anchora, per la unione di tutte le creature lequali hanno in se ragione, nel santissimo sacramento della medesima sostantia sua, io lo possa per mani et authorità dell Santa Chiesa riceuer, accioche esso come Dio PADRE ET SPOSO MIO possi esser da me piu che la vita propria amato, et accioche tutti li membri suoi possino esser in me con infinita CHARITA abbracciate, unite, et conservate."

[63]Kuntz, *Postel: Prophet,* 77-78.

[64]Ibid., 79.

[65]Postel, *Le prime nove,* sig. Giv^v, ". . . quiui in Venetia venesse della Vergine estratta dalla sostanza propria di Iesu Christo, per dar ordine alle cose del Vniverso, quando del tutto appareriano esser disperate. Et per questo non volendo lei esser chiamata da niun luoco, ne manco Venetiana, quantunche IVI descendesse Christo sopra di lei, per molte ragioni io la voglio chiamare et da tutto quanto il mondo essere Chiamata Venetiana . . . cosi anche lei nel suo penultimo avenimento sia chiamata Venetiana per li beneficii della Restitutione dell'universo conferiti da Dio in Venetia, non per Sanque, Carne, o Parenti d'Abrahamo o altro ma per pura gratia et sommi meriti. Imperoche esso havendo conferito il sommo grado delli soi meriti Possanza Sapientia, et Clementia a questa sua Sposa, li cui meriti ha voluto coronar. . . ."

[66]Ibid., sig. H^r-Hii^v.

(1) The beginning of the Reformation of the world will take place in Venice; the Venetian Virgin, although she is the Holy Pope, who has to reform the Church, must not be in the order of Magistracy.

(2) The Minister-Prince of this Papacy will be the most Christian Prince who is most Christian in deeds and not in words alone. [The name of the Prince the Venetian Virgin did not reveal.]

(3) All the Turks will be converted soon, and they will be the best Christians in the world; but if the Christians do not turn to the good life, the Turks will castigate them before they become Christians.

(4) All those who have faith in God, love for all, and the Good Life will be secretly blessed by the Venetian Virgin's Spouse and will be given two bodies, one white in the bread, one red in the wine, which are changed.

(5) The time will come when all who have been lost through Satan will be restored as if the first parents had never sinned. There will be one *Pasqua* or universal *Raccolta* (gathering together).

(6) Human nature will be led to such perfection that all men will be as Christ, except for His Divinity; in men will be seen the living Christ, as root, fount, and trunk.

(7) The Lord of Lords has so ordered His world that it is all made as the nature of the Palm (Thamar) of a perfect substance, immortal and incorruptible like the body of gold or gems. This substance the Lord has made and knows it through His most worthy and first creature, but He has made this creature His own to be known, believed and affirmed to be His very own. In all nature, composite or elementary, life is more noble than simple Being and among the elementary things there is no living thing which produces fruits of most perfect sweetness and nourishment as the palm. The Lord wants to be known through the substance of the Palm, not only because of its sweetness, nourishment, concord, and duration but because of its perfect love. The substance of the Palm is an explanation of the material union of Christ with the palm, as its elementary body through death must be separated from the other two, the celestial and ethereal, and be an immortal part victorious over death; and as the palm will always remain with the two other bodies so the celestial will always remain with the lower part so that by increasing and multiplying new bodies with new souls will be born.

These prophecies of the Venetian Virgin are very significant not only because of what they reveal about Giovanna's concept of herself as prophetess and the vessel of Christ, but also because of the significance attached to Venice in bringing about the "new age" or millenium on earth. The prophecies of the Venetian Virgin influenced Guillaume Postel to the extent that they became for him a platform of restitution and the basis of a universal monarchy under the rule of God. Postel on occasion referred to the Venetian Virgin as "Thamar" (palm), which indicates his belief in the significance of her prophecy.

The establishment of this universal monarchy, according to Postel, was to be the beginning of the millenium.[67] Postel believed that the new golden age was to begin in 1566 and that Venice was the city chosen by God to lead the world to the unity of all mankind under God. Postel's belief that the restitution of the whole world was to begin in 1566 probably was derived from the importance which he placed upon a miracle which occurred in Laon in 1566. Postel was present at an exorcism which took place on the steps of the cathedral of Laon in 1566 during which a demon was exorcised from a young girl, Nicole Obrey, upon sight of the Host.[68] Postel often referred to this "miracle of Laon" as a sign of the power of Christ living within man; he proclaimed that the year 1566 was the year in which the power of the living Christ became manifest universally. The year 1566 also held prophetic implications for Jacopo Tintoretto whom Postel may have known. In Tintoretto's large painting, entitled "Madonna dei Tesorieri," the artist depicted in the left foreground a column upon which is inscribed "unanimis concordiae simbolus 1566." Tintoretto completed this painting in 1566, and he obviously considered the subject matter of the painting, the bringing of the gifts to the Virgin and child by prominent Venetians, a symbol of universal harmony characterized by acts of charity.[69] This painting originally decorated the Magistrato dei Camerlenghi at the Rialto and a little later the Church of Saints John and Paul. Today it is found in the Gallery of the Accademia.

Postel and Tintoretto could have known each other, and it seems likely that they did, although at this moment we have no firm evidence to support this hypothesis. We can ascertain, however, that Postel's millenarian views about Venice were derived in large measure from Giovanna, the Venetian mystic who worked for the poor in Venice and who believed the restitution of all things was imminent. The "miracle of Laon" in 1566 confirmed in

---

[67]See the British Library, Sloane ms. 1411, fol. 338; also Kuntz, *Postel: Prophet,* 144.

[68]See Bibliothèque nationale, fonds lat. 3678, fol. 64ᵛ, fonds lat. 3224; also A. H. Chaubard, *Le Miracle de Laon en Laonnoys. . . A Chambray 1566* (Lyon: Sauvegarde historique, 1955).

[69]Kuntz, "Guillaume Postel e l'idea di Venezia come la magistratura più perfetta" in *Postello, Venezia e il suo mondo,* 176-78.

Postel's mind the prophecies of this mysterious woman and the urgency of their inauguration. So certain was Postel of the imminence of the restitution that he wrote: "In the year 1566 from the creation of the world the key of the instauration of all things will be at hand."[70]

An interesting reversal of sexual roles is observed in the mysteries and prophecies which the Venetian Virgin related to Postel. She had been instructed by God to reveal the divine pronouncements to a chosen "little son" who would also be her spiritual father. In like manner, Postel, the chosen son, proclaimed the teachings of his virgin mother who was also his spiritual daughter.[71] The chaste mother Giovanna entrusted the implementation of her platform of restitution to her chaste son Postel.

Chastity or virginity is an important aspect of the prophecies of Madre Giovanna and of Postel. The virginity of Madre Giovanna is constantly emphasized by the epithet by which Postel describes her – *Vergine Veneziana*. Sexual virginity is only one aspect of Giovanna's chastity, however. True virginity, according to Postel, resides in the one who has a knowledge of the one true God and consequently has obtained restored reason.[72] A chaste person is also the one in whom the spirit of Christ dwells. Postel repeatedly states that Christ lives most fully in Madre Giovanna, and for this reason she is called most virginal, although she also practiced sexual chastity, as did Postel. Sexual chastity is not advocated for all, however, since marriage and familial relationships are necessary for survival. Chastity in the spiritual sense, however, is essential for all mankind in a restored world. Pure love of God clothes men in a virgin body, and "his elements are changed into the whitest Manna."[73] Postel writes that this love of God as demonstrated in the life of Jesus and in the lives of saintly women such as Catherine of Sienna, Joan of Arc, and the Venetian Virgin then "virginifies, Israelifies, and judicifies" the whole world to the extent that all men through charity become virgins and truly restored.[74]

---

[70]"5566.anno a creatione mundi Instaurationis omnium clauis aderit." Bibliothèque nationale, fonds lat., 3678, fol. 64ᵛ.

[71]For additional ideas about sexuality in the thought of Postel see Claude-Gilbert Dubois, "Les métamorphoses mystiques de la sexualité dans la pensée de Guillaume Poste.", *Études françaises* 4, no. 2 (1969): 172-207.

[72]See Bibliothèque nationale, fonds franç. 2115, fol. 102ᵛ.

[73]Bibliothèque nationale, fonds lat. 3399, fol. 13ᵛ, 14. See also Kuntz, "Guillaume Postel and the World State: Restitution and the Universal Monarchy," *History of European Ideas* 4, no. 4, (1983): 449-50.

[74]". . . ibi sanctis desideriis cooperans. Virginificat, Israelificat et Judicificat sensim hunc mundum quousque per Charitatem omnes fiant Virgines et in Integrun restituti sicut antequam, Adam peccasset." Bibliothèque nationale, fonds lat. 3399, fol. 13ᵛ. For a general discussion of chastity in medieval and Renaissance thought see Donald Weinstein and Rudolph M. Bell, *Saints and Society* (Chicago: University of Chicago Press, 1982), 73-99. Also see Carolyn Walker Bynum, *Jesus as Mother. Studies in the Spirituality of the High Middle Ages* (Berkeley:

In a mystical union with God the Venetian Virgin was told that God willed that all reasonable creatures be united into one sheepfold; that there be a General Pardon for all with no exceptions; that peace and harmony of the world were contingent upon the enactment of these principles of restitution for all, union of all peoples and all religions, and a general pardon by a general baptism. Because of the singular merits of the Venetian Virgin, Postel believed that Venice had a providential role in the restitution of all things. He also believed that Venice was the city more beloved by God than all others with the exception of Jerusalem. Because of God's love for Venice, she was chosen to be the administrative center of the united world.[75] Venice enjoyed God's providential care because she had maintained a stable government for more than eight hundred years, contrary to other cities and states where cruelty, violence, and ambition follow the overthrow of princes and governments. According to Postel, a stable government is an essential factor in the establishment of God's kingdom on earth.[76] Because of the stability of her political institutions and because of the purity of her faith and religion Venice was a paradigm for the heavenly state on earth, indeed "the idea of the perfect principate." Postel attached great significance to the geographical position of Venice and noted that all things came from water and from water derived their unity and cohesion. He writes that "civitatem Maris antonomasticum esse Basim Restitutionis omnium."[77]

No small part of Postel's extravagant praise of Venice is derived from the qualities which he attributes to the Venetian Virgin. Most notable was her love of God expressed by her works of charity among the sick, the homeless, and orphans at the Ospedaletto of Saints John and Paul. The charitable deeds of the Venetian Virgin are reflected in the beneficence of Venice which Postel calls the *Publico Bene* and which is demonstrated by the noble care for the sick, the elderly, the poor and the orphans in her *scuole* and in the *luoghi pii*.[78] Postel compares Venice's love of *Publico Bene*

University of California Press, 1982). Also note Postel's words about Christ as Mother: "Sic itaque Restitui omnia necesse est, ut, ex Patre aeterno Jesu qui est VIR virorum, et ex eodem Matre Christo Rege regum seipsum Pontificem abscondente et FOEMINA HAEC VIRVM ILLVM CIRCVNDET. . . ." The British Library, Sloane ms. 1412, fol. 11 v.

[75]Kuntz, "Guillaume Postel e l'idea di Venezia," 165

[76]Ibid., 166. Also see the description of Venice as most hospitable and most stable in *Colloquium of the Seven about Secrets of the Sublime of Jean Bodin,* ed. Kuntz (Princeton: Princeton University Press, 1975), 3.

[77]The British Library, Sloane ms. 1411, fol. 244ᵛ.

[78]Postel says that "*Publico Bene* è il uero fine alquale debbe tendere il uero Cittadino. . .," (sig B), *Il Libro della devina ordinatione.* On the *scuole* of Venice see Brian Pullan, *Rich and Poor in Renaissance Venice* (Cambridge, Mass.: Harvard University Press, 1971).

to the love which God has for Venice, as if she were a *Publico Bene Divino.*[79]

We previously mentioned sexual reversal in the relationship of Postel and the Venetian Virgin. We see a similar analogue in regard to Venice. Venice is called the offspring of male Jerusalem and female Rome. Venice is the female paradigm of Jerusalem who descends as a "bride adorned for her husband and settles in the maternal location of John Mark's final home."[80] The Virgin of Venice evidently used this type of sexual imagery in discussing her role and that of Venice with her designated heir Postel. Madre Giovanna is quoted by Postel as defining her providential role in male terms. She stated:

I am the Signor (Lord) because He lives in me, and because of this I am in Him the Pope, Holy Reformer of the world.[81]

In Postel's translation of the *Zohar* in a passage about the reign of Jehovah as the true Ark of the Covenant, he glosses the text with the words, "Mater mundi et Christus Foemineus latente et circundato masculo."[82] Postel often quotes Jeremiah's prophecy of a restored Israel as being a state in which "woman will surround the man." By this he means that in the reign of Jehovah on earth the perfection of each individual must be realized. When Christ who is complete and therefore feminine as well as masculine lives in the human person, the woman or material nature is said to surround the man. This is mankind's return to the original purity and unity.[83]

Adam in his perfect state contained the unity of male-female. When Eve was drawn from Adam's side, she also contained the unity of female-male. Postel's androgyny implies the unity of the total person which is prerequisite for the restitution of all things. Individual or particular unity must be accomplished before the general restitution of all things can become a reality. The Venetian Virgin is an example of a total unity of person. Christ lives fully and completely in her person, and consequently she reveals God's presence in the world. Hence, she is called the Shechinah, the feminine attribute surrounding the divine presence in the world. The unity of male-female, that is, the unity of form and matter, is the underlying principle in the *renovatio mundi.*

---

[79]*Il Libro della della divina ordinatione,* sig. Bii v.

[80]Kuntz, "Guillaume Postel e l'idea di Venezia," 172-73.

[81]"Io son el Signor per che esso habita in ea, et per questo io sono in esso il Papa Santo Reformatore del mondo." The British Library, Sloane ms. 1410, fol. 51 v. See Kuntz, "Guillaume Postel e l'idea di Venezia," 172.

[82]The British Library, Sloane ms. 1410, fol. 52 v.

[83]Kuntz "Guillaume Postel and the World State: Restitution and the Universal Monarchy," *History of European Ideas* 4, no. 3. (1983): 299-301.

Like the unity of male-female found in the Venetian Virgin, Venice also represents the unity of male-female. The masculine form is the papal magistracy founded by John Mark, when he established his own patriarchy first at Aquileia near Venice; the feminine form is the temporal state which has been preserved by God for more than a thousand years. From the "perennitas" of the Venetian state have developed active virtues of charity, which have been especially defined by the life and example of the Venetian Virgin, the symbol of universal maternity which gives life to the world. Venice in her dual role of feminine temporal magistracy and masculine papal patriarchy represents the union between male and female which produces virtuous sons and daughters. For this reason Venice has been designated the most perfect magistracy and the true form of that "Politia" which must be transferred to the whole world.

According to Postel's millenarian vision Venice would become the center of the legislative affairs of the *Politia universalis,* while Jerusalem would fulfill its providential role as the spiritual center and Paris its judicial capital. The universal monarchy was to be divided into a loose confederation of twelve administrative capitals, the number representing the twelve tribes of Israel, the twelve Apostles and the twelve signs of the zodiac. There would also be twelve additional centers as alternates.[84]

Postel envisions the universal state as an *Ecclesia mundana,* a theocracy whose supreme authority is God. Representing God's authority on earth were to be a king and priest whose duties Postel does not specify. He only states that the priest or Angelic Pope will make no laws but will cooperate with Christ and His faith and that the major responsibility of the king is to ensure the spiritual well-being of the republic of the world. Both king and priest will act as righteous judge along with the six judges chosen from each of the twelve administrative divisions.[85] The functions of priest and king are interdependent. The constitution of the *ecclesia* which the king will uphold is the eternal testament and the law of Moses.[86] The eternal testament is described as the love and praise of the one true God and the practice of universal brotherhood and active works of charity.

When each man is reformed and becomes a complete person, there will be little need for laws, for each man as a son of God will treat every man as his brother. Hence all men of all nations will be joined into one sheepfold, to use the words of Postel's Venetian Virgin and medieval prophecies. In Postel's concept of the millenarian age the teachings of the Venetian Virgin are everywhere evident. However, the influence of Franciscan

---

[84]See The British Library, Sloane ms. 1412, fol. 12ᵛ. See also Kuntz, "Guillaume Postel and the World State," ibid.

[85]"Guillaume Postel and the World State," *History of European Ideas* 4, no. 4 (1983): 454.

[86]Bibliothèque nationale, fonds lat. 3398, fols. 7ᵛ, 8ᵛ, 14.

millenarianism cannot be overlooked in relation to the Virgin of Venice. As we recall, Madre Giovanna's confessor was a Franciscan, probably Francesco Giorgio himself. However, additional Franciscan influences were at work. Venice was rich in Joachimist material, much of which was published by Silvestro Meuccio between 1516 and 1527.[87] Father Rusticianus, a Venetian Dominican who studied Joachimist prophecy, made his own compilation, focusing his work especially on the prophecies of Telesphorus of Cosensa, a fourteenth-century Joachite. Postel, according to his own words, translated the prophecies of Rustician into Italian. In Rustician's compilation are also included the prophecies of Saint Brigida who proclaimed the need for reform of the clergy and all mankind and for the sheep to be gathered into one sheepfold.[88] Saint Brigida, Saint Catherine of Sienna, Saint Hildegard of Bingem, and especially the Blessed Angela da Foligna were admired by Postel and were often cited in his works. The Franciscan tertiary Angela Foligno, as we have indicated, was a paradigm for the spirituality of Postel's Venetian Virgin.

One characteristic which all the mystics cherished by Postel shared was the union of the active and contemplative life. Emphasis on the active life in works of charity was the very heart of the Venetian Virgin's program for renovation and restitution, and the center of Postel's plea for a *republica mundana restaurata* based upon the model of the Venetian republic.

I have recently discovered that Postel had in his possession a manuscript of John de Rupescissa entitled *Divinum opus . . . de philosophiae famulatu. . . .* The opening lines of the manuscript are: "Dixit Salomon Libro sapientiae cap. VII. Deus dedit mihi horum scientiam veram quae sunt ut sciam Dispositionem orbis terrarum. . . ."[89] Postel believed that God had also given to him the knowledge to comprehend the arrangement of the universe by restoring his reason to its pristine state before the Fall. According to Postel, the Venetian Virgin was responsible for his miraculous transformation, since she came to live within him in a spiritual immutation which restored his reason. His transformation was similar to that of the Venetian Virgin in 1540, when Christ came to dwell within her person. Postel ardently believed that man through use of reason and through works of charity could effect God's kingdom on earth. The last half of his life was spent in trying to accomplish this goal.

[87]See Marjorie Reeves, *The Influence of Prophecy in the Later Middle Ages* (Oxford: Clarendon Press, 1969), 262-63, 380-84; also note Bernard McGinn, "Angel Pope and Papal Antichrist," *Church History* 47, no. 2 (June 1978): 158-73; also *Visions of the End. Apocalyptic Traditions in the Middle Ages* (New York: Columbia University Press, 1979).

[88]Biblioteca Marciana, Venezia, Codices latini, Cl III, Cod. CLXXVII (2176).

[89]Biblioteca Marciana, Venezia, Codices latini, Cl VI, Cod. CCLXXXII (2859).

Although in the early part of Postel's career he spoke of a restored Gallic monarchy, after his meeting with the Venetian Virgin at the Ospedaletto of Saints John and Paul Venice became the paradigm of the "most perfect republic." Postel genuinely admired Venetian institutions and the *luoghi pii*. However, the virtues of the Venetian Virgin and her teachings about reform and unity were in large measure responsible for his praise of Venice and his choice of Venice as the administrative center of the *Ecclesia mundana*. For Postel the restitution of all things would begin in Venice, since the life of the Venetian Virgin, who was most fully filled with Christ's spirit, provided an example of how men should live in God's kingdom of earth.

Fantastic as these ideas appear today a long medieval history about a restored world under Christ preceeded them. Postel under the tutelage of the Venetian Virgin took seriously these prophecies. So certain was Postel of the Venetian Virgin's teaching that Venice was the place chosen by God to inaugurate the restitution of all things that he wrote a letter to the Senate and the Doge of Venice in which he urged the Venetians to inaugurate reform by assuming their proper role in the universal monarchy. According to Postel, the universal monarchy or *politia* in a reformed and restored world is the art of arts, and the true artist is she or he who proclaims its establishment and plans its structure. In Postel's speculations the true artist is the Venetian Virgin, the female Pope, and her chosen heir, Postel. The city of art and the place chosen by God for the instauration of the golden age is Venice, the home of the Venetian Virgin and the city of the true art of arts.[90]

---

[90]On the myth of Venice see Eco O.G. Haitsma Mulier, *The Myth of Venice and Dutch Republican Thought in the Seventeenth Century* (Assen: Van Gorcum, 1980); Edward Muir, *Civic Ritual in Renaissance Venice* (Princeton: Princeton University Press, 1981); Kuntz, "The Myth of Venice in the Thought of Guillaume Postel," in *Supplementum Festivum. Studies in Honor of Paul Oskar Kristeller,* ed. James Hankins, John Monfasani, Frederick Purnell, Jr. (Binghamton, NY: Medieval and Renaissance Texts and Studies, State University of New York, 1987), 505-23, with bibliography on the myth of Venice, 505-6, n. 1.

Footnotes to the German Canon: Maria von Wolkenstein and Argula von Grumbach

*Albrecht Classen**

FEMINIST-ORIENTED STUDIES HAVE RECENTLY begun to broaden our perception of the history and role of women through the ages. But while the modern era has provided fertile ground for feminist scholarship, the late Middle Ages and Renaissance have not received equal attention.[1] Although some excellent individual studies have been published in recent years, we still lack a clear overall picture of what women's lives were like in the early modern period.[2] For example, only a few attempts have been made to achieve a better understanding of the role of female authors in the Middle Ages,[3] but the situation is changing.[4] One of the reasons why women of the later Middle Ages have attracted only limited attention has been the decline of women's social, economic, and political position in the

---

*I would like to thank Allison Coudert and Peter E. Medine for helping me with my English. All remaining errors, however, are mine.

[1] A purely historical and rather conservative survey of women in the Middle Ages was written by Edith Ennen, *Frauen im Mittelalter* 2d ed. (Munich: C.H. Beck, 1985); see also *Women in Medieval Society*, ed. with an Introduction by Susan Mosher Stuard (Philadelphia: University of Pennsylvania Press, 1976); Frances and Joseph Gies, *Women in the Middle Ages* (New York: Crowell, 1978); Shulamith Shahar, *The Fourth Estate. A History of Women in the Middle Ages*, trans. Chaya Galai (London and New York: Methuen, 1983); Peter Ketsch, *Frauen im Mittelalter*, ed. Annette Kuhn, 2 vols. (Düsseldorf: Schwan, 1983); Margaret Wade Labarge, *Women in Medieval Life: A Small Sound of the Trumpet* (London: Hamilton, 1986); a very insightful collection of articles was edited by Rosemarie Morewedge, *The Role of Women in the Middle Ages* (Binghamton: University Center at Binghamton, State University Press, 1985); Anna Echols and Marty Williams, *Between Pit and Pedestal. Women in the Middle Ages* (Oxford: Berg Publishing, 1988).

[2] In her "Introduction" to *Women in the Middle Ages and the Renaissance: Literary and Historical Perspectives,* ed. with an introduction by Mary Beth Rose (Syracuse: Syracuse University Press, 1986), xiii, Mary Beth Rose formulates the rhetorical question: "Why do we know so little about women in the Middle Ages and the Renaissance? Until relatively recently, we had never really asked."

[3] See for instance the remarkable body of literary texts by women authors such as Marie de France, Christine de Pisan, Marguereta de Navarre in France, or such as Julian of Norwich, Margery Kempe in England. This list could easily be expanded by the hundreds; in consequence Katherina M. Wilson is presently preparing a *Lexicon of Medieval Women Writers*.

[4] Susan Groag Bell, "Medieval Women Book Owners: Arbiters of Lay Piety and Ambassadors of Culture," in *Women & Power in the Middle Ages,* ed. Mary Erler and Maryanne Kowaleski (Athens: University of Georgia Press, 1988), 149-87; Janel M. Mueller, "Autobiography of a New 'Creature': Female Spirituality, Selfhood, and Authorship in *The Book of Margery Kempe,*" in *The Female Autograph: Theory and Practice of Autobiography from the Tenth to the Twentieth Century,* ed. D.C. Stanton (Chicago: University of Chicago Press, 1984), 57-69.

fifteenth and sixteenth centuries.[5] The economic decline and accompanying intensification of misogynist attitudes proved to be forceful weapons for a male society intent on preserving patriarchy, or rather in establishing it to its full extent.[6] More than ever before male authors relegated women to the role of housewife and thus set the tone for future developments in the battle of the sexes.[7]

Still, the consensus needs to be tested and wherever possible refined. To do so here, I will focus on two remarkable women of the fifteenth and sixteenth centuries. I suggest that the pre-reformation era was not necessarily a time of decline for all women, but instead that it witnessed – even if only in few isolated cases – the emergence of a select group of highly articulate and powerful women.

I

Georg Steinhausen has correctly emphasized that the private letter written by ordinary people became a crucial form of expression in the later Middle Ages. The growth of literacy was accompanied by a need for a more intensified communication, on a business level (merchants' correspondence), political level (political correspondence), and on a private and literary level.[8] In the field of letter-writing women began to occupy a more elevated position, as Maria von Wolkenstein impressively illustrates.[9]

Maria von Wolkenstein has only recently been recognized as a historical personality, that is as a person who can be traced through a remarkable body of literary texts, and who has left her imprint on the historical development of her time. She was one of the daughters of the South Tyrolean poet and politician Oswald von Wolkenstein. Since the early 1960s philologists have acknowledged the grandeur of Oswald's lyric poetry; they now consider his songs to be the most advanced and sophisticated

---

[5]Barbara Becker-Cantarino, *Der lange Weg zur Mündigkeit. Frau und Literatur (1500-1800)* (Stuttgart: Metzler, 1987), 35; Martha C. Howell, *Women, Production, and Patriarchy in Late Medieval Cities,* Women in Culture and Society (Chicago: University of Chicago Press, 1988); a slightly opposing view is defended by Stanley Chojnacki in his article, "The Power of Love: Wives and Husbands in Late Medieval Venice," in Erler and Kowaleski, *Women and Power in the Middle Ages,* 126-48; cf. also Mosher Stuard, "Introduction," to *Women in Medieval History & Historiography,* Middle Ages Series (Philadelphia: University of Pennsylvania Press, 1987), viff.

[6]Hannelore Sachs, *Die Frau in der Renaissance* (Vienna: Anton Schroll, 1971), 42.

[7]Ruth Kelso, *Doctrine for the Lady of the Renaissance* (Urbana: University of Illinois Press, 1956), 78, 274.

[8]Georg Steinhausen, *Geschichte des deutschen Briefes. Zur Kulturgeschichte des deutschen Volkes* (Berlin: Gärtner, 1889-91), 72f.; Stephan Kohl, *Das englische Spätmittelalter. Kulturelle Normen, Lebenspraxis, Texte,* Studien zur englischen Philologie. Neue Folge 24. (Tübingen: Niemeyer, 1986), 98ff.

[9]Cf. Friedrich Heer, *The Medieval World. Europe 1100-1350,* trans. from German by G. Janet Sondheimer (New York: Mentor, 1962), 323; cf. Steinhausen, *Geschichte,* 84.

German poetry of the early fifteenth century.[10] Maria seems to have inherited her father's energetic, somewhat cantankerous character. For example, she clashed openly with the famous Bishop Nicholas of Cues not long after he had become the reformist Bishop of Brixen in 1450.[11] At that time Maria was a member of the Saint Claire convent in Brixen. The monastic discipline of the Brixen convents seems to have declined in the first half of the fifteenth century, at least from the point of view of Nicholas and the higher church administration. Upon the Bishop's recommendation, Pope Nicholas V issued his bull *Inter cetera* on May 12, 1453, in which he demanded the re-establishment of the traditional observance of the Franciscan convent regulation.[12] With this legal weapon in his hands, Nicholas of Cues would soon tackle the resistance in the Brixen convents.

Maria headed a group of nuns in the Saint Claire convent, which first opposed the rule of Abbess Agnes Rasner and later became involved in a bitter conflict with the new Brixen bishop. Nicholas was irate over Maria's impertinent (as he calls it) opposition to him, as he writes to the Saint Claire convent on January 13, 1455:

"das sy ir gelubd halt und der regel und gehorsam genueg tue, wie sy sich selb dar czue verpunden hatt." (Hallauer, 106)

[She should obey her vow and the rules and be obedient, just as she obliged herself to do so by entering the convent.]

Despite a formal agreement between the convent and the bishop to keep peace, the affair soon flared into a military confrontation. Soldiers, employed by Nicholas, forced their way into the convent and separated Maria and three other nuns who had revolted against the bishop from the remaining nuns, which then made it possible for Nicholas to introduce the reform. In the summer of 1455 the Brixen convent was reintegrated

---

[10] Quoted from *Die Lieder Oswalds von Wolkenstein.* Unter Mitwirkung von Walter Weiß und Notburga Wolf, hg. von Karl Kurt Klein. Musikanhang von Walter Salmen. 3d rev. and expanded edition by Hans Moser, Norbert Richard Wolf, and Notburga Wolf. ATB 55 (Tübingen: Niemeyer, 1987); cf. Walter Röll, *Oswald von Wolkenstein,* Erträge der Forschung (Darmstadt: Wissenschaftliche Buchgessellschaft, 1981), 160.

[11] Wilhelm Baum, *Nikolaus Cusanus in Tirol. Das Wirken des Philosphen und Reformators als Fürstbischof von Brixen,* Schriftenreihe des Südtiroler Kulturinstituts 10 (Bozen: Athesia, 1983), 86ff.

[12] This and the following according to Hermann Hallauer, "Nikolaus von Kues und das Brixener Klarissen-Kloster," *Mitteilungen und Forschungsbeiträge der Cusanus-Gesellschaft* 6 (1967): 77ff.; all quotations are taken from his edition of letters.

into the Strassburg Franciscan group of the *observantes*,[13] and soon after Maria appears to have left the cloister.[14]

Two aspects of these events are of particular interest. Although scholars such as Baum and Hallauer criticize Maria for her opposition to the bishop, her example gives an impressive illustration of the power female members of religious orders could employ against high-ranking church administrators. We need to keep in mind that this Wolkenstein daughter had entered the convent not because of a particular religious calling, but because this institution represented an economic safe haven for her as an unmarried woman.

Maria lost against Nicholas, not because she was defeated in this battle of wills, but because, as a woman, she had to rely on the support of her male relatives and local male admirers, and they had insufficient energy and political power to oppose the reforms of the Pope and bishop.[15] Both Agnes von Rasen and Maria, together with two other nuns, signed a letter addressed to Maria's brothers on August 6, 1455, pleading with them to continue their efforts to resist the reform movement.[16] The appeal was apparently to no avail, because Maria finally left the convent, as we have seen, and gave up her battle against the orthodox church administration.

The most fascinating aspect of Maria's character, however, is not her politics so much as her literary abilities. Although she was not allowed to communicate with the outside world without the permission of the abbess, several of her letters have been preserved in the Wolkenstein archives in Nuremberg.[17] These letters furnish ample evidence of Maria's considerable literary gifts. Whatever their political content, whether they present an accurate description of her unjust treatment by Nicholas of Cues or a fabulous fictional portrait of herself and her fellow nuns, the stylistic and structural patterns suggest their high literary quality.

Medieval women, in most cases, did not have the same opportunity as men to acquire the necessary skills to compose courtly poetry, nor were

---

[13]For the history of the reform movement in the Franciscan order cf. Julia A. Hernández, *Studien zum religiös-ethischen Wortschatz der deutschen Mystik,* Philologische Studien und Quellen (Berlin: Schmidt, 1984), 105.

[14]Hallauer, "Nikolaus von Kues," 91, does not know of any information concerning Maria until 1459, when she reappeared in Meran.

[15]Ibid., 86ff.

[16]Ibid., 110ff.; interestingly enough both Hallauer and Baum totally overlooked this.

[17]The fact by itself that these letters could be mailed to the world outside of the convent, either openly by messenger or secretly, indicates the laxness with which the regulations were enforced.

they expected or, in some instances, even allowed to do so.[18] Still, a grammar school education was often available to girls. Not surprisingly, letter-writing became women's favored means of literary expression in the later Middle Ages.[19] It seems that Maria von Wolkenstein learned from her mother, another sophisticated epistolary author, how to employ this personal and intimate form of art.[20] Letters as such have to adhere to a certain literary and generic framework, and this framework is detectable in Maria's letters.[21] Each time she approaches her brothers, for example, she employs the following formula or a slightly modified version of it:

> Mein williges gebet hincz got mit ganczen trewen und mein swesterliche trew wiss alzit. Mein herczen lieber pruder. Daz es dir wol ging an deim gesund und in allen sachen, daz hort ich alzit gern und waer mir ain grose frewd etc. (108).

[Be assured of my obedient prayer to God with all my heart, and of my sisterly loyalty. My heart-loved brother. I hope that you are well in every aspect. It would be a great pleasure for me to hear that all your things go well.]

Almost identical introductions or similar conventional formulaic patterns can be discovered in her other letters. Once this convention has been observed, however, Maria bursts forth into an amazingly emotional and lively account of the political events. Openly and without any reservations, she describes the internal revolt against Nicholas and the bishop's first subtle, but later unrestrained military threats against her and the other nuns:

> Mein herczen lieber pruder. Ich cklag dir und alle frawen den grosen ungerechten gewalt, den der pyssoff mit uns treybt. Er will

[18]Joachim Bumke, *Höfische Kultur. Literatur und Gesellschaft im hohen Mittelalter,* (Munich: Deutscher Taschenbuch Verlag GmbH.) 2: 474ff.; cf. Eileen Power, *Medieval Women,* ed. M. M. Postan (Cambridge: Cambridge University Press, 1975); for the history of German women writers in the Middle Ages, cf. Gisela Brinker-Gabler, *Deutsche Literatur von Frauen,* vol. 1 (Munich: C.H. Beck, 1988); for a broader European perspective, cf. *Medieval Women Writers,* ed. Katharina M. Wilson (Athens: University of Georgia Press, 1984); *Writings of Medieval Women,* ed. Marcelle Thiébaux (New York: Garland, 1986).

[19] Steinhausen, *Geschichte*; see also his edition *Deutsche Privatbriefe des Mittelalters.* Vol. 1: *Fürsten und Magnaten, Edle und Ritter* (Berlin: R. Gaertners Verlagsbuchhandlung, 1899), interestingly he has not included any letter by Maria von Wolkenstein; cf. Classen, "Female Epistolary Literature from Antiquity to the Present: An Introduction," *Studia Neophilogica* 60 (1988): 3-13.

[20]Classen, "Margareta von Schwangau: Epistolary Literature in the German Late Middle Ages," *Medieval Perspectives* 1, no. 1 (Spring, 1986): 41-53.

[21]Wilhelm Grenzmann, "Brief," in *Reallexikon der deutschen Literaturgeschichte,* 2d ed. Werner Kohlschmidt and Wolfgang Mohr, vol. 1 (Berlin: de Gruyter, 1958), 186-93.

uns korn und ra^cnt alles hin aus haben und spricht, daz kloster sey sein, und hat uns daz fleysch verpoten an der panck (108).

[My heart beloved brother. I and all the other women complain to you about the grossly unfair treatment by the bishop. He wants to take away all food and money, and he claims that the cloister belongs to him. Furthermore he forbade us to eat meat at dinner.]

She attacks Nicholas for making false accusations against the nuns, for directing public sermons against their alleged misconduct, and against people who continued to cooperate with the nuns: "und hat sey nit wo^cllen absolfieren die mit uns geret haben oder die zu uns gen etc." (108). [He did not want to absolve those who talked with us or who come to us.] Once the assigned visitor and reformer Albert Büchelbacher arrived from Nuremberg to enforce the reform in the convent, Maria's letters assume a more urgent tone and employ an extremely vivacious, expressive style as she describes the escalating clash between him and the convent's inmates:

Dar nach nam uns der gardian auss unser iiii und sprach, er wolt unpekümmert mit uns iiii sein. Da wolt wir uns von ain ander nit schaiden und sprachen, es pint des pabst priff lich alz wol die edlen alz die unedlen und wolten auch nicht ab noch aufsagen und liessen es alle pey der antwurt sten als ir uns berschriben het (111).

[Then the guardian took us four away and said he did not want to be bothered by us. We did not want to be separated from the rest and said that the Pope's letter would be binding both for the noble and common people. We refused to recant and stood by the response as you had advised us.]

Maria displays a sophisticated epistolary style.[22] She is aware that her letters can only have an effect if she succeeds in convincing her brothers of the plight into which the convent has fallen. Thus she gradually intensifies the pathos of her account, warning them first that all nuns in revolt would have to submit to the pressure exerted by the bishop. The emotional description of her sisters' suffering is an impressive piece of literary blackmail: "und es leit in doch alz hert es mo^ccht aim stain erparmen und aine pey der anderen nit" (111). [They all suffer badly. A stone would cry over this unfair treatment, and all are totally alone by themselves.] Then she incorporates the nuns' outcries for help – almost as a literal quotation: "und sy mo^cchten gancz verczagen und ru^cffen ew an und wir mit samt in, dz ir in und uns zu hilf kummt" (111). [They are about to despair and appeal to you, along

[22] Anton Schwob, in *Oswald von Wolkenstein, eine Biographie.* Schriftenreihe des Südtiroler Kulturinstitute, 4, 3d ed. (Bozen: Athesia, 1979), 256: "Ihre Briefe an die Brüder Leo und Friedrich . . . beweisen, daß sie ebenso gebildet wie beredt gewesen sein muß."

with us, that you come to our help.] In case this still might not have the intended effect, Maria shifts the emphasis of her letter from politics to religious matters and paints a drastic picture of the nuns' actual suffering:

> Wan sol dz lenger weren, so muss wir sterben, wan wir weder essen noch trincken, slaffen noch wachen mucgen von grosem herczen laid von unsern getrewen swestern wegen und die grose smachhait (111).

[If it lasts much longer we all will have to die, because we neither eat nor drink, and we neither want to sleep nor to stay awake because of all the emotional pain we feel for our loyal sisters and because of the extensive injustice.]

She implores her brothers to act like the angels of vengeance who come upon Lucifer: "und erledigt uns alz ir welt dz ew got erledig und erlocss an ewren lesten czeiten" (111). [And help us as you want God to help you to absolve you from all your sins at the time of your death.]

At first glance it remains unclear why Maria claims that all those nuns now in solitary cells and under strict guardianship as in a prison would become crazy if not freed soon: "oder die swestern mocchten unsinnig werden, wan es ist iedlich under ainem sunder sloss" (112). [Or the sisters might become crazy, because all are locked up in isolation.] Her apparent rationale, however, for resorting to these powerful images is to make as strong an appeal as possible to her brothers and other political allies outside the convent. Maria's letter was not a brief note scribbled in haste, but a self-conscious, carefully calculated, and sophisticated document in which she attempts to win support for her cause by a judicious combination of rational and emotional arguments.

Possibly Nicholas and other Church officials were right in their opinion of Maria. After many battles and her total defeat, she finally asks her brother Leo to take her out of the convent because she cannot stand the rigid life and the boredom of the regulated life. Her comments about the new rules are interesting both in terms of the picture they give of life in a fifteenth-century nunnery and in terms of their literary expressions. Maria complains not only about the alien structure imposed on her as a nun, but she also describes the new character of the convent in lively, almost facetious terms, using a combination of dialect expressions, learned rhetoric, and words of direct accusation:

> So sind der zu sacz und der auf sacz so vil, mer wan ander ganczen regl, und ist dez gnuten und dez gnapenn alz vil es mocht ains pumlwiczic werden, und wir sechen sucst nicht geistliche ornung noch geistlichhait dan die stauchen in daugen und denn salck im herczen und wissen wol, soltestu ir ordnung sechen, dz sy dir nit

gefiel dan dz sy sich wol ku͏ᶜnn halten vor der welt und sind doch
grose nequam (116).

[There simply are too many addenda, more than a completely new
set of statutes. There is a critical tone in them, one could become
crazy. But still we do not see spiritual order or spirituality . . .
And you should know, if you saw the new regulations, you would
hate them and that they would not stand up to criticism from the
outside world.]

Not content with condemning the Church authorities, she goes one
step further and attacks the new sisters who have come from Nuremberg
to assist the bishop in enforcing the new law: "Es kan ir aine mer schalkait
dan unser voder vi etc." (116). [Any of them alone knows more to fool
the world than all four of us.] Maria also perceives the various degrees of
religious reformist intentions in different members of the Church. For
instance, she refers, in a facetious way, to the "lange mu͏ᶜnich von Nu͏ᶜrnberg"
as a stern authority.[23] But the real Church inspector ("der rechte visitator")[24]
is described as a formidable threat to the peace not only of the Tyrolean
nuns of the Saint Claire convent but also of the reformed and strict nuns
from Nuremberg: "daz die frawen von Nurnberg selb auf in sorgen und
sprechen, er sey alz hafftig und unparmherczig, dz wunder sey" (117).
[That the Nuremberg women themselves are full of fear and say that he
is pitiless.]

A final letter was sent just before December 1455 to Leo von Wolkenstein.
Maria faced a political dead end, because the last avenues for communication
with the outside world were literally closed up as the cloister was totally
walled in: "Wir lassen dich wissen, dz man die lo͏ᶜcher alle verslagen hat"
(Nr. xvii, 117). [We let you know that all holes have been closed.] Her
letter has lost some of its former stylistic appeal and now sounds relatively
simple and monotonous. Maria reports that she is not allowed to speak out
in public, even when her brother is going to visit her: "Wiss auch, dz wir
ain wort nit tuen reden, oder die mu͏ᶜnich wellen dem pissoff uber uns
klagen etc." (117). [Be informed that we do not dare to express one word,
otherwise the monks would complain about us to the bishop.]

After this letter, Maria von Wolkenstein disappears from historical and
literary records; but her extant letters reveal a surprisingly strong and
vivacious personality, willing to stand up for her own interests and refusing
to accept the Church's demands on her as a nun. Although Nicholas of
Cues is preserved in our memories as an outstanding Church leader, Maria's
correspondence shows her to be comparably strong willed. She lacked

---

[23]Ibid., 116, that is Albert Büchelbach.
[24]Ibid., 117, that is Johannes de Lare.

sufficient support in her community; otherwise she might have succeeded in resisting the bishop. At the very least, her case demonstrates that fifteenth-century women were not all condemned to be submissive and indecisive personalities. As an independent personality, Maria serves as an outstanding example for late medieval women's struggle to preserve their own position in a time when male dominance became increasingly more noticeable throughout all layers of society.[25]

II

Argula von Grumbach (1492-1568?) is another example of a learned and literate woman, representative of the thriving female literary culture which continued to exist even at a time when women were increasingly excluded from literary and humanistic studies.[26] Martin Luther held relatively progressive opinions about women and their lives in a male dominated world, at least in comparison with those views by earlier or contemporary thinkers.[27] His conviction, however, that women should be subordinate to men and relegated to a life of childbearing and household duties considerably determined the future course of women's history in Germany.[28]

Argula von Grumbach, however, defied these new, or rather very old, social ideals for women. Her case dramatically illustrates that learned, strong-willed, and outspoken women did not disappear in German-speaking countries.[29] Her literary work serves as an extremely interesting example of the continuing public presence of women even in the era of the Reformation, a presence corroborated by other scholars.[30]

[25]Cf. Gabriele Becker et al.: "Zum kulturellen Bild und zur realen Situation der Frau im Mittelalter und in der frühen Neuzeit," *Aus der Zeit der Verzweiflung. Zur Genese und Aktualität des Hexenbildes* (Frankfurt a. M.: Suhrkamp, 1980), 11-128.

[26]Heidi Lauterer-Pirner, "Vom *Frauenspiegel* zu Luthers Schrift *Vom ehelichen Leben*. Das Bild der Ehefrau im Spiegel einiger Zeugnisse des 15. und 16. Jahrhunderts," in *Frauen in der Geschichte* vol. 3, ed. Annette Kuhn and Jörn Rüsen. Studien Materialien Band 13. Geschichtsdidaktik. (Düsseldorf: Schwann, 1983), 63-85; Maria Wehrenfennig, "Die Stellung der deutschen Frau um 1450 bis Luthers Einfluß um 1520," (Ph.D. dissertation, University of Vienna, 1939).

[27]Eleanor Commo McLaughlin, "Equality of Souls, Inequality of Sexes: Women in Medieval Theology," *Religion and Sexism,* ed. Rosemary Radford Reuther, (N.Y.: Simon & Schuster, 1974), 216ff.; *Martin Luther: Vom ehelichen Leben und andere Schriften über die Ehe,* ed. Dagmar C.G. Lorenz, Universal-Bibliothek 9896. (Stuttgart: Reclam, 1978), 98f.

[28]Friederike Höher, "Hexe, Maria und Hausmutter – Zur Geschichte der Weiblichkeit im Spätmittelalter," in *Frauen in der Geschichte,* 13-62, particularly 50ff.; Becker-Cantarino, *Der lange Weg,* 41ff.

[29]Becker-Cantarino, *Der lange Weg,* 41ff.

[30]Merry E. Wiesner, *Working Women in Renaissance Germany* (Syracuse: Syracuse University Press, 1986), 8ff.; Hannelore Sachs, *Die Frau in der Renaissance* (Vienna-Munich: Anton Schroll, 1971); Wendy Slatkin, *Women Artists in History. From Antiquity to the 20th Century*

Argula was born in Seefeld in Southern Bavaria ca. 1492 as the daughter of Bernhardin von Stauff, Freiherr zu Ehrenfels, and Katharina von Törring.[31] She dedicated her energies to the study of the Bible, because her father, a fervent supporter of the Reformation, exerted a strong influence on her. After Argula's parents died in 1510, she lived with her uncle Hieronymus Freiherr von Stauff, until she was invited to become a maid of honor at the Bavarian court for the Duchess Kundigunde, wife of Duke Wilhelm of Bavaria. There she met her future husband, Freiherr Friedrich von Grumbach. Soon after their marriage they moved to Dietfurth in Franconia, where he held a position in the government. When a Würzburg priest, Paul Speratus, rekindled her enthusiasm for the Reformation, she soon embarked on an intensive correspondence with such leaders of the Protestant movement as Adrian Osiander, Georg Spalatin, and above all, Martin Luther. Apparently the latter welcomed her advice and her supportive letters. Argula once even went so far as to recommend to Luther that he marry, a suggestion which Luther then reported to Spalatin.[32]

Argula's active participation in the Reformation began when she heard about Arsatius Seehofer, a young scholar at the University of Ingolstadt, who was imprisoned on account of the evangelical belief that he had expressed in seventeen heretical articles. Deeply shocked by the case, Argula sent a letter to the University of Ingolstadt, protesting against its policy – a policy fully in accord with the conservative and rigid rules established by the Bavarian Duke:

> Ach gott wie werdet ihr bestehen mit euer hohen Schuhl, daß ihr so thorecht und gewaltiglich handelt wieder das Wort Gottes, und mit Gewalt zwinget das heilig Evangelium in der Hand zuhalten, dassselbige dazu zuverlaᶜugnen, als ihr dann mit Arsatio Seehofer gethan habt.[33]

(Englewood Cliffs, N.J.: Prentice-Hall, 1985); cf. Lorenz, *Martin Luther,* 86, also refers to the Benedictine authors Barbara von Dalberg and Aleydis Raiskop, Charitas Pirkheimer, Margaretha von Staffel, Duchess Hedwig von Schwaben, among others.

[31]Felix Joseph Lipowsky, *Argula von Grumbach gebohrne Freiin von Stauffen* (Munich: Lindauer, 1801), 10; cf. Classen, "Argula von Grumbach," in *Dictionary of Continental Women Writers,* ed. K.M. Wilson (New York: Garland, forthcoming).

[32]Lipowsky, *Argula von Grumbach,* 17; see *D. Martin Luthers Werke, Kritische Gesamtausgabe. Briefwechsel.* 3d vol. (Weimar-Gratz: Hermann Bohlaus, 1969), 393ff. See also 304 and 365 fn. 1.

[33]Lipowsky, *Argula von Grumbach,* Appendix I: 1. All qutotations will be taken from this source. Unfortunately, Lipowsky does not paginate his appendix. Consequently I will refer to my own numbering, beginning with 1 as the first page of the appendix.

[Oh God, how will you and your university face final judgment, since you have acted so foolishly and violently against God's word, to force Arsatio Seehofer, holding the New Testament in his hands, to renounce it.]

Argula argues both passionately and with the full knowledge of the biblical texts, as her introductory quotations of Saints John, Matthew, and Luke indicate. Her method of criticism is closely modeled on Luther's or Melanchthon's, since she refers to the original text of the Bible and contrasts it with the political realities of her days:

> Ihr hohen Meister, ich finde es an keinem Ort der Bibel, daß Christus noch seine Aposteln oder Propheten gekerckert, gebrennet noch gemoᵉrdet haben (1).

> [You high masters, I do not find any place in the Bible that Christ nor any of his apostles or any prophet have imprisoned, burned or murdered anybody.]

She dares to hint at the scholars' ignorance of the true text of the Bible: "Habt ihr nie gelesen Jeremiaᵉ am ersten, da der Herr saget zu ihm . . ." (2). [Have you never read Jeremiah 1, where the Lord says to them . . .] Her letter appears to be more an elaboration of the prophets and apostles' words than a political or religious debate with her opponents:

> Der Geitz hat euch besessen, ihr moᵉchtet sonst Gottes Wort baß leiden, gieng euch nicht ab, an Vertruckung des Decrets. Das Evangelium traᵉgt nicht so viel Pfenning in seinen Rathschlaᵉgen (2).

> [Greed is possessing you, otherwise you would like God's words better, and you would not have to print the ordinance. The New Testament does not contain as many pennies in its advises.][34]

or:

> Ich bitt euch, vertrauet Gott, er wird uns nicht verlassen, dann er hat alle unsere Haar in acht und gezehlet als Matth. am 10 (2).

> [I beg you, trust in God, he will not abandon us, because he takes care of all our hair and has even counted it.]

She accuses the university officials of violating the law, and of adhering to false, inhumane, and suppressive regulations: "Es ist leicht disputirt, so

---

[34]The full meaning of Argula's proverbial statement is not quite clear. I understand her metaphor as an expression for her belief that money is not the adequate means to learn the true essence of God's words; instead one learns it through God's inspiration only.

man nicht Schrifft, sondern Gewalt brauchet, in solcher Disputation siehe ich nichts anders, dann daß der zuᶜchtiger der gelehrtest ist" (5). [It is easy to argue publicly, when you do not use the Testament, but force. I perceive in such a dispute nothing else than that he who punishes is the most learned person.]

Argula's opponents immediately recognized the threat she posed as a woman thoroughly trained in theology with a detailed knowledge of the biblical text and considerable skill in the rhetorical art of debate. She was convinced that she understood the Bible's essential message, which she constantly quotes as her exclusive source and authority. This gives her a tremendously strong self-confidence, as she says in her letter:

> Gott sey Lob, daß ich das rechte und wahre Licht scheinen siehe. Ich will mein einiges Pfund nicht vergraben, der Herr verleihe mir Gnad (6).

> [God be praised that I perceive the true light. I do not want to be overly modest; the Lord may give me his mercy.]

She bases this statement on the testimony of at least fourteen biblical quotations. Sometimes, however, she fails to distinguish clearly between her own words and those taken from the Bible or from paraphrases of the Biblical text, because she was so thoroughly conversant with it that her own words soon sound like those of the prophets, apostles, and other authors of the Old and New Testaments. Her sharp intellect allows her, however, to go beyond traditional exegetical interpretations to discover in the text arguments supporting a woman's active role in the enlightened and reformed Church: "Dann Hieronymus hat sich nicht geschaᶜmt, und zu den Weibern geschrieben gar viel, als zu Plessila, Paula, Eustachia, etc. etc." (7). [Hieronymus was not embarrassed to write to women such as. . . .]

Having established the legitimacy of women engaging in theological debate, she then proceeds to challenge the Ingolstadt University to a public debate:

> Ich scheu mich nicht, vor euch zukommen, euch zuhoᶜren, auch mit euch zu reden, dann ich kann auch mit Teutsch fragen, Antwort hoᶜren und lesen, aus der Gnade Gottes (7).

> [I am not afraid to come to you, to listen and to talk with you, because I as well can ask in German, give answers and read, thanks to God's mercy.]

In case her plea for a public discussion of the theological issues might be dismissed on the basis of her ignorance of Latin, she admonishes the University professors that

Ihr ko᷄nnt teutsch, in dieser Zung gebohren und erzogen. Ich hab euch nicht arabische Ding zugeschrieben, sondern das Wort Gottes, als ein Glied der Christlichen Kirchen, vor welcher die Pforten der Ho᷄llen nicht bestehen mo᷄gen, aber vor der Ro᷄mischen bestehen sie wohl (8).

[You know German, since you are born with this tongue. I have not written you things in Arabic, but only God's words, as a member of the Christian Church, against which the gates of hell cannot be erected, although they stand in front of the Roman church.]

The official reaction was harsh, repressive and devastating for Argula's family. Leonard von Eck, chancellor of the University of Ingolstadt, read her letter and forwarded it, along with his extremely negative comments, to the Duke.[35] In consequence, her husband was suspended from his offices as administrator, and thus the family had to return to their private estates.[36] Argula did not give up, however, and in a flood of letters continued to pressure other personalities and institutions such as the magistrate of Ingolstadt (10ff.), Duke Wilhelm IV of Bavaria (29ff.), the elector of Saxony Frederick (39ff.), and Johann the count of Palatinate on the Rhine (41ff.) in particular. Yet in the long run her efforts were without avail.

The most interesting of Argula von Grumbach's literary disputes developed when another student from Ingolstadt, Johann von Landshut, sent her a satirical poem "Des Magisters Johann von Landshut Verse gegen die Argula von Grumbach" (12ff.). In this poem he not only tries to ridicule her opinions, her actions, and her literary works, but also outlines the role which women should occupy, according to the characteristic male attitude of that time:

Daß ihr nicht solt disputiren,
Sondern das Haus daheim regieren.
    Und in der Kirchen schweigen still,
    Sehet nur meine liebe Sibill.
Wie ein Frech und wild Thier ihr seyd,
Und wie euch du᷄nkt so gescheut;
    Daß ihr die Heil. Schrifft wollt deuten.[37]

---

[35]Lipowsky, *Argula von Grumbach,* 8f., Letter to Duke Wilhelm IV. from November 1523.

[36]Cf. Ludwig Geiger, "Argula von Grumbach," *Allgemeine Deutsche Biographie* 10 (1879; rpt. Berlin: Duncker & Humbolt, 1968), 7f.

[37]Lipowsky, *Argula von Grumbach,* p. 13. 11. 15-21; the verse count is mine, each time starting on the top of each page anew with number 1.

[You should not dispute, you should manage affairs at home,[38] and be quiet in church, my dear Sibyl. You are a nasty and wild animal, if you think that you are so intelligent as to be able to interpret the New Testament.]

He ridicules her intellectual pretensions and mocks the Reformation, referring derogatorily to "euer Abgott Martin Luther" (v. 31). Then he launches an attack on Argula as a woman. Theological discussions, ecclessiastical issues, political matters, and other subjects were considered to be topics for men exclusively. If a woman attempted to use her skills in these fields, she was immediately suspected of questionable, even sinful, motives. Neither the Catholic theologians nor Luther were free from these prejudices, as the *Frauen-spiegel*, Luther's own reflections on women, and other contemporary texts illustrate.[39] Consequently, Magister Johann considers Argula's theological fervor and her support for Arsatius Seehofer to be sexually motivated:

> Daher kommt auch dein groß Mitleyden
> Und gefaᵉllt dir vielleicht an der Schneiden
> Arsatius im grausen Haar
> Ein Juᵉngling von 18. Jahr.
> Derhalb du ihm sein Sach thust glimpffen.
> Sonst wuᵉrdest dich doch wohl darob
> ruᵉmpffen (14, 35-40)

[Your pity is caused by your physical attraction to the young Arsatius of eighteen years; that is the reason why you defend him; otherwise you would not care.]

He admonishes her to go back to her own domain, to the household and her housework:

> So stell ab dein Muth und Gutdunckel,
> Und spinn davor an deiner Kunckel.
> Oder strick Hauben und wirck Borten,
> Ein Weib soll nicht mit Gottes Worten
> Stolzieren und die Maᵉnner lehren (15, 16-19)

[Stop your arrogance and outspokenness, instead go back to spinning, weaving, knitting. A woman must not pride herself with a knowledge of God's words and should not try to teach men.]

---

[38]The literal translation, however, reads: "to govern at home," which is a bit surprising since the rule at home still was assumed by the patriarch, cf. Howell: *Women, Production, and Patriarchy in Late Medieval Cities*, 180ff.; see also Lawrence Stone: *The Family, Sex and Marriage in England, 1500-1800* (London: Weidenfeld and Nicholson, 1977).

[39]Cf. Lauterer-Pirner, "Vóm *Frauenspiegel*," 67ff.; see especially Sigrid Brauner's article, "Martin Luther on Witchcraft: A True Reformer?" in this volume.

Argula's response is structured in the same formal way: she writes the same type of lyrical verse with a simple rhyme scheme. But even here she cannot refrain from constantly quoting biblical texts, since she gains her strongest arguments from the Bible itself. As her poem illustrates, Argula is a radical supporter of women's rights and a defender of equality between the sexes. Again the Bible serves as her prime authority, because there she reads that God considered women as worthy to receive the Holy Spirit as men:

Daselbst findet ihr also davon
    Nicht ausgeschlossen Weib noch Mann:
Wie Gott sein Geist ausgiessen wo^ell
    Auf alles Fleisch, nicht daß er stell,
Sein Geist in einen engen Stall. (17, 7-11)

[You find that neither man nor woman was excluded from the Holy Spirit when God distributed it to all flesh; he did not place his Holy spirit in a narrow shed.]

Argula adds a further social dimension to her argument, by referring to the peasants who are, as she emphasizes, as much God's creatures as anybody else:

Ist Baur, Weib geschlossen davon,
    Zeigt mir, wo findt ihr geschrieben stohn? (17, 31f.)

[Is the peasant, the woman, excluded from it? Show me, where do you find it written down?]

Argula's energetic public defense both of Lutheranism and of a woman's right to discuss the biblical message in public, together with her belief that peasants and other poor people could be vessels for divine inspiration, are extremely impressive indications of how courageous a woman she was, particularly for a woman living in the early sixteenth century. Her words illustrate why the authorities came to consider her a threat to the public order: she challenged the predominantly patriarchal structure of society, the dominance of the Catholic Church, and even the traditional class stratification of society. She used her theological expertise to support her political and social demands and vice versa. Her religious convictions gave her the strength to approach even the highest authorities as brothers and sisters in God's realm, as in the letter to the city of Ingolstadt: "meine liebe Freund und Bru^cder in Christo" (12), or in her letter to Duke Wilhelm IV: "Ich hab nicht unterlassen moegen. E. F. G.[40] als meinem Bruder in Christo zu schreiben" (33). Over and over again she insisted that

---

[40]Abbreviation for "Eure Fürstliche Gnaden," that is Your Ducal Honor!

she derives her true authority from God, and that this authority overruled all other worldly authorities: "Was ich geschrieben, weiß ich aus go ̈ttlicher Gnaden zu verantworten" (33).[What I wrote I know to take responsibility for through Divine mercy.]

Argula's criticism of the Catholic Church is similar to that of Luther and other Reformers. She protests against the selling of indulgences, the high Church taxes, and the clergy's greed: "dann man siehet, daß sie aus Geitz wieder Gott fechten" (33). [One notices that they fight against God because of their greed for money.] Argula was aware that her "unfeminine" behavior threatened herself and her family. As she says in a letter to her cousin Adam of Törring, governor of Neuburg: "bitt euch kein Beschwerniß zu nehmen, ob ihr ho ̈rt daß man mich scha ̈ndet und verspottet" (36). [I ask you not to worry if you hear that people scoff at me and blame me.] As we have seen, her husband was discharged from his office, because of her activities. As Duke Wilhelm IV writes to his brother Ludwig: "da Er als der man so ̈lche vngeschickte schreiben seinen Weib gar nicht gestatt solt haben, vnd darauf seines Ambz zu stu ̈nd an entsezen" (34). [Because he as a man should not have allowed his wife to write such inappropriate letters, we will discharge him from his office.]

Argula is not a revolutionary, but she does insist on her inalienable rights as a woman to discuss her religious views, to explain her beliefs in public, and to read the Bible in German, all of which, of course, goes against Saint Paul (1 Cor., 14:33-5; 1 Tim. 2:11; Eph. 5:22-33). She goes so far as to claim that she is entitled to her personal interpretations of the holy text, thus establishing a dangerous precedent for both the Protestant and Catholic churches, which, faced with the danger of losing power and control over the individual, could not tolerate Argula's public protests. Asserting her right to her own beliefs, Argula argues convincingly, at least for a modern audience, that even if her husband were to try to force her into a certain belief, she would reject his authority:

> Wo er mich aber Wollte dringen
> Von Gottes Wort treiben und zwingen
>   Daß ich davon nichts halten sollt,
> Welches ir auch gar gern wollt.
>
>   . . . .
>   So ich Gott's Wort verlaugnen sollt,
> Ehe ich das alles verlassen wollt,
>   ja Leib und Leben ergeben frey (27, 15-28).

[If he tried to force me away from God's words, which is exactly what you also want. . . . Instead of recanting God's words, I would rather give up my life.]

Otherwise Argula feels obligated to follow her husband in all domestic matters and to be the best wife possible:

Zu dienen in Gehorsamkeit
Und unsern Mann halten in Ehr'n (27, 4f.).

[To serve obediently and hold our husbands in honor.]

Argula von Grumbach was a controversial figure in the 1520s. We can certainly observe in her an exemplary personality, who not only defied conventional male views about women but even developed, on the basis of her own exegetical interpretation, a revolutionary basis for possible riots of the local peasantry, although, clearly, she had no wish for this to happen. It remains unclear whether she was a rare exception or simply a religiously inspired woman with a more noticeable profile than many other contemporary women.[41] She might, however, function like the tip of the iceberg, and a more thorough historical investigation might lay bare a much wider range of women writers active in public politics, in intellectual matters, and in the liberal arts than has heretofore been known to us. It seems that Argula did not yield to public pressure but continued with her reformist activities. In 1563 she is said to have been imprisoned on the charge of attempting to convert the citizens of Köfing to Protestantism through reading of "revolutionary" books.[42]

The two women discussed here, Maria von Wolkenstein and Argula von Grumbach, illustrate that women could assume a relatively strong position even in the late fifteenth and early sixteenth centuries, stronger at least than has heretofore been observed. Even though women definitely lost some of their influence and were often silenced by the authorities, that did not mean that all doors were shut for them, or that no new doors were opened for women writers and thinkers. A closer look at the historical and literary sources will certainly reveal more women like Maria and Argula. Although women suffered severely from increasing misogyny and the establishment of an all-dominating patriarchy from the later Middle Ages onwards, the impression of late medieval women as totally silenced, anonymous members of their society is a myth which needs to be shattered.

---

[41]Becker-Cantarino, *Der lange Weg,* 47, takes into account only the first option.

[42]Robert Stupperich, *Reformatorenlexikon* (Gütersloh: Gerd Mohn, 1984), 91; Maria Heinsius, *Das unüberwindliche Wort. Frauen der Reformationszeit* (Munich: Chr. Kaiser Verlag, 1951), 158, discusses the scant historical evidence.

Facsimile of letter from Anne of Saxony.

Letters By Women in England, the French Romance, and Dorothy Osborne

James Fitzmaurice and Martine Rey

O N AUGUST 9, 1626, KATHERINE KENDALL TEMPLE wrote to Lady Hester Temple asking for payment of a debt that totalled forty pounds. She described difficulties she was having with her husband and suggested that those difficulties strained her financially, though she did not accuse her husband of stinting her in any way. What makes this letter more than an example of the humdrum of ordinary life in England at the beginning of the reign of Charles I is its literary feel. It is not a monument of great literature, but it shows careful diction, depicts the character of the writer with some detail, and develops narrative tension. The letter, slightly edited for length, reads as follows:

> These [lines] are to intreate you to send the 16 li by this bearer. you know 9 li was due Easter tearme, yet I had not sent soe soon for it, had not I had occason to send for mr Temple, who is at my Sister ffarmers as I thinke ffor I know not how he should come so far as Stowe being so ill provided as he makes himselfe by his strange underthought of jorneys. for when our stuffe, my maide, and the children were gone in the waggaine, and wee makeinge what hast we could out of towne, he said my saddle must be stuffed and to my thinkeing went after the porter, to shew how he would haue it done but he left him and went towarde westminster by water as I heard. I thinking to haue found him at my fathers, brought his horse and came to Acton, but missinge him there I thought it best to goe alonge with my children and the rest of our company and send for him when tyme had worne that whim out of his head which I hope it hath. . . . I would entreate sr Thomas if he thinkes it fitt to wryte to mr Stratford by this bearer. if he may pay us the 40 li here it will save him a jorney of bringinge and wee of fetching it from you, If mr Temple be with you or shall hereafter come in an unfittinge manner I beseech you rather pitty my sufferinges then blame me for that I can noe wayes helpe, thus with my service to your Ladyship I rest
>
> Your obliged
> sister in lawe
> Katherine Temple[1]

---

[1]Katherine Kendall Temple, Letter to Hester (Sandys) Lady Temple. Huntington Library MS 46513 (Temple Family Addenda).

One need not be of a suspicious nature to wonder if Mr. Temple used a ruse to escape from family duties, a possibility raised by Katherine Temple's narrative and which she allows to pass without comment. There are hints that the matter is of little concern, a "whim" that will wear itself out. There are also hints that profound embarrassment will result from the husband's "unfittinge" behavior at Lady Temple's home in Stowe. These carefully chosen words help to give Katherine Temple's story its tension. Lady Temple will have to wait to learn its ending, unless, of course, Mr. Temple is with her. The letter offers a clear picture of its writer. She is burdened down by the responsibilities of a maid and children, out in the countryside and away from home. She knows her husband's haunts and habits. She is also capable of tact, for she does not harangue Mr. Temple and therefore cannot be dismissed as a shrew. Although not quite a Griselde, she accepts her lot with patience.

Dorothy Osborne writes to her future husband within the tradition from which Katherine Temple's letter is drawn.[2] It is a tradition of women writing to women and of women writing as women to men. The tradition involves literary qualities such as those found in the letter to Lady Temple, and it often makes use of a language of its own. Certain words carry special meanings that go beyond ordinary speech, words like "kindness," "friendship," and "freedom." We shall attempt to trace some of the meanings of "kindness" in this essay.

William Temple, Dorothy Osborne's future husband, was by marriage a distant relative of Katherine Temple, but there the connection ends. Osborne's letters to him, produced from 1652 to 1654, have been recognized for a hundred years as having great power, though generally they are seen more as the outpouring of a sensitive heart and less as the product of a conscious artist. As recently as 1987 Kenneth Parker wrote, "Few stories outside the realms of imaginative literature can match that of the love-affair between Dorothy Osborne and William Temple."[3] The letters do provide a warm and touching love story from the seventeenth century in sharp contrast with events like the murder of Sir Thomas Overbury and the trial of Lord Castlehaven. Yet they are much more than a love story, for they, too, contain such elements as careful diction, character development of the writer, and narrative tension that are to be found in Katherine Temple's letter to Lady Temple. Furthermore, Osborne's letters, taken as a whole, constitute a substantial achievement. The earlier letters lay the groundwork for those which follow, and the letters written in the middle period lead logically to what was composed just prior to the time when the marriage contract was settled.

---

[2] G. C. Moore Smith, ed. *The Letters of Dorothy Osborne to William Temple* (Oxford: Clarendon Press, 1928). All quotation will be from this edition.

[3] Kenneth Parker, ed., *Letters to Sir William Temple* by Dorothy Osborne (London: Penguin, 1987), 1.

It is clear that Osborne wrote to be read, not in the sense that she expected her words to appear on the printed page in her lifetime, but, rather, with the knowledge that various people beyond William Temple would see her correspondence. Letters often were considered to be a form of publication, as demonstrated in the detailed account of "manuscript circulation and correspondence networks" in Margaret Ezell's *The Patriarch's Wife*.[4] Osborne sometimes shared letters sent to her with William Temple, and he sometimes reciprocated. She even went so far as to write about the art of the letter as she and others practiced it.

In addition to feeling the influence of the native English tradition, Osborne was aware of the presence of Continental trends. She read and frequently referred to French romances, which often contained epistolary exchanges. She sometimes made light of the implausibilities of the characters of the romance, but the notion that letters make literature was not lost on her. More importantly, she combined the unadorned prose she had learned from the native English tradition with the elegant salon style of the romances. In some places, Osborne even assumes the trappings of a heroine. The result is precisely tuned to the position she held in English society and to the sorts of expectations that she shared with many women in England.

For her to spell out such expectations in so many words would have been pretentious. It would have been like suing for the favors of the powerful or openly setting out to gain privilege in "a class-stratified patronage system."[5] Those activities made sense for unemployed and well-educated young men living in the "bottleneck years" of the 1590s,[6] but they were not so fitting to a woman solidly situated in the upper ranks of the gentry some sixty years later. Nevertheless, Osborne makes some of her expectations clear. She planned to have a comfortable marriage in which she exercised a good deal of domestic authority. Although Lawrence Stone doubts that women of her class were much more than adjuncts to their husbands, others, like Margaret Ezell, have shown that balanced relationships were common. There can be no doubt about Osborne's future husband. He was to be a person who would share major decisions with her and participate in mutual affection. Affection based upon shared responsibility, "kindness," was her *sine qua non*. Her letters demonstrate this fundamental requirement with repeated reference to negative example. Osborne had certain hopes as well, hopes not necessarily important to all of her sisters in the upper

---

[4]Margaret J. M. Ezell, *The Patriarch's Wife: Literary Evidence and the History of the Family* (Chapel Hill: University of North Carolina Press, 1987), 64-83.

[5]Frank Whigham, "The Rhetoric of Elizabethan Suitors' Letters," *Publications of the Modern Language Association (PMLA)* 96 no. 5 (1981): 864-82.

[6]Marilyn L. Williamson, *The Patriarchy of Shakespeare's Comedies* (Detroit: Wayne State University Press, 1986), 14.

gentry. She planned to marry a man who had literary leanings and who would appreciate her own skill with words. She was not disappointed, for William Temple became a noted prose stylist and spent his later years as a mentor to Jonathan Swift. The language of the letter as written by women in England helped Osborne express her practical concerns with marriage. The language of the French romance kept the practical from becoming too mundane.

Genie S. Lerch-Davis examines the unadorned style in Osborne's letters, writing that Osborne "so despised unnaturalness and extravagance because she felt them to be symptoms of insincerity and arrogance – not just in prose, but in all forms of behavior."[7] Lerch-Davis overlooks the high-toned posturing that Osborne engages in from time to time and the elevated style that is its vehicle. A version of the plain style current in the seventeenth century also is described by Annabel Patterson. In her analysis of the letters of James Howell, she shows that transparence is not so transparent. While creating a "chatty, entertaining tone," Howell "cooked" various of his letters; that is, he edited them long after the fact.[8] Even if this were not the case, there is an art at work behind the feeling of spontaneity in much correspondence of the time. Osborne's letters, like Howell's, are entertaining and chatty but they are also calculated for effect. Osborne took care to interweave the more transparent and modest style with its loftier counterpart. As the tension in the love story between Osborne and Temple grows, so does the French influence. When the tide has turned in favor of the lovers, the style of the letters becomes unadorned and more English. A word like "kindness" is more oriented towards "affection" when the French influence is dominant. It partakes of "shared responsibility" when the English style is ascendant.

"Kindness" is defined in *The Oxford English Dictionary* as "kinship, natural affection arising from this." It is also found to be "good natural quality or aptitude," a more modern definition. For women of the late sixteenth and early seventeenth centuries, it had additional associations. Lady Elizabeth Russell uses the language of women in England when looking for a husband for her daughter Bess. She makes kindness a key criterion:

> I love of Wife to marry my daughter to a wise man; that will love
> her, and govern her in Judgment; in the feare of god; according

---

[7]Genie S. Lerch-Davis, "Rebellion Against Public Prose: The Letters of Dorothy Osborne to William Temple (1652-54)," *Texas Studies in Literature and Language* 20 (Fall 1978), 387-415.

[8]Annabel Patterson, *Censorship and Interpretation: The Conditions of Writing and Reading in Early Modern England* (Madison: The University of Wisconsin Press, 1984),

to her worth, and in al kindness and wisdom will deserve her Love: This is what I seeke.[9]

The letter, written late in the 1590s or in the early part of the seventeenth century to Thomas Egerton, does not explicitly define "kindness." Still, the linking of kindness to wisdom and to matters of governance clearly indicates what she has in mind. The husband will feel affection for his wife and will use good "Judgment" in his practical dealings with her so that she will have reason to love him. He will gain this love, not because it is owed to him, but because he "deserves" it. He will treat her according to her "worth," not according to caprice. Unilateral decision-making is precluded.

The language of women was not unknown to men who, like Thomas Egerton, found themselves asked to think in its terms. Thomas Heywood took advantage of the opportunity provided by the word "kindness" to craft an enormously popular play that resonates with its various meanings including those from the world of women. "Kindness" is mainly used in the sense of "good natural quality" in *A Woman Killed with Kindness.* Still, the notion that men "used" their wives with unkindness makes the play what it is, for Frankford is not capable of cruelty. He has the right to subject his adulterous wife to any number of severe measures, and many men of the time would have seen the administration of harsh punishment as his duty. Instead, he showers Anne with so much good treatment that she is filled with remorse and dies. There is never any suggestion that Anne shares responsibilities with Frankford, but he avoids any semblance of self-importance or high-handed behavior. Much of the power of the play comes from its being a fantasy of male graciousness posed in language of women. Men saw themselves as magnanimous. Women relished the public representation of a husband who ran so contrary to what was prescribed in the Puritan conduct books.

Kate Cartwright, in a letter to the Countess of Bridgewater written some twenty or thirty years later, describes family problems, but she happily reports that she and her husband are very "kind" with one another.

> I now let your Ladyship know wee live heare very well and quickly; only my father and mother in law will have some sodayne quirkes some times but I take no notis of them . . . but of jornys . . . my husband & I bee very kind & there is noe faling out on noe side.[10]

[9]Elizabeth Russell, Letters to Thomas Egerton (1595-1604), Huntington Library MS EL 46.

[10]Kate Cartwright, Letter to Countess of Bridgewater (undated). Huntington Library MS EL 6512.

Kate Cartwright may have some of the same problems with an errant husband as does Katherine Temple, but these difficulties have been resolved to her satisfaction. Likewise, there is the possibility that the management of the in-laws could cause a quarrel between husband and wife but it does not. Kate and Mr. Cartwright have worked out a solution agreeable to both, and "there is noe falling out on noe side." A falling out would work both ways, so Mr. Cartwright is no doubt wise to avoid it. Affection and household governance – *otium* and *negotium* if you will – remain in harmony. A similar sharing of responsibilities, of decision-making, is what Osborne wants in her marriage.

In Osborne's early letters, the character of the writer emerges as a mix of savvy young woman, not unlike Katherine Temple, and heroine derived from romance, with emphasis placed on the first of these. The style tends to be unadorned and direct:

> It was nothing that I expected made mee refuse these [other suitors]
> but something I feared, and seriously, I find I want Courage to
> marry where I doe not like. if we should once come to disputes,
> I know who would have the worst on't, and I have not faith
> enough to beleeve a doctrine that is often preached, which is, that
> though at first one has noe kindenesse for them yet it will grow
> strangly after marriage.[11]

The writer does not reject Temple's rivals because they lack a financial or social status to which she aspires. Rather, she demands that kindness be established prior to marriage. If affection based on shared decision-making is not in existence before the nuptials, what can be expected after? There will be "disputes" in which Osborne, as wife, will "have the worst on't." Embedded in the reasoning of the savvy young woman are a few words of the heroine of French romance. The writer makes "Courage" an issue and protests that she writes "seriously."

Three letters later, Osborne brings in a topos from the romance when she claims spontaneity of composition. Women in England sometimes began or closed letters with "written in haste," but they were not likely to develop the point. Osborne pauses to make it an issue:

> This is a strange letter to be sure, I have not time to read it over
> but I have sayed any thing that came in my head.[12]

A character in Mlle de Scudéry's *Clélie* goes into detail on never blotting a line.

---

[11]Letter 4, Moore edition.
[12]Letter 7, Moore edition.

On passe d'une chause a une autre sans aucune contrainte; et ces sortes de Lettres estant a proprement parler une conversation de Personnes absentes. . . . Il faut donc que le stile en soit aisé, naturel, et noble tout ensemble.[13]

[A person goes from one subject to another without any constraint; and these kinds of letters are, properly speaking, a conversation between absent people. . . . It is necessary, therefore, that the style be easy, natural, and noble altogether.]

Such topoi aside, Osborne's early and middle letters generally adhere to the unadorned native English style. She even goes so far as to ridicule a local sheriff who takes fiction too seriously. At the same time she parodies the complicated sentences of romance:

> What has kept him from marryeng all this while, or how the humor com's soe furiously upon him now, I know not, but if hee may bee believ'd, hee is resolved to bee a most Romance Squire and goe in quest of some inchanted Damzell, whome if hee likes, as to her person (for fortune is a thing below him & wee do not reade in History that any knight, or squire, was ever soe discourtious as to inquire what portions theire Lady's had) . . . I doe not see whoe is able to resist him, all that is to be hoped, is, that since hee may reduce whomever hee pleases to his Obedience, hee will bee very Curious in his choise, and then I am secure.[14]

Osborne's negative example helps to define what she desires. She wants affection from a practical man who understands the importance of financial arrangements, and she has no interest in anyone who would "reduce whomever hee pleases to his Obedience." Although her criticism of him is tongue in cheek and based on semifictional depiction, the sheriff is not someone to value kindness.

Six letters farther on, Osborne reintroduces the topic of governance in marriage by way of teasing. She asks Temple to "forbid" her to eat fruit and, in her next letter, chides him for giving her orders:

> Sr.
>   In my opinion you doe not understande the Law's of friendship right; 'tis generaly beleeved it owes it's birth to an agreement & conformity of humors, and that it lives no longer then tis preserved by the Mutuall care of those that bred it, tis wholy Governde by

---

[13]Madeleine de Scudéry, *Artamene, ou le Grand Cyrus* (1656, rpt. Slatkine Reprints, 1972), 2:III; see also Madeleine de Scudéry, quoted in Duchene, Roger. *Realite vecue et art epistolaire* vol. 1: *Madame de Sevigne et la lettre d'Amour.* (Paris: Bordas, 1970).

[14]Letter 21, Moore edition.

Equality, and can there bee such a thing in it, as a distinction of
Power? noe sure, if wee are friends wee must both comande &
both obay alike.[15]

Osborne is being playful, but her point about friendship exactly parallels
her claims for kindness in marriage. It is hard to know whether Osborne
was familiar with Katherine Philips' set of laws for friendship between
women, but Osborne's project is more practical and more oriented towards
men. Should Temple not understand the serious side of Osborne's jest, she
goes on to write of another of her rejected suitors. "Tis most Certaine,
that our Emperour would have bin to mee rather a Jaylor than a husband."
Like the sheriff, the emperor is not one to take much account of kindness.

As might be expected, Osborne and Temple hoped to see one another
from time to time, and by letter number twenty-nine it had been at least
a year since they had done so. The tentative interest they had shown for
each other in the first ten or fifteen letters was now well developed and
openly acknowledged between them. Although Temple's letters to Osborne
are lost, it appears that he urged her to help with arrangements for a
meeting. Should she refuse, she would be using him with unkindness. She
responds with a strong, direct letter:

> Sr.
>
> I can give you leave to doubt any thing but my kindnesse. . . .
> noe, all the kindenesse I have, or ever had, is yours nor shall I ever
> repent it is soe, unlesse you shall ever repent yours; without telling
> you what the inconveniency's of your comeing hither are, you
> may beleeve they are considerable or else I should not deny you
> or my selfe the happinesse of seeing one another, and if you dare
> trust mee where I am Equaly concerned with you, I shall take hold
> of the first opertunity that may either admitt you heer, or bring
> mee neerer you.[16]

Later she will claim that she can love only one man, that she will marry
Temple or remain single. Here she lets him know that she would "repent"
of her affection for him were he to lose his interest in her or were he to
pressure her unduly. She reinforces this independence by refusing to give
him any specific reasons for being unable to arrange the meeting. He will
have to trust her. Although she may not be his equal in other matters, she
has no hesitation in using "Equaly" to describe her position where affection-
based shared decision-making is concerned.

In letter number thirty-six, the savvy woman of the English tradition
begins to abate or, more exactly, to go into hiding. The heroine of French

[15]Letter 28, Moore edition.
[16]Letter 29, Moore edition.

romance asserts herself. Osborne admonishes Temple not to use the word "love," but only after writing that she has read and reread the letter in which it appears:

> As long as your last was, I read it over thrice in lesse than an hower. . . . Love is a Terrible word, and I should blush to death if any thing but a letter accused mee on't, pray be mercifull and lett it run friendship in my next Charge.[17]

It is hard to take her admonition to mere friendship at face value. Rather, she seems to be saying that Temple had better be earnest. Otherwise he is a trifler with emotions, a cad. Like a heroine from fiction, she "blushes" at the thought of love. A "request" becomes a "charge."

The letters build in narrative tension as the strength of the relationship between Osborne and Temple grows. The fact that Osborne's brother disapproves of Temple was less an issue when she and Temple were only friends. By the forty-seventh letter, the two have decided they want to marry. and marriage seems impossible. Osborne sees herself as a thwarted heroine:

> But if as wee have not differd in anything else wee could agree in this too, and resolve upon a friendship that will be much the Perfecter for haveing nothing of passion in it, how happy might wee bee; without soe much as a fear of the Change that any accident could bring, wee might deffye all that fortune could doe.[18]

Without the high-minded resignation in adversity and the elevated language of "perfection," "change," and "accident," the story of Osborne and Temple would not be as powerful as it is. Taken out of the context of French romance, this passage is liable to seem overblown. Left within that elevated tradition, the passage and much of the next letter ride the crest of narrative tension. Will their love be frustrated, or will it be fulfilled?

> Examine your own heart what is fitt for mee to doe, and what you can doe for a Person you Love, and that deserv's your compassion if Nothing Else, A Person that will alway's have an inviolable friendship for you a freindship that shall take up all the roome my Passion held in my heart and govern there as Master till Death come to take possession and turn it out.[19]

Passion, once distrusted and often marked as the undoing of others, is now admitted to have had a home in the heart of Dorothy Osborne. Affection

---

[17]Letter 36, Moore edition.

[18]Letter 47, Moore edition.

[19]Letter 48, Moore edition.

for Temple, once contingent upon his feelings for her and upon his agreement to shared responsibility, is, in its manifestation as friendship, "Master till Death come."

The savvy young woman of the early letters is not entirely effaced in this outpouring of emotion. She reminds us of her existence from time to time. It is an astute correspondent who suggests the contractual nature of her letters to her fiance:

> I will never marry any Other. . . . keep this as a testimony against mee if ever I doe and make mee a reproach . . . by it.[20]

The sentence will haunt Temple, should he ever be tempted to unkindness at some later date. He has proclaimed his kindness often enough that a failure in it would allow "testimony" from his letters to be held as a "reproach" against him. Elsewhere in the letter, Osborne gives way to flourishes from the romance. There is, if not "unnaturalness and extravagance" in Osborne's style, at least a good deal of high-flown thought and language:

> Heer then I declare that you have still the same power in my heart that I gave you at our last parteing . . . that iff ever our fortun's will allow us to marry you shall dispose mee as you please. but this, to deal freely with you, I doe not hope for. noe, tis too great a happinesse, and I that know my self best must acknoledge I deserve crosses and affliction but can never merritt such a blessing.[21]

"Dispose of mee as you please" is the heroine speaking. This passage is especially illuminating because it echoes a section from Mlle de Scudéry's *Le Grand Cyrus*. The cross that Osborne has to bear is only a little less burdensome than that carried by Scudéry's Doralize, who demands that her one love have not ever loved another:

> Ie trouue que de quelque façon que je regarde la chose, il ne faut point aimer celuy qui a déjà aimé . . . la grande difficulté est de trouuer tout ensemble vn honneste homme qui n'ait rien aimé & qui n'aimé rien que moy.[22]

> [I find that no matter from which side I consider the situation, I cannot love at all one who has already loved . . . the big difficulty all together is to find a worthy man who has loved nobody, and who loves nothing but me.]

[20]Letter 53, Moore edition.

[21]Letter 53, Moore edition.

[22]Madeleine de Scudéry, *Artamene, ou le Grand Cyrus.* (1656; rpt. Slatkine Reprints, 1972), Bk. 1, 69-70.

Two letters later, Osborne's style and presentation of herself could not be more different. Marriage negotiations have begun and money is an issue. Although she will return to the style of the romances from time to time, the denouement of Osborne's story is under way and its style is now both direct and unadorned.

> Hee [a foolish suitor] was told that I had thought's of marryeng a Gentleman that had not above two hundred Pound ayeer only out of likeing for his person; and upon that score his vanity allows him to think hee may prettende as farr as another.
>
> (L 56)

Osborne has all the toughness and practicality of Katherine Temple, Elizabeth Russell, and Kate Cartwright. If William Temple wants to marry Osborne he must ask his father for support, difficult as that request will be:

> Tis not likely as you say that you should much perswade your father to what you doe not desyre hee should doe, but it is harde if all the Testimony's of my kindenesse are not enough to satisfye without my Publishing to the world that I can forgett my friends and all my interest to ffollow my Passion . . . and wee that are concerned int can only say twas an act of great kindenesse and somthing Romance.
>
> (L 56)

If he fails to ask his father, they become no more than characters out of a fiction and their "kindenesse" no more than affection.

The remaining letters are more relaxed, and, although they continue with hard-nosed financial negotiations, the marriage is a foregone conclusion. It is no small irony that Osborne had to rely on her once-reviled brother to make the formal arrangements. She writes in letter seventy-five, two letters before the correspondence concludes, "But if your father out of humor shall refuse to treate with such friends as I have, let them bee what they will, it must End hear." It did not end except in marriage.

It is customary to trace the development of unadorned prose style in the letter as an adjunct to the anti-Ciceronian movement. Certainly when Osborne writes in favor of plainness, she is in line with what is to be found in Angel Day's *English secretorie* (1586). Gary R. Grund, perhaps inadvertently, points to another important influence when he writes of "native bourgeois writers."[23] Women in England managed to develop a plain style with a language of its own. That style goes back to the Paston women in the

---

[23]Gary R. Grund, "From Formulary to Fiction: The Epistle and the English Anti-Ciceronian Movement." *Texas Studies in Literature and Language* 17 (1975): 379-95, esp. 381.

middle of the fifteenth century.[24] They also delineated character with precision and often with fictional elements.

A great many letters written by the women who followed the Pastons remain to be read for their literary value. This is not to ignore the fact that the letters served immediate and nonliterary ends. Nor is it to say that their literary value frees them from the culture in which they were generated. Rather, the tradition of women writing to women and to men as women is part and parcel of a society that allowed women to write in some circumstances and on some topics while restricting their writing elsewhere. Translations of secular works, as with Mary Sidney Herbert's rendering of Garnier's *Marc Antoine,* were allowed. Likewise, religious writing by women as discussed in Margaret Hannay's collection, *Silent But for the Word,* was widespread.[25] Letters enjoyed a similar exemption presumably because they were viewed then, as they sometimes are now, as something less than a form of art. Serious consideration of *ars dictaminis,* was something else and left to men like Erasmus and More. With this license to compose, women developed a tradition of writing of their own, one which is literary and which possessed usefulness for those who employed it.

Although it is not unusual to read about the "radical otherness of the past,"[26] in descriptions of twentieth-century inability to come to terms with the Renaissance, the letters of Dorothy Osborne do not seem so very alien. The feel we have for Osborne's life is, however, a literary feel. That is, we may identify with the fiction of Osborne as a heroine from the French romances, a high-minded idealist struggling against a tyrannical brother. On the other hand, we may admire the hardheaded woman, who knows what sort of marriage she wants. We should remember, too, the writer who created these images.

[24]Norman Davis, "The *Litera Troili* and English Letters," *Reviews of English Studies* 63 (1965): 233-44.

[25]Margaret Hannay, *Silent But For the Word: Tudor Women as Patrons, Translators, and Writers of Religious Works.* (Kent, Ohio: Kent State University Press, 1985).

[26]Jean E. Howard, "The New Historicism in Renaissance Studies," *Renaissance Historicism: Selections from English Literary Renaissance,* ed. Arthur F. Kinney and Dan S. Collins. (Amherst: The University of Massachusetts Press, 1987), 2-33, esp. 11.

The Authors and Editors

JAMES L. BRAIN is Professor Emeritus in Anthropology at the State University of New York at New Paltz.

———————— • • ● • • ————————

SIGRID BRAUNER is Assistant Professor of German at the University of Massachusetts, Amherst.

———————— • • ● • • ————————

JEAN R. BRINK is Associate Professor of English at Arizona State University, Tempe, and director of the Arizona Center for Medieval and Renaissance Studies in Tempe.

———————— • • ● • • ————————

ALBRECHT CLASSEN is Associate Professor of German at the University of Arizona, Tucson.

———————— • • ● • • ————————

VIVIANA COMENSOLI is Assistant Professor of English at Wilfrid Laurier University, Waterloo, Ontario.

———————— • • ● • • ————————

ALLISON COUDERT is is a lecturer in the Honors College at Arizona State University, Tempe.

———————— • • ● • • ————————

JAMES FITZMAURICE is Associate Professor of English at Northern Arizona University in Flagstaff.

———————— • • ● • • ————————

MARYANNE C. HOROWITZ is chair of the History Department at Occidental College, Los Angeles.

———————— • • ● • • ————————

MARION L. KUNTZ is Regents Professor of Classics at Georgia State University, Atlanta.

——————————————— • • ● • • ———————————————

CAROLE LEVIN is Associate Professor of History at the State University of New York at New Paltz.

——————————————— • • ● • • ———————————————

WILLIAM MONTER is Professor of History at Northwestern University, Evanston, Illinois.

——————————————— • • ● • • ———————————————

MARTINE REY is currently working on a Ph.D. in Comparative Literature at the University of North Carolina, Chapel Hill.

Index